JUDGING IN THE ISLAMIC, JEWISH AND ZOROASTRIAN LEGAL TRADITIONS

Cultural Diversity and Law

Series Editor:
Prakash Shah, School of Law, Queen Mary, University of London, UK

Around the world, most states are faced with difficult issues arising out of cultural diversity in their territories. Within the legal field, such issues span across matters of private law through to public and constitutional law. At international level too there is now considerable jurisprudence regarding ethnic, religious and cultural diversity. In addition, there are several layers of legal control – from communal and religious regulation to state and international regulation. This multiplicity of norm setting has been variously termed legal pluralism, inter-legality or inter-normativity and provides a fascinating lens for academic analysis that links up to cultural diversity in new and interesting ways. The umbrella of cultural diversity encompasses various population groups throughout the world ranging from national, ethnic, religious or indigenous groupings. This series particularly welcomes work that is of comparative interest, concerning various state jurisdictions as well as different population groups.

Also in the series

Socio-Legal Integration
Polish Post-2004 EU Enlargement Migrants in the United Kingdom
Agnieszka Kubal
ISBN 978-1-4094-3700-0

Law, Religious Freedoms and Education in Europe
Edited by Myriam Hunter-Henin
ISBN 978-1-4094-2730-8

Islamic Law in Europe?
Legal Pluralism and its Limits in European Family Laws
Andrea Büchler
ISBN 978-1-4094-2849-7

The Challenges of Justice in Diverse Societies
Constitutionalism and Pluralism
Meena K. Bhamra
ISBN 978-1-4094-1928-0

Judging in the Islamic, Jewish and Zoroastrian Legal Traditions

A Comparison of Theory and Practice

JANOS JANY
Pázmány Péter Catholic University, Hungary

Routledge
Taylor & Francis Group
LONDON AND NEW YORK

First published 2012 by Ashgate Publishing

Published 2016 by Routledge
2 Park Square, Milton Park, Abingdon, Oxon OX14 4RN
711 Third Avenue, New York, NY 10017, USA

First issued in paperback 2017

Routledge is an imprint of the Taylor & Francis Group, an informa business

British Library Cataloguing in Publication Data
Jany, Janos.
Judging in the Islamic, Jewish and Zoroastrian legal traditions : a comparison of theory and practice. –
(Cultural diversity and law)
1. Judicial process (Islamic law) 2. Judicial process (Jewish law) 3. Zoroastrian law. 4. Religion and law–Cross-cultural studies. 5. Culture and law.
I. Title II. Series
347'.014-dc23

Library of Congress Cataloging-in-Publication Data
Jany, Janos.
Judging in the Islamic, Jewish and Zoroastrian legal traditions : a comparison of theory and practice / by Janos Jany.
p. cm. — (Cultural diversity and law)
Includes bibliographical references and index.
ISBN 978-1-4094-3716-1 (hardback : alk. paper)
1. Islamic law. 2. Jewish law. 3. Zoroastrian law. 4. Comparative law. I. Title.
KB190.J36 2012
347'.014—dc23

ISBN 13: 978-1-138-11697-9 (pbk)
ISBN 13: 978-1-4094-3716-1 (hbk)

Contents

List of Tables

Acknowledgements

My special thanks go to Dr Gáthy Veronika, scholar and friend, for helping me to put this work into readable English and for her numerous comments and suggestions during the long hours we worked together.

I would also like to thank Dr Prakash Shah, the Cultural Diversity and Law Series Editor, for including this book in the series.

The writing of this book was sponsored by the TAMOP 4.2.1 B-11/2/KMR grant from the Hungarian government and the European Union.

Introduction

Subject and Aim

The subject of the present work is a comparative analysis of the Islamic, Jewish and Zoroastrian legal systems, highlighting the function of the judiciary, the social standing of the judges in their respective societies and their relations vis-à-vis jurisprudence. Since these legal systems are called 'religious' in legal literature, giving the impression that it is religion which is their most important feature, it is necessary to compare postulations of legal theory to legal practice in order to show the relationship between theory and practice.

We can find in the works of some authors of comparative law (e.g. Sola Cañizares, Adolf Schnitzer and René David)[1] the concept of religious legal system, although the definition of religion itself is rather complex and subject to various interpretations. To refer to just one obvious example, there is hardly any similarity between the Chinese concepts of religion (universalism, Taoism, yin-yang school etc.) and those of the revealed religions (the religions of the book). Moreover, there are so many schools and interpretations within Hinduism that one can hardly speak about any uniform 'ism'. If religious foundations taken for granted in legal literature are so diverse and complex, how much more the legal systems built on them would be. Thus, it is problematic to put such different legal systems under the aegis of one rather enigmatic category. With some exceptions, however, these considerations are not present in comparative legal literature since in the majority of cases it is the erudition and interest of the author and limited space which determine what comes under the aegis of religious legal systems. Hindu law and Islamic law are always discussed in comparative legal works because of their importance, influence and the great number of their followers. By contrast, Jewish and Canon law are discussed very briefly, if not omitted altogether; meanwhile Zoroastrian law is considered as not worth mentioning. Consequently, not only the definition of the term 'religious legal system' is missing, but also the exact enumeration of the individual legal systems covered by this category.

This issue was the topic of a conference in 2000, dedicated to the memory of David Daube, a scholar of reputation both as a Talmudist and as a Romanist. The participants, authorities in comparative law and experts in religious legal systems, were not able to reach a consensus on the meaning and definition of religious law.[2] The net result of the discussion was put by Jacques Vanderlinden: 'there are

1 These and other taxonomies are discussed in Varga 2005: 219–37.

2 For the discussion see Huxley 2002: 148–56.

as many comparative laws as there are comparative lawyers'.[3] Perhaps no more tangible results could be expected, for what are those characteristic features that link Canon law to Islamic, Jewish or, for that matter, Hindu law?

The present author agrees with Werner Menski, an authority on Hindu law, who claims that religious legal system as a concept is useless. He argues that this concept is an implementation of a Europe-centred worldview on law which considers the entire world from its own perspective, regardless of genuine legal thinking. According to this understanding, Menski argues, the term 'religious legal system' is composed of legal systems which are considered traditional, incapable of change, backward and irrational.[4] As such an approach is no longer acceptable; the term reflecting this understanding is also useless. This is the reason why this book has dropped the term religious legal system throughout, including from its title – which resulted, admittedly, in a somewhat artificial wording.

Despite all this, religion does have important functions in Islamic, Jewish and Zoroastrian law, both in legal theory and, in a more restricted sense, in substantive law. It is the aim of the present work to understand the real functions of religion in these legal systems, regardless of the dogmatic postulations of these religions. In order to do this one has to depart from ideals of the religious-legal texts and put social practice, everyday legal mechanisms and their social, political and economic background under scrutiny, finding the proper place of religion in the respective societies.

For this purpose the judiciary was made the focus of this enquiry since it is the judge who has the obligation to adjust to legal texts yet, at the same time, consider social realities being sometimes at variance with religious ethics and legal rules deriving from them. In addition, since the judge is also a theologian, a wise man of learning in various extra-judicial fields and a teacher of enormous social prestige, his social functions are more extensive, more articulate and colourful than in the continental or common law legal systems, where the function of the judge is limited to the solution of legal cases. As the religious elite tried to monopolize the administration of justice in order to assert the ethical principles represented by them, the office of the judge became a key issue for both the state and that elite.

At the same time, judges and legal scholars were also the driving force behind legal development, for they had the uneasy task of implementing legal rules deriving from religious postulations into an ever-changing social reality. Judges have been esteemed members of their society who eminently knew daily life and could see the danger of a rigid implementation of religious rules leading to social dysfunction. This consideration has led to various legal methods and techniques of argumentation that are far more characteristic of a legal system than the external history of law. The subtitle of this book (*A Comparison of Theory and Practice*) refers to this contradiction as an essential element of its content. Yet, at the same

3 Vanderlinden 2002: 166.

4 Menski 2002: 110–11.

time it is in accordance with the view of Alan Watson, who sees procedural law as one of the most important engines of legal development.[5]

Obviously, in pre-modern societies not only courts bore the burden of adjudicating disputes; there were other institutions and social mechanisms which were at play, too. As W. B. Hallaq demonstrated in relation to Muslim societies, procedures at a law court dealt with only a restricted number of cases, while others were discussed and solved by organs of micro-communities such as the extended family, the clan and the tribe, the neighbourhood and the guilds. Since the legal maxim 'amicable settlement is the best verdict' is deeply rooted in Muslim societies, arbitration and mediation were sometimes more important social mechanisms to solve a conflict than formal procedures at a law court.[6] Jewish law endorsed the same attitude towards social mechanisms other than formal litigation, and Sasanian society did not differ from Jewish and Muslim societies either. This attitude is, therefore, the broad social framework where formal litigation should be placed. This is why this is the subject of the present study and hence other mechanisms were dealt with only when necessary.

Naturally, it has to be clarified why the study covers Islamic, Jewish and Zoroastrian law while omitting others. Historical, cultural and phenomenological considerations figure equally among the factors supporting the comparison of these legal systems. Common linguistic, ethnic and social background (of the Jews and Arabs), a multitude of cultural interactions throughout a long history (of all three systems) and a legal system based on similar theoretical considerations (also of all three systems) are objective factors making comparisons possible and meaningful. Thus, the focus is on the Middle East. Therefore, the Hindu legal system is mentioned only occasionally. Although it does share some common features with Islamic, Jewish and Zoroastrian law, essential similarities, however, can be found only in relation to Zoroastrian law supported by an early common history and cultural background. But this could be the subject of further research.

As far as the time frame of the study is concerned, it does not go back beyond late Antiquity and only rarely stretches beyond the thirteenth century, omitting the Ottoman period altogether. The sixth and the seventh centuries are among the most interesting and most decisive periods in the history of law, although this is not emphasized in comparative legal literature. The sixth century was the time of Emperor Justinian and of the codification of Roman law during his reign. During the reign of his contemporary and rival, King Khusraw of Persia, the Iranian state witnessed a cultural flourishing not experienced in the previous centuries. It was the time when the Awesta, the holy book of Zoroastrianism, was codified after several centuries (millennia?) of oral tradition. It was also the century when the codification of the Babylonian Talmūd, which became the most important document of the Jews after the Torāh, was completed in Mesopotamia under Persian political and administrative control. Thus, within a couple of decades three

5 Watson 1999: 91.

6 Hallaq 2009: 160–64.

cultures of hoary past – the Roman, the Jewish and the Persian – codified their own legal heritage, which makes the period rather remarkable in itself.

The seventh century is of no less significance: legal codification was continued both in Persia and among the Jews. The law book *Mādigān ī Hazār Dādestān* (MHD+A),[7] compiled probably in the first decades of the seventh century, is a collection of judgments and legal rulings of scholars, and thus a source of utmost importance for students of Zoroastrian law. Meanwhile the Jewish Academies continued to work on their masterpiece, the Babylonian Talmūd, on which Persian influence could be discerned in the level of legal terms. The second part of the century witnessed the emergence of Islamic law, which fundamentally transformed the (legal) history of the Mediterranean and of the Middle East. Thus in 100 years one can witness the codification of Roman and Jewish law, the heyday of Zoroastrian law and the birth of Islamic law.

The significance of the next two centuries is different between the legal cultures under discussion. During that period Jewish legal scholars primarily restricted themselves to commenting on Talmudic wisdom, and no major work similar to the Talmūd was produced. The works of some outstanding authors (such as Saᶜadya Ga'ōn) refined the inherited tradition in many respects. Zoroastrianism, no longer the official religion of Persia, was losing ground during that period, yet the ninth and tenth centuries witnessed the birth of important religious and legal works (the so-called *riwāyas*) which adjusted the legal tradition to the changing historical context. As far as Islamic law is concerned, the first centuries were of utmost importance, during which generations of legal scholars established both the theoretical framework and the rules of a new legal system.

To avoid this work being more complex than it already is, focus is restricted to Sunnī legal tradition. Shiᶜī law, admittedly, is distinct from the Sunnī legal understanding, but only concerning questions which are irrelevant for the purpose of the present study. Important aspects such as the *uṣūlī-akhbarī* disputes, the emergence of the various titles of the legal scholars and their relation to each other (*Ayat Allāh, Hujjat al-Islām* etc) and the concept of *welāyat-e faqīh* are the results of the modern period and bear no imprint on the legal understanding of the pre-modern period.[8]

This book is about comparative law. Therefore, it leans on the results of previous researches by outstanding experts on Islamic and Jewish law. Concerning Zoroastrian law, however, it does contain original research material since Zoroastrian law is a less frequently studied field and belongs to the particular field of research of the present author. But comparative law might be misleading because it is not positive law which is compared here but rather the social and

7 The text was edited and translated into German as well as English by Macuch 1981; 1993 and Perikhanian–Garsoian 1997.

8 For shiᶜī legal theory see Löschner 1971; modern trends are analysed in Mallat 1993.

cultural environment of the legal systems in which they operate. Therefore, comparative legal culture seems to be a better designation.

Principles and Methods

To accomplish the aim outlined above meant facing innumerable difficulties, hence it is necessary to define the principles and methods of research.

The present work was written expressly for a scholarly purpose hence its approach is markedly secular. Stressing the secular approach is important because one may study a religious system also as a believer, and then, naturally, the result will not be the same. Jewish, Islamic and Zoroastrian law is being practised, taught and applied even today, primarily by Rabbis, scholars and priestly individuals. Their approach, however, is obviously different from that of secular lawyers. To clarify the matter, Jewish law offers a good example: *halakah* and *mishpat Ivri* are not identical concepts (though one may translate both as 'Jewish law'), as the first reflects the Talmudist approach, insisting on tradition, whereas the second is that of the modern lawyer. The main difference between the two is that the modern lawyer is not satisfied with the analytical method, which is practically the only means of the Talmudist, but approaches the issue historically and applies the method of legal comparison, too.[9]

It is impossible to describe these legal systems with the terminology of Western legal systems, whether civil or common law. As the founder of the *ᶜādat* legal school, Cornelis van Vollenhoven correctly emphasized, one has to view Oriental law in an Oriental manner. This principle, marking a breakaway from the ethnocentric approach, is an outstanding intellectual foundation of his school which it insists upon to this day.[10] Sadly enough, it also means that the reader has to find their way in the ocean of Middle Persian, Aramaic, Hebrew and Arabic legal terms, which would, at first sight, make the task more difficult than easy.

There is, hopefully, no sign of 'parallelomania' (Jacob Neusner) in the work since it does not want to show similarities at all costs. Moreover, since similarities in themselves prove no 'legal transplants' (Alan Watson), this study does not want to complicate matters with historic speculations about 'who borrowed what from whom' because such transplants, in the majority of cases, cannot be proven for certain. Omitting such speculations one can discover a series of structural similarities in the legal systems studied here, the results of which will, hopefully, stimulate more research in this field of comparative law.

It is important to note that the present study is the result of multidisciplinary research and, therefore, has no method of its own, but rather applies methods of philology, history, sociology, religious and legal history. In other words, while it

9 Shilo 1982: 97.

10 Fikentscher 1980: 99.

touches on the area of several, not interrelated disciplines, it does not belong to the main trend of research of any of them.

This complexity explains why this research has hardly any antecedents. As far as the author is aware Jewish, Islamic and Zoroastrian law has never been compared in a single work, either conceptually or in details of substantive law. Naturally, a comparison of certain aspects of Islam and the Jewish religion is available but Zoroastrianism has been exempt from these studies. Zoroastrianism is either compared to the Jewish religion (primarily in the field of dualism, cosmology and soteriology) or its influence on Islam has been studied. It is Jacob Neusner who has devoted several works to the comparison of Jewish and Zoroastrian religious texts and to their analysis, unveiling the social position of the Jews in Sasanian Persia.[11]

To carry out more research in this important field the Irano-Judaica programme was launched in the 1990s, embodied in a series of conferences. It puts emphasis on the interactions between Iranian and Jewish cultures, comparative legal history not missing from its agenda, primarily due to the works of Maria Macuch and Yaakov Elman. Legal terms of Persian origin found in the Babylonian Talmūd not only testify to Persian legal influence on Jews, but also prove at the same time that members of the Jewish Academies knew the language and rules of Zoroastrian Persian law, and sometimes made use of them in their works.[12]

A systematic comparison of the Zoroastrian and Islamic legal systems is only a desideratum at the moment. Legal institutions of similar nature where the adaptation of an earlier Persian model is most probable, such as charitable foundations (*waqf*) and the *mutʿa* marriage, were studied and compared already during the 1980s,[13] while a comparison of the legal theory of these legal systems has been done only recently.[14]

Attempts have been made to compare Jewish and Islamic law already at the beginning of the 20th century; the first work worth mentioning among the early writings is that of Robert Roberts.[15] Among the results of the more recent literature the paper of Judith Wegner is worth mentioning. She argues for a kind of Talmudic synthesis in the sources of Islamic law and assumes a Jewish legal background in the legal theory of Islam.[16] The book by Jacob Neusner and Tamara Sonn is rather a textual and not a historical comparison, and their work primarily tries to explore

11 The situation of Jews and Christians in Sasanian Persia and their relationship to Zoroastrianism is analysed in detail by Neusner 1990. A comparison of the major Jewish and Zoroastrian religious texts is in Neusner 1993. The situation of Jews in Sasanian Persia is discussed at length in Neusner 1965, 1966, 1968, 1969, 1970 and in a shorter version by the same author (Neusner 1984).

12 See Macuch 1999, 2002, 2003; Elman 2003; Jany 2009.

13 Macuch 1994; Macuch 1985.

14 Jany 2005, 2008.

15 Roberts 1925.

16 Wegner 1982.

the similarities between the two legal systems in general.[17] Gideon Libson in his most recent study compares the influence of social practice in both Jewish and Islamic law and convincingly argues for similarities and interactions.[18]

In the majority of cases these studies primarily compare individual legal institutions in an analytical way, argue for a general interrelationship or possible historical connections, but do not approach the topic from the perspective of sociology and anthropology. An exception is the work of Irene Schneider, who studied the Muslim judges of the classical period in her pioneering book in a sociological approach.[19] A criticism of the Weberian model is given in another work of Schneider, but it again concentrates only on Islamic law, omitting a comparative perspective completely.[20] A valuable contribution to the field of legal anthropology is the work of Lawrence Rosen, who concentrates on the Moroccan judicial practice with the help of his field work; the comparative approach, however, was not on his agenda.[21]

What follows does not discuss the topics in chronological order but according to their significance. This is why it is not Jewish law (as historically the oldest one) which would be the starting point in a case when the problem under scrutiny is of marginal importance in this legal system. In such cases the study will discuss first that legal system which offers the best opportunity to unveil the problem in its entirety and only then will attention turn to the other two systems.

In contrast to the methods of modern sociology, where questionnaires, field work and statistics are of great importance for the researcher, here the only possible way is to study the sources. It is therefore necessary to clarify the approach to the sources, the 'golden mean' being the best solution here, too. A naïve and uncritical following of sources is just as harmful as a hypercritical approach which regards every statement of the sources with suspicion. As sources reflect the imprint of the circumstances of their genesis it would be unwise not to acknowledge this fact. Moreover, some sources are expressly religious texts whose aim is not to explore reality but to record the 'theory' and, as such, to cover up reality at times. Thus, it is not easy sometimes to explore social reality and to separate it from the religious-legal ideal beyond it. For example, works on Islamic legal theory in general and the *adab al-qāḍī* literature in particular are about the ideal of a legal scholar and a judge, a picture which could be far from social realities at times – which demands caution. By contrast, *fatwā* collections, the ongoing legal disputes in the Talmūd and the legal cases presented in the Persian law book, are closer to contemporary legal practice and have nothing to do with the ideal of a legal scholar. As a result, these are more reliable sources for a historic understanding than works on theories.

17 Neusner-Sonn 1999.
18 Libson 2003.
19 Schneider 1990.
20 Schneider 1993.
21 Rosen 1989.

Notes on Transcription

Symbols: ā, ē, ī, ō, ū indicate long vowels; to transliterate Middle Persian names and words MacKenzie's method is used with some minor modifications.[22] Concerning words which have found their way into English vocabulary (such as 'Islam') this study avoids applying rigid rules of transcription and transliteration (which would result in 'Islām') to make the work easier to read.

Table I.1 Transliteration of Arabic names and terms

Script	Transliteration	Pronunciation	Script	Transliteration	Pronunciation
ء	'	Glottal stop	ض	ḍ	Emphatic d
ا	ā	Long a or glottal stop, depending on context	ط	ṭ	Emphatic t
ب	b	b	ظ	ẓ	Emphatic z
ت	t	t	ع	c	Voiced pharyngeal fricative
ث	th	th in 'thin'	غ	gh	French r
ج	j	j in 'joke'	ف	f	f
ح	ḥ	h (voiceless pharyngeal fricative)	ق	q	Voiceless uvular stop
خ	kh	German ch	ك	k	k
د	d	d	ل	l	l
ذ	dh	th in 'then'	م	m	m
ر	r	r	ن	n	n
ز	z	z	و	w; ū	w; ū like oo in 'school'
س	s	s	ه	h	h
ش	sh	sh	ی	y; ī	y in 'yes'; ī like ee in 'deer'
ص	ṣ	Emphatic s			

22 MacKenzie 1971.

Table I.2 Transliteration of Hebrew and Aramaic names and terms

Script	Transliteration	Pronunciation	Script	Transliteration	Pronunciation
א	ʾ	a or glottal stop, depending on context	מ	m	m
ב	b	b or v	נ	n	n
ג	g	g or gh	ס	s	s
ד	d	d or dh	ע	ᶜ	Voiced pharyngeal fricative
ה	h	h, o, a, e	פ	p	p, f
ו	w	w, o, u	צ	ṣ	Emphatic s
ז	z	z	ק	q	Voiceless uvular stop
ח	ḥ	German ch	ר	r	r
ט	ṭ	Emphatic t	שׂ	ś	s
י	y, ī	y, i, e	שׁ	sh	sh
כ	k	k or kh	ת	t	t or th
ל	l	l			

PART ONE
THEORY

Chapter 1
Historical Overview

It is not the intention here to give a detailed overview of the history of Islamic, Jewish and Zoroastrian law since it is an impossible task to do in such a short chapter and has been done prudently by others.[1] This chapter restricts itself, therefore, to things which are necessary to understand the argument of this book and are relevant to the topic of the present research.

Jewish Law

Traditionally the history of Jewish law is divided into two periods, the pre-Talmudic and the post-Talmudic, each of which is subdivided into shorter periods. The pre-Talmudic period consists of the following sub-periods:

1. the Old Testament up to the activities of Ezra and Nehemiah;
2. from Nehemiah to the 'pairs' (*zugōt*), to the middle of the second century BCE;
3. from the pairs to the period of the *tannaim*;
4. the period of the *tannaim* (from the age of Jesus to the early third century), which begins with the activities of Rabban Gamalī'el, grandson of Hillel, and lasts up to the compilation of the Mishnah;
5. the age of *amoraim* (third to fifth centuries) – the intellectual result of this period is the Jerusalem and Babylonian Talmūd;
6. the age of *saboraim* (up to the seventh century), when the final text of the Talmūd was completed.

The post-Talmudic period is also divided into sub-periods, among which the age of the *ge'onīm* (up to the eleventh century) is important here. This period was marked by the dominance of the Babylonian Academies, the heads of which (*ga'ōn*) gave the name to this age. At the end of the period of the *ge'onīm* Babylon had lost its pre-eminence in Jewish learning and gave way to local intellectual centres throughout Europe and the Islamic world.

1 Concerning Jewish law a valuable historic introduction is Hecht–Jackson–Passamaneck–Piattelli–Rabello 1996; for Islamic law the latest books are Vikor 2006 and Hallaq 2009. For Zoroastrian legal history no book is available for now, but a short overview is to be found in Jany 2011.

The period of the Old Testament itself is divided into further sub-periods but there is no need to discuss them in detail. Suffice it to say in respect of the judiciary that the early judges were not heads of any law court, despite the fact that they gave their name to a separate book in the Bible (the Book of Judges). By contrast, persons called 'judges' were charismatic leaders who led the people and commanded military action. The stories of legendary persons (such as Samson) only further confirm this impression. In reality the administration of law was not in the hands of these judges but was the responsibility of a court of elders situated at the gates of cities, implementing customary law known by all.[2]

With the birth of the monarchy a more elaborated organization of the judiciary emerged. The local courts of elders continued to exist but a judiciary operated by royal officials also appeared. The king was regarded as supreme judge particularly in difficult cases (see Solomon's judgment).[3] The interrelationship of these courts cannot be identified precisely; at any rate, the king was not only an appellate forum but also could interfere in cases at any time if he considered it desirable for some reason (corruption, misuse of power etc.).[4] At the same time the king functioned also as an appellate forum when mistakes and injustices of the administration of justice had to be corrected. Many scholars suppose that stories that can be read in different books of the Old Testament were invented to legitimize organizational changes in the juridical system. These are: the model suggested by Jethro to Moses (to appoint judges from among the leaders of thousands, hundreds, fifties and tens – which suggests an expressly military pattern: Ex. 18.13–26); the decision taken by Moses to appoint the chiefs of tribes according to Deut. 1.9–17; while, according to a third tradition, he appointed judges from among 70 elders and officials (the figures are significant because of the later rabbinic tradition). It is important to note that no traces of priestly judicial activity can be found in any of these traditions; priestly administration of justice operated inside the temple at best.[5]

The event known as the reform of Yosiah was a turning point in the history of Jewish law. It is reported on twice in the Old Testament: the backbone of the tradition is identical; only some details are given differently (2 Kings 22–3.30; 2 Chronicles 34–6). Accordingly, in the 18th year of the reign of King Yosiah (622 BCE) a 'book of law' was found in the temple during some reconstruction work. The text was read out immediately to the king, who turned to Prophetess Hulda to confirm the significance of the law book – which she did. Next Josiah called the people to read out the law and he took a vow that from then on he would submit himself to the stipulations of the law in every respect. This is how it happened: he had several shrines demolished, and then he celebrated Passover in keeping with the rulings of the law.

2 Ruth 4.1–12.

3 Westbrook 1996: 3.

4 Westbrook 1988: 134.

5 Westbrook 1996: 9.

Obviously, the most important question is what was 'found' during the work? The majority of scholars think that the law referred to was the Deuteronomy, or a part of it.[6] Maxwell Miller and John Hayes think that the original material of the Deuteronomy is in chapters 12–26 of the present Deuteronomy, which was expanded in the light of Yahwist theology and anti-Assyrian ideology only later. This second, enlarged part could be the text found during the reign of Yosiah. It is important to note that there is no reference to Moses, or to the idea of the covenant with God.[7] On the other hand, Morton Smith considers the circumstances of the 'finding' extremely suspicious and holds that the work 'found' was probably that of High Priest Hilkīah (the finder) instead, reflecting the interests of the Jerusalem priesthood. The fact that the text was checked by Hulda, a little-known Prophetess, is a circumstance as good cause for suspicion. In his view all this was an effort of a minority, which he calls the Yahweh-alone party. This effort, however, was not a success at that time in the light of the catastrophic foreign policy of the young and not too talented king, sealed by his consequent death.[8]

The reform of Yosiah fits into the circumstances of the eighth century when Yahwist theology was gaining an increasingly emphatic role in religious and legal life. It was at that time the process Rainer Albertz called 'the theologization of law' (*die Theologisierung des Rechts*) started. In this process law was being increasingly projected as a requirement of Yahweh which addressed not only priests and elders but was regarded as the legal rule and moral standard for all Israelis. The ethical principles corresponding to the Yahwist concept lent reformist content to law-making which was primarily manifested in the protection of the poor (maximization of the duration of debt slavery, prohibition of collecting interest etc.). The reform of Yosiah fits well into this process where the king is no longer the lawmaker; the monarch only 'finds' the law that does not originate from him but from Moses. Thus the king is subordinated to the 'laws of Moses'; his only task is to implement them. The role of Moses was to ensure stronger legitimacy to a more and more theologized law through a direct revelation by God. As there was no Israeli kingdom at Moses' time the law based on his authority was of stronger legitimacy than royal law. Regarding legal life the role of the king was not abolished, but transformed into law enforcement since it was one of the most important royal duties to guarantee justice and order. This change of concept was expressed by the transformation of the central judiciary, which was originally established as a royal court of law in the ninth century to solve the more difficult cases. As a result of the reform this court became the most important institution of the judiciary which functioned as its supreme court, with directives being compulsory for lower courts of law (Deut. 17.8–13). Parallel to this, cultic

6 Westbrook 1996: 3.

7 Miller–Hayes 1986: 394.

8 Smith 1971: 40–51.

activities were also centralized; sacrifices were concentrated in Jerusalem, while all kinds of religious syncretism was threatened by capital punishment.[9]

The Persian period is the next important turning point in the history of Jewish law. After Cyrus II put an end to the Babylonian captivity of the Jews the Second Temple period began (see above). The activities of Ezra and Nehemiah, which are narrated by two separate books of the Old Testament, are our starting points. According to the Old Testament Ezra set out from Babylon to Jerusalem on the order of the Persian King Artaxerxes (it is still disputed whether it was the first or the second Persian monarch of the same name). The king's order is repeated word by word in the Old Testament (7 Ezra 12–26) and there is a difference of opinion about its authenticity and content.

Interpretation of verse 26 is subject to scholarly dispute. Accordingly, those who do not observe 'the law of your God and the laws of the kingdom' may be punished by death, exile or confiscation of property. The quotation raises two problems: are the two laws identical and which law is involved? The heart of the matter is the interpretation of 'and' in the above quoted phrase, which can be understood as of an explanatory nature (in this case the two laws are identical) or in a mutually exclusive sense (in which case the two laws are two different norms).

Peter Frei postulates the identity of the two laws and is of the view, therefore, that the Persian ruler lent imperial authority to the law of the Jews.[10] As a result he exercised a kind of 'constitutional' control over Jews who otherwise had relative autonomy.[11] Joseph Blenkinsopp had serious reservations concerning this thesis and called attention to the fact that Frei's hypothesis was based merely on the interpretation of a short sentence and is insufficient to prove this claim. Though Blenkinsopp does not deny the possibility that the approval of the Persian authorities was necessary for the law to come into force, he does not see it proved at all. Blenkinsopp considers it probable that divisions among the Jews may have led to requests for confirmation from the Persian ruler, and in this case the rigorist party had availed themselves of this opportunity.[12] Similarly to Blenkinsopp, Gary Knoppers also sees two separate laws in the quoted passage.[13]

The relationship between Ezra's law and the Pentatheucus is subject to debate in modern scholarship. According to the Old Testament, Ezra was a wise man in the laws of Moses – who also taught that law (7 Ezra 6,10.). As the laws of Moses were destroyed in the siege of Jerusalem, or were forgotten for some other reason, Jewish tradition sees the renewer of the law in his person.[14] Based on this tradition Wellhausen thought that the Pentatheucus was actually made in Babylon and was

9 Albertz 1997: 120–27.

10 Frei 2001: 12.

11 Frei 2001: 38.

12 Blenkinsopp 2001: 54–62.

13 Knoppers 2001: 122–3.

14 Giving such emphasis to the person of Ezra is characteristic of later rabbinic literature.

taken to Judea by Ezra. Though today this view is not supported by consensus, the majority of scholars still date the origin of the Pentatheucus to the Persian period, some also accepting the identity of Ezra's law and the Pentatheucus.[15] By contrast, according to Morton Smith, Ezra's law disappeared from history together with the person.[16] Despite these disputes the majority of scholars think that the Pentatheucus was already known in its present form by the end of the Persian period (early fourth century BCE);[17] moreover, David Freedman is of the view that we have to deal with a textual tradition already closed down before the age of Ezra.[18]

According to the order of Artaxerxes Ezra had the right to appoint judges and elders who knew the law and were entitled to decide on cases of litigation (7 Ezra 25). This comes as a surprise since Ezra was not the satrap of the province. According to Lisbeth Fried, however, this is precisely what reveals the core of Ezra's mission: as a special agent of the king he was entitled to appoint judges independently of the satrap. As the royal officials were not directly appointed by the Persian ruler but through his representatives, no extraordinary authorization can be seen in Ezra's commission. Moreover, since the Persian king did not delegate the appointment of local officials to the satrap, he exercised control over these governors constantly striving for autonomy. Thus Ezra's mission was the following: to appoint royal judges, Persians by birth, in the province as royal agents who were not responsible to him but to the governors and the Persian king.[19]

Lester Grabbe, however, does not accept anything of this theory because he holds that it is practically unimaginable that Ezra could appoint judges or assert the law while ignoring the provincial satrap. According to Grabbe Ezra's most important mission was to teach the law; but even in this respect he was not a unique figure, only one among those who had accepted and taught the law. Had it been otherwise it would be impossible to understand why so many traditions had forgotten about Ezra's person. On the other hand he accepts that the 'laws of Moses' were crystallized in their present form by the end of the Persian period due to the activities of Ezra and similar personalities.[20]

Establishing the 'laws of Moses', however, did not stop legal pluralism, and different attitudes to law prevailed. We can witness during the Second Temple period various interpretations of law which resulted later in 'legal schools'. It was this period when the Pharisees and the Sadducees, with their different attitudes to law, emerged. This was also this period when we can witness the separation of the

---

15 Blenkinsopp 2001: 56–62. According to Blenkinsopp the various social groups may have had different legal compilations, consequently the simple identification of the two bodies of law cannot be accepted (59).

16 Smith 1971: 125.

17 Grabbe 2001: 100, 111; Piattelli–Jackson 1996: 25.

18 Freedman 1990: 317.

19 Fried 2001: 84.

20 Grabbe 2001: 112–13.

Qumran community and the activities of John the Baptist and Jesus. Law and its interpretation were of basic importance for all these groups and persons. While everyone acknowledged the Pentatheucus, the Sadducees adhered exclusively to the laws of Moses and rejected everything that was not itemized in those books. This assumed attitude of the Sadducees would later on lead to a conflict with the Pharisees (we will return to this issue later). The Qumran community had its own legal norms (see, among others, the texts of the Damascus Covenant, the Temple Scroll, Community Rule and the War Scroll), which were also based on the laws of Moses. John the Baptist had to die because he warned even the ruler to respect the law (Mark 6.14–29), and the Pharisees constantly put questions to Jesus which were in the foreground of contemporary legal discourse (what kind of work can be done on *Shabbāt*, the obligation to wash hands before eating, giving wages to labourers etc.). The *Sanhedrīn* was formed in the Second Temple period, too. *Sanhedrīn* is a name of Greek origin designating a court situated in Jerusalem as the supreme forum of the administration of justice. The *Sanhedrīn* dealt with cases of importance and sometimes politics was also involved (details will be discussed in Chapter 3 on Jewish procedural law).

The Pharisees are believed to be a politico-religious group emerging after the Hasmonean Revolt. Their name – originating from the root 'p-r-sh', meaning 'to separate' – is meant to indicate the separate standing of that group. They believed in corporal resurrection and divine providence, both rejected by the Sadduceans representing priestly circles. The Pharisees attributed outstanding significance to issues of ritual purity and stressed the importance of teaching, particularly the teaching of law. According to the Pharisees Moses was also given an oral customary law, while the Sadduceans rejecting the customary law of the Pharisees denied that God had revealed anything else besides the written law.[21] According to Josephus Flavius the Pharisees were filled with pride because of their knowledge of the law, pretended to be the favourites of the Lord, resisted political authorities and were also ready to fight against them.[22]

The Pharisees were thought to be members of a highly influential political group for decades, but now this well-known thesis is subject to debate. According to Ellis Rivkin the term '*p^e^rūshīm*' does not refer to the Pharisees in many cases but to ascetics and other 'isolationists', therefore data pertaining to the Pharisees should be reconsidered.[23] E. P. Sanders claims that the Pharisees were dominant during the short reign of Salome Alexandra (76–67 BCE) but not under Herod (37–34) and the Roman occupation.[24] Jacob Neusner applied a different method: he tried to explore the peculiarities of the Pharisees on the basis of well-known traditions referring to the Pharisees. He summarized his results in a three-volume work in which he sees the Pharisees as a '*pure food club*' to whom the most

21 Piattelli–Jackson 1996: 44.

22 Josephus XVII: 38–42.

23 Referred to in Sanders 1990: 152–4, agreeing with him.

24 Sanders 1990: 101.

important question was ritual purity and particularly eating daily food according to the norms of priestly purity. In his view this group was transformed into a 'table society' by Hillel.[25] In other words, in contrast with accepted wisdom, the Pharisees did not constitute a politically influential group holding positions of religious or public authority. Sanders agrees with Neusner insofar that the old wisdom according to which the Pharisees were the most important political group of this period should be discarded; at the same time he believes that one should not see an isolated and withdrawn group in them, the truth being somewhere in between.[26]

The Sadduceans (*Ṣedūqīm*), whose name originated presumably from the high priest Ñādoq, were members of an influential aristocratic group consisting mainly of priests and merchants. Their theological and legal teaching was at variance with the doctrines of the Pharisees. They denied corporal resurrection, the immortality of the soul and the existence of angels. Since they did not accept anything outside the Torāh, they did not acknowledge the validity of the oral law of the Pharisees either. The Sadduceans dominated the *Sanhedrīn* for a long time, since its head was the high priest, also a Sadducean. As they were primarily linked to the temple they were not only stressing the importance of prayer and learning, but also attributing a more significant role to cult than the Pharisees did. This unpopular group cultivated good relations with the Roman political elite, and was also an advocate of harsher measures against the Christians.[27]

The interpretation of the law by the Sadduceans was believed for a long time as narrow and rigid, insisting on the literal meaning. David Daube, however, has convincingly demonstrated that this accepted wisdom should be challenged. He argued that since our sources about the Sadduceans were produced by Pharisee-rabbinic authors, they could be misleading. The fact, he continues, that the Sadduceans did not accept the doctrine of the Pharisees about oral law does not necessarily mean that they insisted on the literal meaning of texts. By contrast, the Sadduceans insisted on the rules set by the text, and it was the Pharisees who diverted from the text by innovations. Thus, it was not the Sadduceans who had interpreted the law narrow-mindedly but the Pharisees who diverted from written law, and to a significant extent in many cases. That the legal interpretation of the Sadduceans was not literal is proved by the fact that they were ready to interpret legal rulings broadly, even to their own detriment. An example of this thesis offered by Daube is the biblical rule pertaining to the responsibility of the owner of animals which was interpreted by the Sadduceans as a rule to be applied to damage caused by slaves as well. This interpretation is not only extensive

25 Neusner 1971: III: 305.

26 Sanders would rather replace the term 'food club' introduced by Neusner with 'purity club' as he suggests that the significance of food rules merged into stressing the rules of purity as a framework of a more general approach: Sanders 1990: 242–5.

27 Sadducees in *Encyclopedia Judaica*: 14, Keter Publishing House, Jerusalem, 620–22 (Menachem Mansoor).

but is also clearly detrimental to the interest of the Sadduceans because, as rich merchants, they had the largest number of slaves. Yet they were capable of making themselves independent of group interest when interpreting the law.[28]

Sanders continues the line set by Daube and draws the conclusion that the statement of the Sadduceans according to which they did not accept any rule outside the Bible was of a rhetorical nature because they did in fact accept traditions without textual foundation. These traditions emerged for centuries during the Persian and the Second Temple periods and everybody accepted them, irrespective of their relationship to the Bible. An example of this is the calendar accepted by both the Pharisees and the Sadduceans which was not based on the Bible. If it were true that the Sadduceans did not accept anything else but the rulings of the Bible then they could not have agreed with the Pharisees on this issue, which they did. Those who disagreed, the members of the Qumran community, did have a separate calendar. Thus Sanders came to the conclusion that the Pharisees acknowledged having extra-biblical traditions, whereas the Sadduceans did not.[29]

Although different in interpretations and in details of law, the Pharisees and the Sadducees respected each other's stand. There is no trace to qualify each other as ritually impure although they observed different norms. Neither the Sadducean high priest nor the sacrifice offered by him was declared impure and invalid by the Pharisees. Surely there were minor skirmishes. There is a narrative telling us that a leader of the Pharisees, Yōḥanān ben Zakk'ay, slit an ear of the Sadducean high priest just preparing for the sacrifice, trying to hinder him by this act in offering the sacrifice by making him impure (Yōḥanān's deed also shows that the high priest was to be considered ritually pure without this act).[30] This was not the rule but the exception since disputes were restricted to intellectual debates, the place of which was the *Sanhedrīn*. The day when a fully Pharisaic *Sanhedrīn* emerged is celebrated as a special occasion by the rabbinic tradition.[31]

The *Sanhedrīn* was in fact the forum of debates. Not only legal, but religious, political and practical considerations also came to the fore in its sessions. This could be seen in legal actions taken against Christians: while the Sadduceans proposed rigorous punishment of the Apostles, Gamalī'el (the elder), a respected leader of the Pharisees, convinced the members of the court to refrain from bloodshed. As a result of his arguments Peter and his followers were released after having been flogged.[32] As David Daube put it, it is unlikely that Gamalī'el was influenced by sympathy towards Christians since it was under the leadership of his grandson, Rabban Gamalī'el, head of the Academy of Yabneh, that the condemnation of Christians and other heretics was included among the daily Eighteen Benedictions.

28 Daube 1960: 182–9.

29 Sanders 1990: 103–7.

30 Daube 1960a: 431.

31 Daube 1960: 187

32 Acts 5.17–42.

Gamalī'el was primarily terrified by the irreversibility of capital punishment.[33] His view is in harmony with the effort of the Rabbis to limit acts calling for punishment and to humanize punishment. This attitude is best expressed by a saying attributed to Rabbi ᶜAqībah and Rabbi Ṭarfōn (second century): 'Were we members of a Sanhedrīn no person would even be put to death.'[34]

Leading Pharisean legal scholars of this period were called 'pairs' (*zugōt*) by the rabbinic tradition, and played a central role in transmitting their legal tradition. According to rabbinic teaching oral law reached Shimᶜeōn and Anṭīgonus through Moses, Yosiah, the elders and the Prophets; and from that time on the pairs mediated legal tradition to the Pharisees and Rabbis. Thus it is the continuity of tradition which attributes outstanding significance to the pairs. The two persons at the end of the chain of five pairs (Yōsē b. Yoezer-Yōsē b. Yōḥanān; Yoshuᶜa b. Perahiah-Nitt'ay; Yūdah b. Tabbay-Shimᶜeōn b. Shetaḥ; Shemᶜaīah-'Abtalīōn; Hillel-Shamm'ay),[35] Hillel and Shamm'ay, are said to be the founders of two legal schools named after them. Thus, at this juncture the unity of Pharisaic legal tradition ended (if there was unity at all previously) and legal development was determined primarily by the scholarly debates between these two camps.

Barely a few of the personal disputes of the two founder scholars were preserved, but their followers are believed to dispute about 350 legal problems concerning details of positive law. These disputes can be dated to the period between the destruction of the temple and the Yabneh period. As the leaders of the Yabneh Academy were the followers of Hillel the corpus of the positive rules of law, accepted only later, contains in huge numbers the doctrines of this school. Because of tolerated legal pluralism, however, the doctrines of both schools were accepted and regarded as valid during the first centuries CE. As they believed, both were the voice of the living God; but today it is impossible to tell what the differences between the schools were.[36] The view that Hillel's school was more lenient while the school of Shamm'ay interpreted the law rigorously was already widespread as early as the age of the *tannaim*, but this is only an oversimplification of the matter. Some scholars assumed that there were social differences between the schools. Thus, while the followers of Shamm'ay may have been representative of the upper and richer middle classes, followers of Hillel came rather from the lower social strata. This and similar other generalizations do not explain the essence of the doctrines of the schools. At any rate, these disputes, no matter how they had been pitched, were limited to the field of law: the schools acknowledged

---

33 Daube 1971: 40.

34 The saying is quoted in Kirschenbaum 1991: 141.

35 The full list of the chain of handing down tradition, consisting of 40 generations and starting from Moses, is given by the introduction of the Mishneh Torāh of Maimonides (Maimonides 1981a: 3a).

36 The later rabbinic tradition makes the unmerited disciples of the two masters responsible for the extensive spread of disputes which resulted in the emergence of disagreement in Israel: Tos Sanh 7:1; T Sanh 88b.

each other as equals, which is indicated by a relatively high number of marriages between families of these schools.[37]

The period of the *tannaim* (*tanna* means 'reciter of the law') brought about political chaos and decades of sufferings, yet legal development could be witnessed even during these harsh circumstances. The destruction of the temple did not terminate legal discourse, yet at the same time the disappearance of the Sadduceans practically opened up the way towards the hegemony of the Pharisaic legal tradition. The survival of the *Sanhedrīn* and the emergence of new scholarly centres called Academies ensured institutional background to this.

Usually the expressions *bēt midrāsh* or *bēt talmud* were used to indicate institutions translated as Academies; the currently widespread *yeshībah* is only a latecomer. These Academies were established for teaching the next generations and were open to boys above the age of 13 who wanted to acquire a more profound knowledge of Jewish tradition and law. The schools of Hillel and Shamm'ay, lacking any institutional structure, could not be regarded as such Academies; they existed only on the level of a master–disciple relationship. The only exception could be the Academy at the seat of the *nāśī*, for it was in direct contact with the judiciary (*yeshībah* originally meant law court and it was the contact of the Academy with the law court which made the alteration of the meaning of this term possible). Yabneh and Usha – later on Caesarea, Sepphoris and Tiberias – became homes of the Academies, of which it was the *bēt midrāsh* of Tiberias that functioned up to the Islamic period.[38] In the period of the *tannaim* a new leader of the Pharisaic community, the *nāśī*, emerged, who headed the *Sanhedrīn* and was a political leader at the same time.

The period of the *tannaim* was hallmarked by outstanding scholars such as Rabban Gamalī'el, Yōḥanān ben Zakk'ay, R. 'Elīᶜezer ben Hyrcanus (who was ultimately excommunicated for his doctrines), R. ᶜAqībah (participating personally in the Bar Kokba' revolt and cruelly executed by the Romans) and Rabbi Yūdah (also acting as *nāśī*). These and other legal scholars perfected the inherited legal tradition by interpreting the existing norms and by formulating new legal doctrines. Undoubtedly Rabbi Yūdah ha-Nāśī was the most famous scholar among his colleagues and was referred to as *the* Rabbi. As the compiler of the Mishnah he left an indelible imprint on the history of Jewish law. His personal achievement is not overshadowed even by the finding of modern scholarship which does not regard the Mishnah as his personal work, but the result of a group of legal scholars headed by R. Yūdah. This assumption also explains why a stylistic mark of a single person cannot be identified in the Mishnah.[39]

---

37 Bet Hillel and Bet Shammai in *Encyclopedia Judaica*: 4B, 737–40 (Shmuel Safrai).

38 Stemberger 1996: 8–10.

39 Stemberger 1996: 138.

The Mishnah (from the Hebrew verb *shanah* – 'to repeat, to teach') is defined as a compilation of oral customary law discussing legal material by subject.[40] The work is arranged in six orders (*sedarīm*), which are comprised of tractates (*masektōt*). The individual orders are about a comprehensive area of law, while the tractates deal with issues of detail concerning them. Needless to say, these legal areas have nothing to do with modern concepts of the branches of law, as becomes clear by the following survey of the orders:

1. *Zerāīm* (seeds): rules related to agriculture;
2. *Mōᶜēd* (festivals): rules related to religious festivals;
3. *Nashīm* (women): rules related to family law;
4. *Nezikīn* (damages): rules of private law and procedure;
5. *Qodashīm* (sacred things): temple rules;
6. *Tohorōt* (purities): rules of purification.

This classification does not show the original arrangement, because it was subsequently rearranged in keeping with the demands of the scholars of later ages.[41]

The aim and subject of the Mishnah is subject to debate in modern scholarship. It was taken for granted for a long time that there was an unbroken continuity between the Pharisaic and rabbinic traditions. It was Jacob Neusner who challenged this view and who has shown that the continuity between the Pharisee and rabbinic (legal) tradition is not so obvious. In his view the Mishnah can be traced back to the Yabneh Academy. Its legal material was developed by the works of subsequent generations of legal scholars during the period of the *tannaim*. It was the disciples of R. ᶜAqībah who played the most important role in this development and only the canonization of the final texts is linked to the name of R. Yūdah. In a later work he goes even further and sees in the Mishnah the metaphysical worldview of a social group which expressed its own values in a coded language, but this theory met with refusal.[42]

Stemberger also argues for a late emergence of the Mishnahic material since the earliest legal scholar quoted in it lived in the first century, whereas other tractates reflect a time after the destruction of the Temple. In addition he also warns that it is impossible to date the entire work, but the various tractates should be studied separately instead if the interpolations are also considered.[43] Next to the

---

40 The aim of the Mishnah is disputed. According to Albeck the work is a compilation of academic interest, an eclectic collection containing legal material known by its compiler. Goldberg sees educational material in it which does not reflect the legal practice of the age. In contrast to these opinions, Epstein expressly sees a code in the text which contains the actual legal practice. The debate is analysed in detail in Stemberger 1996: 133–9.

41 Stemberger 1996: 121.

42 For more on this subject see Sanders 1990: 309–31.

43 Stemberger 1996: 128–9.

Mishnah the Tōsefta', another important work of the rabbinic legal tradition, soon appeared. The Tōsefta' is a subsidiary work compared to the Mishnah because it supplements and comments on the rules contained in the Mishnah. The subsidiary nature of the Tōsefta' is also shown by its arrangement because it corresponds to the structure of the Mishnah.[44]

The development beginning with the recording of the Mishnah and continued by the compilation of the Tōsefta' reached its climax with the birth of the Talmūd. The Talmūd (teaching) is a repository of issues, polemics and doctrines emerging during the learning and study of the Mishnah, hence it is usually characterized as a commentary on the Mishnah.

The compilation of the two Talmūdīm (the Palestinian and the Babylonian) reflects the changes which had taken place in Jewish history in late Antiquity. After the third century CE, the supremacy of the Palestinian centres was challenged by scholars living in Mesopotamia. According to ga'ōnic traditions the first Babylonian Academies emerged in the third century: the Sura Academy was founded by Rab, a younger contemporary of R. Yūdah, while the Academy of Nahardea was founded by Mār Shamū'el. After the destruction of the Academy of Nahardea the Academy of Pumbedita replaced it in the middle of the third century. In the beginning the Babylonian Academies were barely more than a network of some prominent masters and disciples gathering around them, although later sources project realities of their own times back to earlier centuries.[45]

Presumably the Jerusalem or Palestinian Talmūd (PT) was compiled in the fourth or fifth century, most probably in Tiberias. The innumerable repetitions and self-contradictions led some researchers to see in it only a collection of materials loosely put together, lacking any editorial work. According to the majority of scholars certain editorial work could not be denied, but surely not in the modern sense of the term.[46]

The Babylonian Talmūd (BT) raises similar problems. Since there are linguistic differences in the text, the BT is surely a compilation of materials originating from various geographic areas, produced in different historical periods. Some scholars believe that the linguistic differences could be explained by geographical differences (part of the material was produced in Sura and texts from Pumbedita were added to it). Others believe that the BT reached its final form over a long period and it is the outcome of continuous editing and interpolation. As a result, part of a text reflecting a different state of the language is the product of another historical period. Leaving behind these problems it is certain that the BT is more than a commentary on the Mishnah – rather a kind of an encyclopaedic work: in addition to legal arguments it also contains the legendary biography of Rabbis, anecdotes and legends, and mathematical, biological and astronomical

44 For details see Stemberger 1996: 151–8.

45 Goodblatt 1975: 267–72; Stemberger 1996: 11.

46 Stemberger 1996: 164–86 discusses the problem at length.

observations. Consequently it is larger in scale than the PT and due to these features significantly precedes it in popularity and importance.[47]

Coming to the judiciary, in Palestine it was the right of the *nāśī* to appoint judges – this being part of the more and more restricted legal autonomy ensured for the Jews by the Romans. In Babylonia the *rēsh galūta'*, the Mesopotamian leader of the Jews, had similar prerogatives both in Parthian (250 BCE–226 CE) and Sasanian (226–651) times. If he was also a legal scholar he exercised a presidential function in his own court.[48] Both in Palestine and Babylonia a twofold judicial organization can be observed: the political leader and the judges appointed by him can be regarded as official forums of the administration of justice, while the authority of the Academies of legal scholars was primarily ensured by the social prestige of their members. It is repeatedly stressed in rabbinic literature that the parties should turn to Jewish law courts and avoid the courts of foreigners – that is, the Roman or Persian law courts – in order to secure the continuity of Jewish legal tradition. This, however, occasionally demanded serious self-restraint from the parties, particularly if they or one of the parties enjoyed a more advantageous position in foreign law than in the Jewish court (for instance, for a female litigant Roman law was more advantageous than Jewish law ensuring a more rigorous patriarchal order).[49] A similar problem would emerge later on with respect to the Muslim judicial authorities.

While the legal status of Jews living in Sasanian Persia did not change significantly, the legal autonomy of those living in the Roman Empire was continuously narrowing. From the fourth century only religious issues were left within the competency of the Jewish courts, criminal and civil law being the privilege of the Roman courts. At the same time the parties could continue to turn to the law courts of the Academies as arbitrators.[50]

The Talmudic period was followed by the period of the *saboraīm* and the *ge'ōnīm*. In the period of the *saboraīm* the final redaction of the Talmūd was still in progress; therefore the final redactors of the Talmūd should be sought among the *saboraīm*. After the Muslim conquest of ᶜIrāq Jews living there became subjects of their new Muslim masters. Independently from this global change in politics an internal transformation also took place by which the Babylonian Academies lost their pre-eminence in Jewish scholarly life. For some time the Babylonian Academies remained the intellectual centres for Jews living as far away as Europe and Hispania. This is proven by the fact that emissaries were sent from great distances to Babylon in order to learn their scholarly opinion about legal cases the community or the parties were divided on. Consequently, judges of those distant regions did not participate in scholarly activity the same way judges had

47 The disputes about the origin of the BT are summarized by Stemberger 1996: 191–7.

48 Lifshitz 1996: 170–74.

49 Lifshitz 1996: 171.

50 Rabello 1996: 153–4.

up to the period of the Talmūd in Babylonia. On the other hand, as it could not be kept up for long that everyone turned continually to the Babylonian Academies for help, soon local intellectual and scholarly centres emerged. The decline of the Babylonian Academies can be traced back to the advent of local centres of learning which became successful in the long run, particularly in territories which are nowadays Spain, France and Germany. As a result, local judges could learn law and continue their studies in their own places of residence and were no longer 'Babylon-dependent'.

Zoroastrian Law

Persian law is not identical to Zoroastrian law, although there is obviously a strong correlation between the two. Persian customary law preceded Zoroastrian law for centuries and it was this legal tradition which was transformed into a legal system dominated by Zoroastrian ethics, ritual and legal concepts.

At the beginning of the Achaemenid period (sixth to fourth centuries BCE), Persian customary law existed as a custom of the Persian tribes proven by Herodotus, who recalls some aspects of Persian customs he found interesting.[51] This corpus of law remained the custom of the Persians, who did not attempt to enlarge its scale to the entire empire, securing limited legal autonomy to the conquered people. Some researchers (e.g. Olmstead)[52] believed that Darius I had made a law book along the lines of Hammurabi's Code, although not a single line of this assumed code has survived. Since the Persians ensured legal and religious autonomy for subjected people the emergence of a unified imperial law seems unlikely.[53]

Herodotus informs us about Persian customs very briefly. According to him judges were appointed and dismissed by the king from among the men who were well versed in Persian law. We also learn from him that they hold their office for life, or until they were found guilty of some misconduct. All disputes were decided by their ruling and at the same time they were the interpreters of the old laws, too.[54] There is no mention of priestly judiciary, temple courts or priestly legal interpretation. The Persian legal system was, therefore, secular both in the composition of the court and the law enforced by it.

Persian judiciary was, however, not independent but subject to the king's political and personal influence, proven by a short report of Herodotus telling of

51 Herodotus: Book I, 131–40.

52 Olmstead 1948: 119–35.

53 Dandamaev–Lukonin 1989: 118–30. Blenkinsopp 2001: 46 also thinks that the Achaemenids only interfered in the life of a province if it was necessary. Fried's book, however, means a serious challenge for representatives of this widespread view (Fried 2004: 233).

54 Herodotus: Book III, 31.

the alleged crime of the young Cambyses. According to this the young king fell in love with his own sister and wanted to marry her. For this reason he called the royal judges and asked them if there was any law permitting this marriage. The judges – who did not want to contradict the ruler and risk their office and life – answered that although there was no rule establishing the right of a brother to marry his sister, the king could do whatever he wished.[55] Irrespective of its historical credibility, this brief story shows the personal dependency of the royal judges on the ruler.

Since according to Persian understanding (and Zoroastrian ethics) to tell the truth was an ethical imperative of utmost importance, judges were expected to decide fairly and impartially. Perhaps this requirement led to the widespread public belief already in Antiquity that the skin of a judge condemned for unjust judgment was peeled off and his successor in office was made to sit on a chair made of that skin. The existence of this custom was refuted by the fourth-century historian Ammianus Marcellinus,[56] yet at the same time he stressed that only experienced and honest people who did not have to rely on the advice of others were appointed as judges.[57]

The accession of the Sasanians to power (224 CE) altered the structure and ideology of the Iranian state fundamentally. Since Ardakhshēr (224–240) acceded to power by open revolt, defeating the last Parthian king in the battle of Hormizdagan, the legitimacy of his rule was based on shaky foundations. Since his reference to Sāsān – a mythical ancestor related to the Achaemenids – did not ensure sufficient legitimacy for the new dynasty, they were in need of ideological support, which was presented by the Zoroastrian priesthood.[58]

Tansar and Kardēr, two powerful high priests of the third century, contributed considerably to the consolidation of Sasanian power, yet at the same time organized the Zoroastrian Church into a hierarchical system never experienced before.[59] High priest Kardēr's extraordinary power is indicated by the fact that he was the only person outside the royal dynasty who could have made his own inscription near the rock edicts of the rulers.

Though Shābuhr I continued the liberal policy of the Achaemenids and supported other religions too (Mani), as Zoroastrianism became the official religion of the Sasanian state, religious tolerance disappeared more and more under his successors to the throne. As a result, law, legal theory and the judiciary were reformed and transferred to the Zoroastrian Church. Persian law, formerly

55 Herodotus: Book III, 31.

56 Marcellinus: Book XXIII, 6:82.

57 Ibid.

58 Several traditions survive in later historical and literary works about the relations between Sāsān and Ardakhshēr, all of them knowing about a different degree of relationship; but all versions contradict the law of the day. See Jany 2001.

59 The transformation of the relationship between the state and religion is discussed in detail by Gnoli 1989: 129–83.

interpreted by secular persons of learning, became the domain of a new elite – scholars and leaders of the Zoroastrian Church. As a result, state and Church were increasingly intertwined – as expressed by a famous saying according to which state and religion were twins born from the same womb, never to be separated.[60]

The Zoroastrian Church, as such, was the result of developments of Sasanian history since no such entity existed previously. The new Church was shaped into a hierarchical organization, its structure being adjusted to that of the state: upon the analogy of the great king (*shāhan shāh*) there was the *mōbedān mōbed* heading the Zoroastrian priesthood and being ex officio the legal advisor to the ruler. As there were provinces and provincial governors, provincial *mōbed*s also emerged. Besides the *mōbed*s, *rad*s and ērbeds were also important dignitaries of the Zoroastrian Church. The judiciary was in the hands of the *mōbed*s and the *rad*s, whereas the ērbeds were charged with educating young priests.[61]

Since sources reveal little about the structure of the judiciary, details are unknown. It seems probable that the priesthood exercised judicial power not exclusively, because there is sporadic information also about royal judges.[62] As a result competencies were confused and the struggle for authority begun. Stronger rulers (such as Khosraw I) tried to get rid of the influence of the clergy and nobility, who by turn did not refrain from dethroning and jailing some kings of lesser authority (like Hormizd, son of Khosraw I).[63] In addition to rivalry there are also examples of political cooperation when political and social events violated the interests of both the priesthood and the monarch. Such an event was undoubtedly the appearance and spread of Christianity in Iran, which violated the interests of the Zoroastrian Church and of the state built on Zoroastrian ideology which waged numerous wars against the Romans. As a consequence the priesthood happily assisted the king in procedures against Christians driven by both political considerations and religious fanaticism (for details see the chapter on criminal procedure).

In the second part of the Sasanian period legal schools emerged as a result of legal debates, mostly in the field of ritual law. The schools of Abarag and

---

60 The most concise wording of this theory is preserved in the Letter of Tansar: '*Dīn ū mulk har dō beyek shekam zādand dūside, hargez az yekdigar jodā neshawand.*' Ibn Isfandiyār 1942: 17 – 'For Church and State were born of the one womb, joined together and never to be sundered.' Boyce 1968: 33–4. It is worth mentioning that centuries later al-Ghazālī, one of the greatest scholars of classical Islam of Iranian origin, repeats it almost word for word, applying it to the Islamic Caliphate: '*Dīn u pādshāhī čūn dō barādar-and az yek shekam-e mādar āmade*': al-Ghazālī: 1351: 106: 'Religion and kingdom are two brothers originating from the same womb.'

61 Both the Syriac Acts of Martyrs and Shāyast-nē-shāyast proves the judicial authority of *mōbed*s and *rad*s.

62 The compiler of the Mādigān ī Hazār Dādestān (MHD+A), Farrokhmard ī Wahrāmān, seems to be such a lay judge: see Macuch 1993: 12.

63 Nöldeke 1879: 264–75.

Mēdōmāh resembled their early counterparts in Jewish legal history since they are to be understood rather as a master–disciple relationship lacking any institutional structure. In these debates between the schools and their individual members, basic legal institutions and religious–legal values were not subject to discussion; but hair-splitting methods were applied to resolve issues of minor importance, some of them being raised only in hypothetical cases. Since some of the persons belonging to these schools are also known as commentators on the Awesta (provided these names refer to the same persons), leading intellectuals of the learned priesthood participated in the interpretation of Zoroastrian law because of their religious authority and mastery in law and ritual. By contrast, at the present stage of knowledge we cannot determine whether judges were members of these schools or not.[64]

As a result of a more complex legal life, both in theory and practice, it is possible to witness legal literature emerging at the end of the Sasanian period. The Mādigān ī Hazār Dādestān (The Book of a Thousand Judgements, MHD+A) already mentioned in the Introduction is a compilation of difficult cases the compiler had excess to, whether through his personal experience, by using archives or both. This work, compiled in the first part of the seventh century, confronts the researcher with innumerable philological and interpretational difficulties, yet is of utmost importance as the only source which allows some insight into contemporary legal practice. To discuss legal problems on a case-to-case basis is not the sole terrain of the MHD+A; other works written presumably at the same time also apply this method. Casuistic works discussing some issues of detail of ritual and law in a somewhat boring manner are Shāyast-nē-shāyast,[65] Nērangestān and Ērbedestān.[66]

After the fall of the Sasanians Zoroastrian law was no longer the law of the Iranian state but was transformed into regulations of the Zoroastrian community, still existing but losing more and more followers to Islam. Therefore, social functions of law altered drastically, focusing on preserving and upholding legal traditions. Days of superiority being over, the former refinement of legal tradition became forgotten; the legal schools disappeared together with their scholarly legal disputes and the magistrates of the Zoroastrian Church. It was a new priestly leader of the community, the *dastūr* who, as a priest, was charged with leading the religious life of the community and preserving the basic institutions of Zoroastrian legal tradition. Being a learned man also in law, members of the community turned to him for legal advice pertaining to their daily life. Typical questions and answers given to them were subsequently collected and put in writing. This is how the *riwāyat*s, a new legal genre in the Zoroastrian Pehlevi literature, came into being during the ninth and tenth centuries. The Riwāyat-i Ēmēd-i Ashawahishtān (REA)

64 Concerning the emergence of the schools and their methods see Jany 2006: 295–311.

65 Text editions: Tavadia 1930 and Kotwal 1969.

66 Text editions: Kotwal–Kreyenbroek 1992, 1995, 2003; and Humbach–Elfenbein 1990.

of the high priest Ēmēd and the *riwāyat* accompanying the Dādestān ī Dēnīg (PRDd) became the most important of them.[67]

Islamic Law

Islamic law – as a new legal system – was established, elaborated and refined by subsequent generations of legal scholars in the formative period, that is, the first three centuries AH. Since according to classical Islamic legal theory neither the Caliph nor any other political authority has the right to make law, only scholars of law were entitled to formulate legal doctrines and interpret existing norms.

The first generations of scholars and Muslim intellectuals did not have too much material at their disposal to build upon. Previous customs of the pre-Islamic era were known to all but these were at some points at variance with the ethical principles of the new religion. Legal rules established in the Qur'ān regulate family matters and some problems of inheritance on a rather case-to-case basis, but are far from being a complete guide for everyday legal life. Thus further rules were needed if the first generation of Muslims were not content with the modification of existing customs but wanted to establish a new legal system.

The first Caliphs supplemented commonly known norms in some cases. In so doing they invested themselves with legislative authority which they did not possess according to later classical theories. An example is the Qur'ānic prohibition of drinking wine, for which no legal sanction was specified in the text (2.219; 5.90). This was made *lex perfecta* when the punishment was established first by Abū Bakr at 40 strokes, which was increased to 80 by ᶜUmar and ᶜAlī – arguing that this was analogous to the false accusation of adultery, which was punishable by 80 strokes.[68]

It was the administration of justice which was among the most important functions of the early Caliphs. Historical reports clearly show that the early Caliphs decided personally about questions and complaints presented to them. It was family law and the law of inheritance which caused them a lot of headache because Qur'ānic law brought basic changes in these fields compared to previous customs.[69] Precedents known as the Minbariyya and Ḥimāriyya case show the uncertainties of the early Caliphs in complicated legal cases.[70]

Soon, however, the Caliphs appointed the first *qāḍīs* to share the burden of legal administration. Already the Prophet appointed some of his most faithful followers to judge in disputed cases in his place. He sent, among others, one of his companions, Muᶜādh b. Jabal, to Yemen and authorized him, according to tradition, to decide on the basis of the Qur'ān, prophetic tradition and his personal

67 Text editions: Safa–Isfehani 1980 and Williams 1990.

68 Hallaq 1997: 8.

69 Powers 1986: 209–16.

70 The outline of the cases is given in Coulson 1964: 24–5.

opinion.[71] Though this is obviously the result of a later interpolation, the case nevertheless documents the early practice of appointment.

The appointment of the first judges was the result of successful military conquests and the need to administer new territories which had little to do with the religious law of Islam. At the beginning local judges dealt with the problems of the Arab-Muslim troops stationed in the conquered territories (e.g. Egypt), while local cases remained within the competencies of the Egyptian authorities left in office. Slowly, as the establishment of the Caliph's local governance brought along a new public and legal administration, the competencies of the judges were increased from military issues to the legal administration of everyday life, too. In doing so the judges began also to consider local customs in their judgments.[72] Some elements of these legal customs were incorporated into the prophetic traditions later on.[73]

At the beginning judges were not independent but subordinated officials of the local governors. As their office slowly became independent of the military and the governor's authority their respect and self-confidence grew. They were more and more unwilling to accept their replacement from one office to another by governors (for instance it was not an exception to place a formerly appointed judge in a scribe's job). At the same time they expanded their competency to areas previously excluded from their power (among others to supervise the *waqf*s) on their own initiative. In the second part of the Umayyad period the judges were no longer subordinated military and administrative officials, but members of the elite, learned in law and dedicating their lives to the religious teaching of Islam.[74]

A letter of disputed authenticity but attributed to Caliph ᶜUmar shows what values were expected of judges. This letter – formally addressed to a judge in ᶜIrāq, Abū Mūsā al-Ashᶜarī (who was in reality a governor) – contains admonitions of proper behaviour which highlight partly pre-Islamic customs, partly new expectations. Accordingly:

1. The administration of justice is a tradition existing for long (*sunna*).
2. Impartiality is compulsory in the case of noblemen (*sharīf*) as well.
3. The plaintiff bears the burden of proof.
4. An agreement can be concluded any time save, what is legal became prohibited and what is prohibited became legal.
5. If the issue is not clear one should rather strive to achieve the agreement of the parties.
6. A judgment may be based also on the judge's opinion if sources are missing.
7. Special attention should be paid to foreigners so that their case could be settled as soon as possible, before they went home.

---

71 Hallaq 1997: 106.

72 Simonsen 1995: 78–9.

73 Hallaq 1997: 13.

74 Coulson 1964: 29–35.

Since Abū Mūsā al-Ashᶜarī was a member of an eminent dynasty serving as *amīr* and ᶜāmil in various regions of ᶜIrāq, it shows that not only judges but also provincial governors were among the administrators of justice in the early period.[75]

What role judges and governors played in legal development in the first century is subject to debate in modern scholarship. According to Schacht, the contribution of governors and judges was of primary importance. In his view, the social customs of the Umayyad period were decisive in respect of marriage and divorce, while the administrative rules of the Caliphate covered far broader areas. Thus *zakāt* was also extended to horses in the field of finances; the blood money of Muslims and non-Muslims was stipulated by criminal law; and rules concerning escaped slaves and the principles of martial jurisdiction were also laid down. The extent of the share of soldiers in the spoils of war was determined in law pertaining to war.[76]

Coulson is of a similar view. He believes that the judges were influenced in their decisions by the customs of the territory of their operation. Cultural, social and economic differences between regions were therefore embodied in the judges' rulings. Thus, for instance, in ᶜIrāq the position of women was entirely different from their legal status in traditional Medina due to earlier Persian influence and the cosmopolitan atmosphere there. In brief, early judges, Coulson argues, supplemented legal gaps with their individual opinions and local customs, which resulted in contradictions and at times significant differences in law. Thus the different legal practice of the regions can be traced back partly to earlier customs and partly to the early discretion of judges.[77] John Burton, too, thinks that Islamic jurisprudence was formed on a regional basis.[78]

The results of Harald Motzki's research, however, offer a different explanation. According to Motzki's opinion judges and governors played a marginal role in developing Islamic law, which was elaborated by legal scholars instead. Rules formulated this way were later justified by prophetic traditions.[79] Motzki's findings are confirmed by the most recent results of Peter Hennigan, according to whom law developed on the basis of the opinion of scholars, and rules thus produced were made to be accepted later in the form of prophetic maxims and traditions.[80] In short, there is consensus among Western scholars that Islamic legal doctrines were elaborated in the first century by individuals whose doctrines were traced back to the accepted sources only later on. What is disputed is whether governors and judges or legal scholars were the dominant actors.

This now presents the problem of the legal sources of Islamic law. Obviously, as the source of primary importance the Qur'ān comes to mind, but its role in the first century is disputed in modern scholarship, too. According to Joseph Schacht

75 Serjeant 1991: 65–78.

76 Schacht 1950: 190–213.

77 Coulson 1964: 30–31.

78 Burton 1990: 17–18.

79 Motzki 2002: 295–7.

80 Hennigan 2004: 107–14, 178–86.

Islamic law only began to develop one century after the death of the Prophet, and references to the Qur'ān were only of secondary development.[81] In Schacht's theory the secondary nature of Qur'ānic law is also shown by the fact that he dedicated only four pages to the Qur'ān in his monograph on the origin of Islamic jurisprudence.[82]

His view is now challenged by a number of scholars. According to Wael B. Hallaq the implementation of the Qur'ān is not a late development in Islamic law, but began already in the age of the Prophet and continued unbroken after his death. Thus, in the earliest times the newly organized Muslim community truly relied on two sources: the Qur'ān and the customs of pre-Islamic Arabia.[83] Hallaq's opinion is supported by earlier results of Goitein.[84] Harald Motzki also argues for an early writing down of the Qur'ān and its implementation in legal life. He recalls that reference to the Qur'ān is given even in the work of such an early legal scholar as ᶜAṭā', which proves not only that the contents of the verses were known at that time, but presumably that their arrangement in suras was also completed.[85]

The emergence of prophetic tradition which later became the second source of Islamic law was also considered by Schacht a later development, to be dated to the early eighth century. The assumed narratives of sayings and deeds (*ḥadīth*) attributed to the Prophet were works of later generations aimed at canonizing and subsequently legalizing the already developed doctrines. With this view Schacht follows the opinion of the Hungarian scholar Ignác Goldziher.[86] According to Goldziher the *sunna* is the result of the development of jurisprudence, and Islamic law did not develop from the Qur'ān and the *sunna*, only individual opinions of scholars (*ra'y*) were legitimized subsequently with their help. In his view the emergence of Islamic jurisprudence can be dated to the accession to power of the ᶜAbbāsīds and its centre was ᶜIrāq, not Arabia.[87]

In contrast to the opinion of Goldziher and Schacht, who were highly critical concerning the authenticity of the *ḥadīth* Vesey–Fitzgerald considered it possible that the text (*matn*) may contain the Prophet's authentic words and deeds, notwithstanding his doubting the authenticity of the chain of transmitters (*isnād*).[88] Coulson was of a similar opinion. He believed that though the chain of transmitters could in fact be subject to criticism, nevertheless the traditions related to daily life and the explanation of Qur'ānic rules may go back to the Prophet and was preserved by oral tradition.[89] According to Nabia Abbott, however, the *ḥadīth* were

81 Schacht 1950: 224.
82 Schacht 1950: 224–7.
83 Hallaq 1997: 3–10.
84 Referred to in Hallaq 1994: 65.
85 Motzki 2002: 111, 115, 117.
86 Schacht 1950: 40–61; Schacht 1970: 542–3; Goldziher 1890: 258–81.
87 Goldziher 1927: 102.
88 Vesey–Fitzgerald 1955: 93–4.
89 Coulson 1964: 64–5.

handed down both orally and in writing right from the first years of the history of Islam, and a blossoming of this literature in the eighth and ninth centuries was not due to falsification but to a meeting of traditions that had originally spread independently of each other. Fuat Sezgin and David Powers also came to the same conclusion.[90] According to G.H.A. Juynboll the possibility cannot be excluded that some reports in fact contain what the Prophet had said or done, but now it is impossible to develop a method by which the authenticity of the traditions could be proved beyond doubt. It cannot be denied that the followers of the Prophet spoke about him and his deeds after his death, but a formalized transfer of these traditions did not begin earlier than the 670s.[91]

What scholars think about the emergence of Islamic law and their sources also determines their views concerning its later development. According to Schacht governors and judges, and later on private individuals well versed in law, incorporated administrative practice and local customs into law. Due to differences in local customs differences emerged in various local centres. As a result the first schools ('ancient schools of law') emerged in the early eighth century, having their own doctrines and methods. Thus the doctrines of the schools slowly crystallized and the 'living tradition' of the school was born. As these doctrines lacked textual foundations, the schools began to trace their teachings back to respected persons known by all. At first the 'tradition' of the Prophet's Companions emerged, to be followed later by the Prophet's tradition as an ultimate point of reference. Schacht understood the difference between schools on a geographic basis: there were the ᶜIrāqī schools (including Kūfa and Baṣra) and the schools of Medina and of Syria.[92] Parallel to this development, legal and religious specialists, as Schacht called them, acquired an increasingly central role, whereas governors and judges were squeezed out of shaping the contents of law. Consequently Islamic law began to lose its relationship with living reality and became an expression of the ideal of the above-mentioned religious elite.[93]

These early schools were transformed later into personal schools. As a result of this transformation the school of Kūfa became the Ḥanafite school; the school of Medina, merging with the school of Mecca, became the Mālikite school. This development was completed by the early ninth century.[94] Meanwhile schools of later origin like the Ḥanbalite and the Shafiᶜīte were organized as personal schools right from the beginning. At this juncture two tendencies met each other: one is the transformation of the geographic schools into personal schools; the other is to trace the doctrines of the schools back to respected persons and leaders of the early history of Islam. Since both developments can be witnessed in ᶜIrāq, the birth of

90 For these and other interpretations and their critiques see Powers 1986: 4–8.

91 Juynboll 1983: 3–10.

92 Schacht 1970: 550–56.

93 Schacht 1970: 549.

94 Schacht 1950: 7–10.

Islamic jurisprudence should also be located in ᶜIrāq and not in Arabia. Thus the earlier view of Goldziher of similar content was confirmed by Schacht.[95]

Among modern scholars it is Christopher Melchert who follows the footsteps of Schacht. While Schacht established the transformation of the schools from geographic to personal entities, Melchert also explores the reasons behind this. According to him the controversy between the *aṣḥāb al-ra'y* and the *aṣḥāb al-ḥadīth* was of importance here. The *aṣḥāb al-ra'y* were scholars who deduced their doctrines through *ra'y*, rational thinking. Originally *ra'y* (opinion, view, from the verb 'to view') was not an arbitrary opinion based on individual discretion but a well-founded claim deducted logically by rational arguments. Every scholar of the early period applied *ra'y*, albeit in various degrees. The early lawyers of Mecca such as ᶜAbd Allāh ibn al-ᶜAbbās, ᶜAṭā' ibn abī Rabāḥ and their followers made use of it just as much as those of Medina (Mālik) and of ᶜIrāq, primarily Abū Ḥanīfa. Since there were enormous gaps in the law and legal sources as known today were not yet established, governors, judges and the early representatives of the schools turned to *ra'y* – and ultimately to their own reason, sense of justice and life experience – for help when nothing else could be found to offer them guidance. Thus according to the *aṣḥāb al-ra'y*, law can also be deduced from the reasonable assessment of a person authorized to do so (judge, legal scholar) provided the result is not arbitrary but can be proved logically. The supporters of this thought attributed less significance to prophetic or other traditions.

By contrast, *aṣḥāb al-ḥadīth*, representatives of the *ḥadīth*, stressed the decisive importance of traditions. According to them law can be deducted from the prophetic tradition because the Prophet's acts and sayings do not contradict revelation, and legislative shortcomings can be supplemented by rules identified by the example of the Prophet's deeds. In this line of argument rational thinking ranks second in importance because the decisive element is the normative content of the tradition, whether it could be buttressed by logic or not. Just as representatives of *ra'y* were present in every early school, similarly traditionalists, too, could be found in every school. Therefore it is not possible to say that one school represented *ra'y* and another *ḥadīth*. Centuries later the pro-traditionalists gained the upper hand in the debate and from then on *ra'y* lost its earlier content of positive meaning and stood for arbitrary, unjustified and unfounded opinion which was neither based on textual sources nor on tradition.[96] It is the reason why – according to Melchert – the transformation of the early schools into personal schools began. Members of the ᶜIrāqī schools, but primarily that of Kūfa, favoured argumentation on *ra'y*. They increasingly became the focus of the traditionalists' attacks, who saw self-conceit and arrogance in the formation of individual opinion. In order to avoid attacks members of the school slowly gave up reference to *ra'y* and traced their teaching back to Abū Ḥanīfa, a teacher of the school. Thus, besides traditions that could be traced back to the Prophet, his Companions and followers the doctrine

95 Schacht 1950: 223.

96 Melchert 1997: 1–8; Melchert 1999: 329–31; Melchert 2001: 385–93.

of Abū Ḥanīfa was born. This was still different from prophetic tradition but was closer to the traditionalist way of thinking than to rational argumentation.[97] In his later writing Melchert argued that the doctrine going back to Abū Ḥanīfa was ultimately not born in Kūfa but in Baṣra and Baghdad, while the original legal tradition of the Kūfa school was forgotten.[98]

Schacht's theory is now subject to dispute. W. B. Hallaq formulated serious criticism concerning his thesis, pointing out the following weak points of the theory: (1) it presupposes the existence of a generally accepted ᶜIrāqī doctrine that could be later transformed into the corpus juris of Abū Ḥanīfa, but there is no trace of it; (2) if anyone wanted to trace back the teachings of the school subsequently to one person then Abū Ḥanīfa was a miscalculation because of his preference for *ra'y* and indifference towards traditions. As a result, he was perhaps one of the most unacceptable personalities for the traditionalists. Therefore, had this tracing back actually happened it would have referred to other, far more authentic persons such as al-Shaybānī. In Hallaq's view there were never regional schools, therefore it would be in vain to search for their common doctrine. These early schools lacked any doctrinal unity and cohesion, thus there was no accepted, common doctrine either. By contrast, it was always the doctrine of individual legal scholars that was quoted. In Kūfa, for instance, there lived a number of famous legal scholars – such as Ibn Abī Laylā, Abū Ḥanīfa, Abū Yūsuf, al-Shaybānī, Zufar and Sufyān al-Thawrī – yet not all of them were members of the Ḥanafite school. There were such substantial differences between Abū Ḥanīfa and Abī Laylā that the latter was not regarded as a member of the Ḥanafite school. Sufyān al-Thawrī was also outside the Ḥanafite school and later became the founder of his own school. The situation was similar in the Mālikite and Shāfiᶜīte schools. Sources talk about a certain region and its inhabitants (*ahl*) but never about the law and jurisprudence of that region. According to Hallaq, Schacht was misled by his sources which mention the inhabitants (*ahl*) but not the schools. Obviously scholars lived in ᶜIrāq, Medina or elsewhere but this provides no reason to discuss an ᶜIrāqī school. For instance, Ibn Abī Laylā, Abū Ḥanīfa, Abū Yūsuf, al-Shaybānī and Sufyān al-Thawrī spent their entire life in ᶜIrāq and therefore they are all regarded as ᶜIrāqīs; but there was no common doctrine which could be called the teaching of the ᶜIrāqī school. These scholars developed their own methods and doctrines which were not compulsory even for their disciples to follow. Thus, lacking any structure, doctrinal unity and common ground, it is not possible to speak about schools in the eighth century, only about a master–disciple relationship.[99]

Independently of Hallaq's results Nimrod Hurvitz came to the same conclusion. In his view Schacht's theory on the 'ancient schools of law' is an artificial category of historiography which has nothing to do with reality. There were no such schools; instead scholars in various centres of the Islamic world worked independently of

97 Melchert 1997: 32–47.

98 Melchert 1999: 347.

99 Hallaq 2001: 1–21.

each another, and young men, desirous of learning, joined them. This relationship of master and disciple does not constitute a school as Schacht believed.[100] Thus, both Hallaq and Hurvitz convincingly argue that in the beginning no doctrinal schools existed; schools developed only later, based on the original master–disciple relationship.

In Medina the school was organized around local tradition (*ᶜamal*), which was represented in the masterpiece of its founder, Mālik ibn Anas. His work, the Muwaṭṭa', is a basic text for the Mālikite school – creating precedent both by its style and structure – and subsequent generations passed it down and supplied commentaries on it. The Muwaṭṭa' is not a code, but a thematic systematization of the prophetic traditions and local customs known and accepted by Mālik, who occasionally also added his own opinion to them. Due to the casuistic nature of tradition and customs the work contains a selection of rules, while the abstract elaboration of principles is missing. Thus the Muwaṭṭa' reflects the first period of the development of Islamic law, the time of the growth of positive law and the first attempts at its systematization, and describes law as it was used in daily practice in Medina.[101]

In ᶜIrāq the school organized around Abū Ḥanīfa, a member of the Kūfa school, became prominent. His extraordinary role and his raising to the *eponym* of the school are somewhat puzzling to modern scholarship because he did not enjoy such a privileged position in his lifetime. No written work is known from Abū Ḥanīfa and some of his teachings were preserved only by his disciples, who often refer to their master in their work. Abū Yūsuf, stepping into the footsteps of his master, dedicated a separate book to the differences between the teachings of his master and those of Ibn Abī Laylā, his contemporary (Kitāb ikhtilāf Abī Ḥanīfa wa Ibn Abī Laylā). Next to Abū Yūsuf another disciple, al-Shaybānī, also often refers to the teachings of Abū Ḥanīfa. Methods of Abū Yūsuf and al-Shaybānī differed from that of their master in that they preferred the prophetic traditions and applied *ra'y* less frequently. This tendency can be observed particularly in the case of al-Shaybānī. Contrary to the Medinese lawyers who, Wheeler argues, could identify local customs with prophetic tradition, the ᶜIrāqī lawyers had to develop their own methods because the Prophet never entered ᶜIrāq. While in Medina there was a relatively uniform practice embodied in the Muwaṭṭa' mentioned above; in ᶜIrāq the situation was just the opposite. Here a great number of scholars developed their own doctrines, and legal pluralism prevailed. As a result they had to select the tradition they held relevant in order to secure common ground. In doing so an emphatic role was attributed to the personal qualities of a legal scholar referred to, and to logic as an important factor. Thus the scholars of ᶜIrāq created a more complex epistemological background for their work.[102]

---

100 Hurvitz 2000: 41–67.

101 Text edition: Mālik 1987; English translation: Mālik 1989.

102 Wheeler 1996: 32–40.

The reliance on both logic and traditions changed the argumentation of the Ḥanafites: *ra'y* was replaced by reliance on tradition; at the same time logic remained the decisive criterion for selecting the relevant tradition. Thus tracing back the teaching of the school began in ᶜIrāq: members of the Kūfa school traced back their doctrine for the first time to Ibrāhīm al-Nakhaᶜī, whose generation represented the first scholars of law.[103] The ever greater reliance on prophetic traditions beginning with Ibrāhīm al-Nakhaᶜī, Ḥammād ibn Abī Sulaymān and Ibn Abī Laylā reached its climax with the work of al-Shaybānī in which reference to prophetic traditions became even more underlined. His understanding is discernible in his work written on the law of war and peace in which he unfolds the traditions relevant to the topic, and the exposure of the topic only begins afterwards in the form of a dialogue.[104] Al-Shaybānī was the first ᶜIrāqī scholar to claim that no rule can be valid if it is not based on a written source, under which the Qur'ān and the prophetic tradition should be understood.[105] Simultaneously *ra'y* was increasingly dropped from the language of discourse because the meaning of arbitrary opinion was (wrongly) attached to it, to be supplemented by *qiyās* and *ijtihād* – designating methods of logical deduction strictly deriving from texts.[106]

Thus the rivalry between the *ahl al-ra'y* and *ahl al-ḥadīth* was decided to the detriment of the former. At the same time the argumentation of extreme traditionalists – that the reliance on rationalistic thinking should be dispelled from the world of legal issues – could not be supported either, particularly in complicated legal problems. The elaboration of a compromise between the two camps, between traditionalists and rationalists, was realized in the work of al-Shāfiᶜī, long regarded as the founder of Islamic legal theory – a claim now subject to challenge.[107]

Muḥammad b. Idrīs al-Shāfiᶜī (767–820) was at first a student of the Mālikite school and was a personal disciple of Mālik ibn Anas. During his stay in ᶜIrāq he had close contact with al-Shaybānī. At the end of his life he lived in Egypt, where his major works were produced. His father was a member of the Quraysh tribe; his ancestors were relatives of the Prophet and participated actively in the early episodes of the emergence of Islam. This prophetic relationship raised al-Shāfiᶜī's authority, but this was not the reason why ultimately his theory was accepted. His most important work, establishing the theoretical foundations of jurisprudence, is the Kitāb al-risāla fī uṣūl al-fiqh. He wrote two works under this title – one while he was still in ᶜIrāq, but it was lost. The second work of the same title was written in Egypt during the last years of his life; hence it contains the final, mature variant of his thinking.[108] Positive legal norms figure in it only as examples because he

103 Hallaq 1997: 17.
104 Shaybānī 1966: 75–94.
105 Hallaq 1997: 18.
106 Hallaq 1997: 19.
107 For the reassessment of al-Shāfiᶜī's role see Hallaq 1993.
108 Khadduri 1961: 8–16.

did not aim at unfolding the details of positive law, but was primarily interested in establishing what constitutes the sources of Islamic law.

In al-Shāfiʿī's work great importance was attached to prophetic traditions in general and to their significance in legal reasoning in particular. As we have seen, argumentation based on *sunna* was not a novelty in that period; moreover, the *ahl al-ḥadīth* treated it as the most important legal source (after the Qur'ān). Al-Shāfiʿī accepted the prophetic traditions as legal source, at the same time he limited it to the sphere of authentic traditions. Since in his time the teachings of various schools, the doctrines of individual legal scholars and some customs of a particular area began to take the form of prophetic tradition, al-Shāfiʿī regarded their separation from the authentic traditions as necessary. According to him authentic tradition was obligatory and occupied second place in the hierarchy of legal sources after the Qur'ān, whereas other traditions containing the Prophet's Companions' or some leading legal scholars' opinion were not obligatory; they only served to facilitate the understanding of some passages more difficult to understand.[109]

Al-Shāfiʿī dedicated two separate chapters to traditions in his work: in chapter five he offered the explanation of the compulsory nature of traditions, whereas in the much longer chapter nine he discussed issues of detail related to tradition. As belief in Allāh cannot be separated from belief in the Prophet, he argued, the observance of the rules of the Qur'ān cannot be separated from the observance of the Prophet's *sunna*. Unfortunately for him, the Qur'ān does not contain direct reference to the Prophet's *sunna* as legal source, but speaks about wisdom in general. Referring to verse 4.113 of the Qur'ān, al-Shāfiʿī identified 'wisdom' mentioned in the verse with prophetic tradition saying that this derives from the commandment of obeying the Prophet. Hence obligations derive from the Qur'ān and the prophetic tradition, and the function of the latter is to make God's intention clear. This order of religious authorities (God, Prophet) also determines the order of legal sources that can be linked to them: Qur'ān, *sunna*.[110] With this argumentation al-Shāfiʿī not only placed prophetic tradition in the system of legal sources, but also lent divine legitimacy to it. Thus al-Shāfiʿī's theory was closer to the traditionalist's agenda because prophetic tradition was the second most important legal source to him, whereas rational argumentation ended up at the bottom of the legal sources in the form of *qiyas*, meaning not only analogy but also *a fortiori* arguments (e.g. *a maiore ad minus*; *a minore ad maius*).[111]

The Ḥanbalite school grew out of the circle of traditionalists of Baghdad, who doubted the role of reason in the system of the sources of Islamic law. Ibn Ḥanbal himself condemned not only al-Shāfiʿī but also the role of analogy, though in very exceptional cases he did not refrain from its use – in contrast to Dāwūd al-Ẓāhirī, another famous traditionalist legal scholar who categorically rejected analogy.

109 Khadduri 1961: 36.

110 Shāfiʿī 1940: 79ff; Khadduri 1961: 109–12.

111 For these modes of argumentation see Hallaq 1997: 96–9.

Ibn Ḥanbal was one of the leading figures among the ninth-century traditionalists whose interest primarily extended to the *ḥadīth*. No comprehensive legal work survives under his name; his only writing discusses issues of ritual prayer. He acknowledged the Prophet's and his Companions' tradition as authentic and did not care much for the opinion of legal scholars because it could not necessarily be right. This was the reason why Abū Ḥanīfa and the method of *ra'y* were unacceptable to Ibn Ḥanbal and his followers, who continually attacked representatives of rational argumentation. But the same reason led Ibn Ḥanbal also to prohibit his followers to put down and preserve his legal opinions. Thus his disciples acted against his will when, after his death, they compiled his teachings. Ibn Ḥanbal's teaching was compiled by Abū Bakr al-Khallāl, criticized by his fellow companions for disobeying their master's will. This 20-volume work, called al-Jāmiᶜ li-ᶜulūm Aḥmad ibn Ḥanbal, is regarded as the basic text of the school even today.[112]

At the end of the formative period the foundations of legal theory, legal institutions and rules of substantive law were established. Although Islamic legal history remains somewhat turbulent in the coming centuries, too, this study does not follow it but turns its attention to questions of legal theory instead.

112 For the formation of the Ḥanbalite school see Melchert 1997: 137–55.

Chapter 2
Legal Theory

After this rather short but necessary historical overview attention now turns to the legal theories of Islamic, Jewish and Zoroastrian law in order to distinguish historical reality from theoretical postulations of legal theory. In doing so, this chapter first discusses the underlying principles of the legal systems, followed by conclusions which compare postulations of jurisprudence with the findings of modern legal history.

Jewish and Islamic Law

As seen in the previous chapter, the formation of an autonomous Jewish kingdom had no reality after the return from Babylonian captivity. What Jews could realize for themselves was a limited autonomy within the framework of the Achaemenid Empire. The house of David, however, symbolized the independent kingdom, the restoration of which was an impossible end to achieve. As argued by Freedman, Ezra therefore reorganized the Jews around Moses, another outstanding hero of Jewish history whose name was not linked to the monarchy and hence was acceptable to both the Jews and the Persian authorities. Obviously, traditions related to Moses were not the work of Ezra because they go back centuries. At the same time, by shifting the focus from David and the kingdom to Moses and his work Ezra ensured a new cohesive force for Jews now living within the boundaries of the Persian Empire. As a result, society was no longer organized around the state and its head in a single political community, but by law related to Moses and known by divine revelation. Thus the laws of Moses did not go back to Moses the lawmaker as a king (he was never referred to as king) but to Moses the mediator of law ('a prophet'), since the origin of norms is ultimately divine revelation. Here the idea of the covenant which created an alliance between God and His people is of importance because it makes obedience to God necessary. Yet obedience to God is not to be separated from obedience to the revealed legal norms for which state and its institutional structure is not a necessary precondition. As a result of Ezra's work the historical aspect survived (David and his house continued to be a dynasty enjoying great authority and ultimately the Messiah would also come from his house), but was pushed into the background and the legal aspect came to the foreground. The observance of law which was learned through Moses ensured the covenant with God.[1]

1 Freedman 1990: 317–29.

As a result, already existing norms acquired divine legitimacy and became a new cohesive force to the community. These norms were either part of customary law going back centuries or were introduced by legislation during the monarchy, when the king had the right to legislate. In other words, legal norms were linked to Moses later and the assumption that the laws of Moses were known in their present form in that period is a historical anachronism,[2] although it shares common topics (e.g. the goring ox) and rules with the major law collections of the Ancient Near East.[3]

As the turning point in Jewish law was the activity of Ezra, so the beginning of a new understanding of Islamic law could be linked to the name of al-Shāfiʿī, a process which Rainer Albertz called 'die Theologisierung des Rechts' in respect of Jewish law. Although al-Shāfiʿī made every effort to prove the divine sanction of the prophetic traditions and to show that legal rulings were formulated either on the Qur'ān or on the *sunna*, just the opposite happened. To put it differently, legal norms historically precede the Prophet's *sunna*, yet theoretically they derive from it. In fact we are facing a subsequent theologization of an already existing corpus of norms in which the key element is the norm's relationship to the *sunna*: if a norm is based on a prophetic *sunna* it is regarded a rule of Islamic law, irrespective of its origin. Thus, *sunna* guarantees the validity of a great number of already existing rules, while in terms of historical reality it is not their source.

The theologization of law was a long process surrounded by debates among Muslim scholars for centuries. The work of al-Shāfiʿī had almost no influence in his own age and his contemporary, Ibn Ḥanbal, branded the work of al-Shāfiʿī as not even worth reading.[4] It was unacceptable to the traditionalists because he allocated a significant role to the set of rational arguments; at the same time the rationalists did not support him either because of his basic tenet about the central role of the *sunna* and the secondary nature of rational argumentation compared to it. In the decades following his death no commentaries were written to his work. It is important because respect and acceptance of a work were manifested in commentaries written by members of the subsequent generations. By contrast, lack of such works was a tacit sign of dismissal. Moreover, he had only a handful of followers and few of his disciples remained faithful to him. One century later, however, we can witness just the opposite happening. He was referred to as the founder of legal theory, the number of his followers increased rapidly, his works were copied in numbers and commentaries were written on them. Thus there was a fundamental change in the assessment of al-Shāfiʿī within one century. The reason, according to W. B. Hallaq, was the change in the intellectual environment: while the debate between the rationalists and traditionalists was under way, no one paid attention to the intermediate theory of al-Shāfiʿī. As the debate was resolved in favour of the traditionalists, yet at the same time extreme traditionalism was

2 Westbrook 1996: 2.

3 For a comparative study see Westbrook 1988.

4 Melchert 1997: 71.

pushed to the background, the almost forgotten theory of al-Shāfiʿī stressing a synthesis of rationalism and traditionalism was discovered: a compromise of the two major camps, with greater emphasis on tradition. The work of Ibn Surayj, one of the greatest scholars of the Shāfiʿīte school, also contributed to this development which significantly promoted interest in al-Shāfiʿī and his understanding of *uṣūl al-fiqh*. Thus both intellectual movements and the work of outstanding scholars contributed to making al-Shāfiʿī one of the most outstanding authors of jurisprudence in the ninth century.[5]

Norman Calder has found another explanation. According to him all the works written by the most eminent figures of the early period of Islamic law (Saḥnūn: Mudawwana; Mālik: Muwaṭṭa'; al-Shāfiʿī: Kitāb al-Umm; Muzanī: Mukhtaṣar; Abū Yūsuf: Kitāb al-Kharāj) were produced continuously by handing down texts and by textual inserts of later generations ('organic process'). Therefore, these texts cannot be linked to persons who are indicated as authors of those works. This process can be observed in relation to the work of al-Shāfiʿī, too: the theory of law by which he became famous was inserted later and the work known now is the product of the Shāfiʿīte school, probably around 300 AH.[6]

For legal historians it is evidently an important question when and under what historical circumstances the theory linked to the name of al-Shāfiʿī emerged; but currently what matters is that the sources of Islamic law were defined by a post-event theologization of an already existing corpus of norms – a theory that was attached, wrongly or not, to an outstanding legal scholar. Studying these sources was the task and privilege of the legal scholars and, therefore, Islamic law was further elaborated by men of learning and not by law making. Thus, Islamic law evolved as a jurists' law, as Schacht correctly observed.[7]

The summary of the achievements of both al-Shāfiʿī and Ezra – or, properly speaking, theories attached to their names – is the posterior divine legitimization of already existing norms of customary origin on the authority of a prophet accepted by all. Though historical circumstances were different and, consequently, different motivations were behind this intellectual achievement, the final outcome is the same in both legal systems. As a result, law moved to a central position in religious life as a set of norms which leads the believers to God and guarantees the maintenance of the covenant, provided obedience to God and His laws is observed. As a result, studying law became the most eminent activity and those who devoted their entire life to it shared their prestige with that of their subject. It is small wonder that in such an intellectual environment other subjects (like philosophy) were pushed into the background.

Jewish law has a different attitude to revealed norms than Islamic law. Jewish law differs from its Islamic counterpart in two issues: it acknowledges

5 Hallaq 1993: 587–601.

6 Calder 1993: 241–3. Lowry, however, doubts that al-Shāfiʿī had elaborated a theory of four sources of law at all, see Lowry 2002.

7 Schacht 1964: 209.

the possibility of legislation within a limited sphere (*takkanah*); and distinguishes between written and oral law. The possibility of legislation was ensured by a distinction between norms dealing with ritual issues (*issura'*) and those of social coexistence (*mamōna'*). Obviously a clear-cut caesura cannot be drawn between these two areas, yet the acknowledgement of the relative autonomy of these fields resulted in two consequences. First, legislation in the field of *mamōna'* was accepted and manifest while it had only a marginal role in ritual law. Second, within these two areas of law different principles were asserted and, therefore, no inferences could be drawn from the norms of social coexistence to the norms of ritual law and vice versa.[8] Yet the rightfulness of legislation posed a question to Jewish legal scholars and there was disagreement among Rabbis concerning rabbinic legislation. But independently of theoretical disputes they did not accept rabbinic legislation only as a mere possibility but put it into practice, proven by innumerable pieces of *takkanah* (*gezerah*) from Antiquity to this day.[9]

Oral law (*Torāh shebeᶜal peh*) is not oral because it was not committed to writing; here writing reflects the Bible, therefore oral law is every norm that cannot be found in the Bible. Consequently rules in the Mishnah and the Talmūd qualify as oral law just as much as interpretation or the corpus of rules produced by *takkanah*. According to rabbinic tradition even oral law is part of the revelation at Sinai, and Moses received it together with the written law during the course of revelation. It includes not only legal norms but also methods of legal exegesis, with the help of which further rules may be derived from already existing norms. Persons in the chain of transmitters from Moses to the Pairs – discussed in the previous chapter – guarantee the authentic transmission of the entire text of oral law and its meaning. According to tradition the law reached Shimᶜeōn and Anṭīgonus through Moses, Joshua, the elders and the prophets, and from then on the Pairs transmitted the legal tradition to the Pharisees and the Rabbis. This chain relates only to oral law because written law is not to be handed down in this way.[10]

It does not mean, however, that Jewish law was incapable of change. As indicated above, it was the legal scholars who had the right to formulate new norms. Contrary to Islamic law, where the consensus of the scholars is needed to enlarge the body of norms (*ijmāᶜ* being the third source in al-Shāfiᶜī's theory), in Jewish law consensus is not a precondition since a majority vote is sufficient to establish a norm of *halakah*. It is not the agreement in itself, but the doctrine

8 Elon 1974: 5–6.

9 The difference between *takkanah* and *gezerah* is disputed even in Jewish jurisprudence: according to the dominant view *takkanah* was an ordinance of positive action, whereas *gezerah* means prohibition; this view is refuted by Mantel 1965: 228–31. According to Cohen, referring to Rambam, *gezerah* is a prohibition the aim of which is to protect the Torāh and maintain religious morality, whereas *takkanah* is a rule facilitating social coexistence and for general public good (Cohen 1991: 62–7). For legislation, documents and legal problems discussed in them see Elon 1994: 490–880.

10 Elon 1994: vol. I, 191–3; see also Chapter 1 note 35 supra and related text.

of oral law that guarantees the validity of the norm. Thus, ultimately, *halakah* identified this way is indirectly linked to revelation. Obviously, Rabbis were aware that rules specified in this way could, sometimes, be rather far away from the biblical rules.[11] As they put it, some rules are '*as mountains hanging by a hair*', because there were lots of rules and few written supports.[12] The well-known story of Moses appearing in R. ᶜAqībah's lecture also comes to mind here: accordingly, Moses visited the Academy of ᶜAqībah but did not understand the discussion there. On seeing his embarrassment R. ᶜAqībah assured him that the opinion discussed had been given to Moses; on hearing this Moses was reassured and left.[13]

If a norm was not to be legitimized this way, a method called *asmakta* (support) came to the assistance of legal scholars. The aim of this method was to link a rule to written law when it was not a rule of written law and was not even produced by its interpretation but was derived from independent sources, such as customs. Thus *asmakta* was a posterior link between a rule and its assumed source, while the historical origin of the norm should be looked for elsewhere.[14] The emergence of *asmakta* as a legal technique can be dated to the fifth century because rabbinic lawmaking emerged in increasing number during this century.[15] *Asmakta* as a legal technique in its own right is unknown to Islamic law; its function was partly taken over by *sunna*. What was called by Goldziher and Schacht the subsequent modification of the *sunna* is the linking of the existing rules to the revealed sources. As the *asmakta* technique was unknown, the only opportunity to legitimize a norm of obscure origin (local practice, etc.) was to encapsulate it into a Prophetic *sunna*.

In sum, both Jewish and Islamic law could be regarded as jurists' law, elaborated by subsequent generations of legal scholars. Legal pluralism, an underlying principle of both legal cultures, assured the validity of various doctrines formulated by legal scholars. In Islamic law consensus – that is, consensus of legal scholars – was regarded as the third source of law, while in Jewish law a norm established by majority rule also qualifies as *halakah*. Moreover, Rabbis had the power to enact regulations, too – a licence not shared by their Muslim fellows.

Zoroastrian Law

Zoroastrian legal theory differs from the Jewish-Islamic legal thinking because it is not based on revelation from God mediated to society by a prophet and, consequently, the idea of a covenant between God and His people is also missing.

---

11 It is disputed whether rabbinic tradition goes back to the tradition of the Pharisees or not; see Sanders 1990: 97–130.

12 Quoted in Sanders 1990: 119.

13 Sanders 1990: 125.

14 Elon 1994: vol I, 302–5; see also Halivni 1986: 13–16; Cohen 1991: 61.

15 Halivni 1991: 14–15.

No doubt Zoroastrianism also knows revelation since Wohu Manah revealed his intentions to the Prophet Zarat.ushtra. This revelation, however, does not contain legal norms, but the ethical foundations of the new religion represented by Zarat.ushtra. Thus the Gāthās (parts of the Awesta which are believed to be composed by the Prophet himself) basically differ from the contents of the Bible and the Qur'ān, which contain not only ethical principles but also legal rules of normative force.

The idea that some rules are of divine origin is not alien to the Iranian tradition either. The daiwa inscription of Xerxes clearly proves this when reminding the faithful to 'have respect for that law which Auramazdā has established', because 'the man who has respect for that law which Auramazdā has established, and worships Auramazdā and Arta reverent(ly), he both becomes happy while living and becomes blessed when dead.'[16]

The law ordered by Auramazdā, however, is not specified in this text or in any other source as the Bible and the Qur'ān have it. Perhaps the reason is that the term *dātā* (law) has a dual meaning: it means divine law (whatever it might be) and also the law of a ruler.[17] Darius repeatedly refers to *dātā* as his own law representing his own will.[18] Thus the king's will had the force of law. This is confirmed by Herodotus, according to whom the judges answered Cambyses that the king did what he deemed right;[19] in other words, the monarch was above the law, while there was no reference whatsoever to the relationship with the laws of Auramazdā. In Middle Persian literature *dād* (corresponding to *dātā* in Old Persian) continues to be attached to religion. This is clear in the rule found in the Riwāyat accompanying the Dādestān ī Dēnīg (PRDd) defining apostasy: a person commits apostasy (a capital crime) when he or she 'is deserting the law of the Good Religion and is taking up this bad law'.[20] The wording of the text is interesting because it reflects an understanding of religion which is close to

16 Kent 1953: 151–3. The translation and interpretation of *artāčā brazmaniya* figuring in the text is subject to debate. The question is whether čā means 'and', and as such it links the two as wedged between Auramazdā and *arta*, or it reflects the *artā-hačā*, closer to the Elamite transcription, meaning 'in keeping with *arta*'. Kent accepts the former interpretation and thinks that *arta* as an abstract principle and Auramazdā should be worshipped on an equal footing. Other interpretations are discussed by Skjaervo in *Encyclopedia Iranica* I: 696.

17 The Old Persian expression *dātā* entered various languages of the ancient Near East: Aramaic, Hebrew and Syrian. The order of *Artaxerxes*, which is supposed to be preserved word by word in the Book of Ezra, also uses this expression in both senses: the law of God and the law of the king.

18 Darius I Behistun inscription I. 23: 'by the favour of Auramazdā these countries showed respect toward my law; as was said to them, thus it was done' (Kent 1953: 117). Darius I Naqsh-I rustam inscription. 21: 'my law – that held them firm' (Kent 1953: 137).

19 Herodotus III: 31.

20 PRDd 7.2; Williams 1990: Part I, 47; Part II, 9.

Islamic and Jewish interpretation: Zoroastrian law is a personal law, too, following the *Personalitätsprinzip* – therefore, it is not territorial.

Arta (Awestan *asha*) is an ancient concept of the Indo-Iranian period which can be found both in the Gāthās and the Vedas. The interpretation of *arta* has been subject to debate among Iranists for decades but will not be entered into here. Some scholars interpret it merely as truth, while others as cosmic order. Whether cosmic order regulating everything in the world or simply truth – that is, an underlying principle of social coexistence and human behaviour – both interpretations have a common element: *arta* is the conceptual framework of social coexistence and norms regulating human behaviour.[21]

A man who lives according to *arta* is *artawan* (*ashavan*). *Ashavan* is a human being who walks on the path of *asha*, is pious and just and whose salvation will be assured. Only those recognized as *ashavan* could enter Paradise which, in turn, depends on his/her mode of conduct and behaviour.[22] The divine protector of *arta* was originally Waruna, a deity charged with upholding physical and moral order. Later Mithra, a well-known deity of the ancient Indo-Iranian pantheon, came to be associated with *asha*, too.[23] Since in the long run Mithra gained prominence while Waruna disappeared almost entirely in Iranian tradition (in India just the opposite happened), Mithra became the protector of *arta*; therefore everyone who was the enemy of *arta* (a liar) was at the same time the enemy of Mithra, that is, a *mithrō-druj*.

Thus, *arta* as an underlying principle was connected to its divine protector, a god belonging to the remote past of the Indo-Iranian religious worldview who was incorporated later into the Zoroastrian religion, too. Here, however, Mithra's functions end: whether a god of friendship or that of contract,[24] he merely supervises the maintenance of the right order (truth) but does not tell mankind how to do it, leaving this task to humanity. In short, neither Mithra nor any god reveals legal norms, only ethical principles are defined in a rather vague manner. The so-called three words, a concise summary of Zoroastrian worldview – good thought, good talk and good deed (*humat*, *huwarsht*, *hukht*) – are not legal norms either but ethical norms of how to implement truth in society. As a result, Zarat. ushtra – in contrast to Muḥammad and Moses – did not mediate any legal norm to humanity or to his followers, his mission focusing predominantly on ethical and not on legal aspects of religion. It is the reason why the Gāthās contain no

---

21 Following Lüders, Gershevitch 1959: 6 interprets *arta* as truth; Schlerath agrees, see 'Asha' in *Encyclopedia Iranica* I: 694-5. Boyce, however, thinks that although the term *asha* could not be translated into any other language; its meaning is more complex and cannot be reduced to truth and it stands for cosmic and moral order, see Boyce 1975: 27.

22 Gnoli: 'Ashavan' in *Encyclopedia Iranica* I.

23 Gershevitch 1959: 4–8.

24 The meaning of the name of Mithra is subject to debate. It was interpreted as contract for the first time by Meillet in 1907 and was followed by Gershevitch 1959: 26; Lentz 1970: 245–53; and Boyce 1975: 27 (the author agrees with this interpretation).

legal rules. The present Awesta, it is true, contains some legal precepts, but only in one of its books, the Wīdēwdād. But the Wīdēwdād is not a code, not a law book but a collection of very different topics, some aspects of law being a part of it. Chapter 4, for example (Fragard IV), is written in the form of a dialogue between the Prophet and Ohrmazd (Ahura Mazdā) concerning some questions of contractual obligations and the punishments of those who break these contracts. This dialogue, and particularly the answers of Ohrmazd, cannot be considered as a revelation of legal norms; it is only a literary form, a common feature of Zoroastrian texts. Contemporary Zoroastrians, too, do not look on these texts as part of divine revelation; they consider them only as part of an ancient tradition. It is proven by the arguments of Dastūr Kotwal, High Priest and scholar, in a Bombay debate concerning marriage laws. According to his argumentation the observance of tradition is as important as religion, therefore mixed marriages must not be permitted.[25]

The emergence of the idea of revealed legal norms was presumably hindered because Zoroastrianism is not a monotheist religion like Islam and Judaism. In addition to Auramazdā other gods (such as Mithra) found their place in the pantheon just as much as the Yazatas or the Amesha Spentas. Though Auramazdā is the supreme god his position is fundamentally different from that of YḤWH or of Allāh. It is the principle of truth and cosmic order (*arta*) and not a supreme god which regulates human behaviour and, therefore, there is no need for a revealed law. Thus, in contrast to Jewish and Islamic thinking, in Zoroastrianism there was no covenant between God and man which was to be guaranteed by the respect of law. The role of obedience to norms was taken over by rites: the commitment of a faithful Zoroastrian was not expressed in his submission to law – and particularly not in studying law – but in observing rites, saying prayers and keeping the rules of purity in every detail.

Based on *arta*, only the ethical foundations of the social order were ensured, leaving more freedom to the wording of legal norms for authorities – above all, the king. With a freedom to lawmaking, interpretation of existing norms was of lesser significance than in the Islamic and Jewish legal systems. In this respect the Zoroastrian legal system is markedly different from the Jewish and Islamic legal systems. In such a religious context lawmaking is possible for the king or any other civic authority. Consequently secular laws and religious demands may collide, which raises the issue of which enjoys primacy. Surprisingly there is no clear-cut answer to this question.

In the sixth book of the Dēnkard an attempt was made to resolve the contradiction between a religious obligation and royal edict. Here the question is raised of what the faithful is supposed to do if a deed of greatest virtue (*mahist kirbag*) is prohibited by the ruler for some reason not specified in the text. The answer is to follow the ruler's order; otherwise performing the ritual act would become a sin since it would result in the destruction of royal authority (*dehbadīh*

25 Hjerrild 1992: 192–4.

wishuft bāwed).[26] There is, however, a passage in the third book of the same work which contradicts the above answer both in its content and spirit. The wisdom describing the ten most important characteristics of Zoroastrian law acknowledges a decision made by the ruler only as of lower rank than religious law, for it is the servant (*bandag*) of law.[27] Consequently it is not royal decision but religious law that is to be followed in case of contradiction. Since one may read two fully contradictory decisions in two different chapters of the same work, the issue was seemingly not resolved in Zoroastrian theory of law.

Finally, to say some words about the legal doctrines of legal scholars as a source of law is in order. As seen above, in Islamic law legal disputes came to an end when legal scholars reached a consensus about the matter in question, and consensus was regarded as the third source of law. In Jewish law this was achieved by a majority decision. In Zoroastrian law, too, a judgment could be pronounced on the consensus of the learned (*hamdādestānīh ī wēhān*) – but we are left in the dark concerning the mechanism of how it was established. According to the Dēnkard, a judge should judge from the Awesta and Zand (its commentary) or from the consensus of the learned;[28] that is, consensus was regarded as the second source of the law. But it is by far not evident what consensus means, since we have evidence for a variety of its interpretations: MHD 41.5–8 refers to the consensus of three scholars; 42.5–9 has the agreement of only two scholars; MHDA 11.12–17 mentions the consensus of the majority; and MHD 46. 14–15 refers to the consensus of all the sages. It seems, therefore, that it was not established in late Sasanian times what exactly consensus was, but it was not a unanimous consensus of the legal scholars or a majority view. The same doctrine of two or three legal scholars was considered solid enough on which a judgement could be pronounced, a practice alien to both Jewish and Islamic law.[29]

Despite these differences, Zoroastrian law shows essential similarities with Jewish and Islamic law. In all three legal systems rules were regarded as customs known to all and followed by the entire society, disputes being settled by the traditional and secular elite (elders sitting at the city gates, sheykhs, arbiters, royal judges). The theologization of law – that is, a new ideology by which divine sanction was attached to *existing corpus iuris* – was a later development in all three legal systems, due to different historical conditions: the necessity to reorganize society after the Babylonian captivity in Jewish law; the dispute between the traditionalists and the rationalists in Islamic law; the emergence of the Zoroastrian Church and its close alliance with the Persian state. When the long process of theologization was completed and accepted by both legal scholars and

26 Dēnkard VI, 232–4: Shaked 1979: 91

27 Dēnkard III, 197: de Menasce 1973: 205–6.

28 *Dādwar wizīr az awistāg ud zand kunishn ayāb az ham-dādestānīh ī wehān*; quoted in Macuch 1993: 12.

29 On the role of consensus in Zoroastrian law see Jany 2005: 295–303.

the respective societies, no new theory or paradigm emerged since it would result in the complete denial of legal theories.

Different in details and developed under different historical circumstances, but similar in the essence of their new, religious-minded ideology: this is the short summary of findings up to now concerning all three legal systems. Next, attention turns to legal practice, above all to the judiciary, in order to find out how legal theories were implemented in everyday legal life.

PART TWO
PRACTICE

Chapter 3
Institutions

Judicial Procedure in Zoroastrian Law

Since there are no sources concerning legal procedures from the Achaemenid and Parthian periods, rules and social practice of these centuries remain in darkness. It is only the Sasanian period which is documented in this respect. In the Sasanian period private and criminal procedural law were distinguished in practice, though not in theory. There were different rules governing these two fields of procedure and, what is more, there were different legal terms for technical details, too. For instance, protocols produced in a civil procedure were called *sakhwan nāmag*, while protocols of criminal procedure were *pursishn nāmag*.

But here, too, there is no law regulating procedures available, whether civil or criminal, and studies cannot determine at present whether there was any at all. What is at hand is the Mādigān I Hazār Dādestān (MHD+A) containing hundreds of civil cases and their sometimes very terse description. Based on these judgments one can only infer by way of induction to rules being behind particular decisions. We can have at least a general overview of Zoroastrian private procedural law only when generalizing and sometimes conceptualizing the particularities of this ocean of casuistry. Since the MHD+A contains only minimal references to criminal cases, the source used to reconstruct criminal procedure is the Syriac Acts of Martyrs, which contains several criminal procedures against Iranian Christians. Although it is not a legal code but rather a religious work highlighting the sufferings and steadfastness of the Christian martyrs, it reflects the criminal procedural practice of the day.

Private Procedural Law[1]

The compiler of MHD+A, Farrokhmard ī Wahrāmān, is well acquainted with rules of procedure and the contemporary judicial practice of the courts. Perhaps it is because he was a judge himself, presumably in Pārs province, incorporating numerous cases from this area into his work.

As witnessed in various archaic societies, litigation was not looked at positively and attempts were made to avoid it if possible. Launching a lawsuit was regarded as a condition invalidating several contracts already concluded between

1 This section is based on previous work on private procedural law published in *Iranica Antiqua*, see Jany 2010.

the parties;[2] sometimes the right to launch a lawsuit was abandoned in exchange for compensation.[3] Women were particularly safeguarded against the turbulence and honour-breaking debates of a lawsuit and were kept at a distance from courts as much as possible.

Organs of Procedure

The judiciary consisted of a rather complex set of institutions. Unfortunately, not every detail is known, though Farrokhmard ī Wahrāmān dedicated a separate chapter to the issue. Nevertheless, it seems that several forums of different competencies and power existed and operated parallel to each other.

The designation of a judge was *dādwar* but occasionally there are references to subcategories such as *dādwar ī keh* (literally: small judge) and *dādwar ī meh* (great judge). Perhaps the *dādwar ī keh* was, as indicated by his designation, a judge of lower grade, while the *dādwar ī meh* meant a forum of appeal.[4] A verdict passed by the *dādwar* could be revised by the *mōbed*s representing the next level in the hierarchy of the judiciary.[5] There is one reference (MHDA 12.11) to the *dādwar ī pasēmār* and the *dādwar ī pēshēmār*, who are literally the judges of the defendant and the plaintiff respectively. Perhaps an arbitrate court is indicated, as Maria Macuch rightly observes,[6] where both parties delegated equal members to represent their interests and decide the case. If this assumption is correct, we can witness an official judiciary operating, perhaps, on three instances; and parallel to this an unofficial body composed of unofficial judges was also accessible to the parties, applying less rigid rules of procedure and opening the door to compromises.

Rad and *mōbed*, two priests of the Zoroastrian clergy, had judicial competencies, too. The *mōbed* was both an appellate forum of the regular court of the *dādwar* and a separate court. As a next instance above the *dādwar* he could proceed in all issues that fell under the competency of the *dādwar*.[7] As a separate court he could decide issues that other organs had no competency to deal with, most importantly to appoint a *stūr* for a man and a *sālār* (guardian) for a family.[8] The *mōbed*, however, was not only a judge of the highest standing but had other judicial functions as well. Authenticating documents may rather be regarded nowadays as a notary's task but naturally it was not so sharply separated in that period. The reference according to which the *mōbed* also functioned as an authority of public administration, and particularly in the supervision of revenue administration and

2 MHDA 33. 3–7, 11–14.

3 MHDA 17. 4–7, 22. 1–7.

4 Macuch 1981: 14.

5 MHD 3. 6–8; MHD 110. 13–15; Macuch 1993: 660; MHDA 12. 12–13.

6 Macuch 1981: 14 suggests a procedure of a chosen court.

7 MHDA 26. 14–15; MHD 110. 13–15.

8 MHDA 26. 12–16. See also notes 355–6 and related text.

of the fire temples, is more difficult to interpret.[9] As there are no more texts at our disposal it is not possible to say more about this issue. The function of the *rad* was similar to that of the *mōbed*, with the significant difference that the choice of the person for the *sālār* and the *stūr* was outside his competency.[10]

The hierarchy of the judiciary was headed by the *mōbedān mōbed* and no further appeal was possible against his judgment.[11] Unfortunately it is not possible to determine how many levels the system was composed of. There was, however, a distinction made in respect of appeal – whether the judgment was made according to the *kardag* (legal custom of the courts) or to the čāshtag (legal doctrine). As a judgment passed on *kardag* was not regarded as 'sure' (ēwar), an appeal against it also meant that the appellate court did not proceed according to *kardag* but according to the norms of čāshtag, and it was up to the parties to decide.[12] In exceptional cases the *mōbedān mōbed* could also participate in the procedure as a witness but not as a judge. His statement as witness qualified as absolutely reliable and did not have to be confirmed by oath, and even proved to be stronger than an oath.[13]

The *hamārgar*, an office going back to the Achaemenid period, was a legal representative of the monarch in a lawsuit, an authority of public administration and a judge – his function depending on the case he dealt with. As representative of the royal treasury he represented the state (the ruler) in a lawsuit if the subject of the dispute was an item of goods belonging to the royal treasury. As an officer of public administration he was responsible for collecting taxes, and as judge he could fine those who damaged property belonging to the royal treasury.[14]

Some auxiliary personnel whose task was to help a judge conducting a lawsuit are known. The *war sālār* was charged with managing and supervising the complex procedure of oath-taking. In doing so he had to present the text of the oath, say the necessary recitations and produce the oath-taking protocol.[15] The taking of the oath was performed outside the courtroom in a procedure having its own rules and the lawsuit itself continued after the taking of the oath was completed. Finally, the clerks (*dibīr*), who played an important role in preparing the protocols, should also be mentioned. The number of clerks was set at a maximum of four per court.[16]

The number of law courts was determined by districts (*rōstāg*) in a royal decree. These buildings of the judiciary were called *mānāgān*.[17] Unfortunately the text of the MHD+A is damaged exactly where the number of law courts organized

9 MHDA 26. 12–16.
10 MHDA 26. 17–27. 4.
11 MHDA 27. 4–5.
12 MHDA 13. 8–9.
13 MHDA 28. 6–7.
14 MHDA 27. 13–28. 3.
15 MHDA 27. 7–9.
16 MHD 78. 4.
17 MHD 78. 2–11.

in districts is mentioned, therefore, it is not possible to state the exact number of law courts per district. The province of the court seems to be determined by the residence of the defendant,[18] but problems emerged when nomads were among the parties. In this case every court was competent to proceed in the province where nomads resided at least on one occasion;[19] thus in the case of nomads the province of the courts was defined very flexibly in order not to hinder judicial procedure.

Judicial organs had their own seals to prove their authority and competence. The use of seals was introduced for the *mōbed*s and *hamārgar*s during the reign of *Kawād ī Pērōzān* (CE 488–531), and for the *dādwar*s only under *Khusraw ī Kawādān* (CE 531–79).[20] Only documents sealed by the authorities were considered official, this seal being regarded as the 'valid seal' (*muhrigān wāwarīgān*), in contrast to the seal of a private individual.[21] It seems to have been a widespread custom for private individuals to seal documents instead of signing them,[22] but this was not a substitute for the seal of the authorities.

Legal representation was not alien to Sasanian legal practice, and Farrokhmard dedicated a separate though short chapter to this issue (MHD 74.12–76.3). A legal representative was called *jādag-gōw*, a term expressing precisely the role he performed during the lawsuit: a person speaking in the case. As it seems he was not a barrister or a person well versed in law, he only represented a party, acting on their behalf and perhaps using his talent in rhetoric. Legal representation was the duty of the guardian of a family. Sasanian law elaborated rules to prevent the guardian misusing his position and gaining material or legal benefit from his position when a clash of interests between the family and its guardian representative emerged.

The 'representative of the poor' (*driyōshān jādag-gōw*) was a particular though somewhat puzzling institution or honorary title. Presumably it goes back to the Awestan tradition where the Prophet is mentioned as the protector of the poor.[23] Its religious connotation could be discerned in the Sasanian period, too, because this title was put on the seal of the *mōbedān mōbed*, the high priest of Pārs province.[24] Archaeology, however, proves that this title was widespread in Iran and was not limited to a single province.[25] Unfortunately, nothing is known about his activity in a lawsuit or outside litigation, while the complete wording of the title is embarrassing: in fact the *driyōshān jādag-gōw ud dādwar* means the 'representative of the poor and judge'. Perry thinks that it was not only an honorary title but also a function of a high-ranking official,[26] but it is difficult to

18 MHD 5. 5–8.
19 MHD 99. 8–10, 11–13.
20 MHD 93. 4–9.
21 MHD 99. 1–3; see also Macuch 1993: 628.
22 MHD 99. 3–8.
23 Perikhanian–Garsoian 1997: 354.
24 MHD 93. 7–9.
25 Macuch 1993: 600 with further references.
26 Perry 1978: 205.

see how to combine these functions in one and the same person during a trial. The institution was deeply embedded in Iranian tradition since it survived in Islamic times in the form of *wākil al-raʿāyā*, though naturally this function was no longer performed by the Zoroastrian priesthood.[27]

Private Procedure

A lawsuit started with the plaintiff bringing an action against the defendant, but the plaintiff was left alone against a defendant unwilling to appear at court and no official help to overcome this problem seems to have been at his disposal.

Persons of full legal capacity could be parties on either side, but there were some exceptions. Women and slaves could be litigants in their own right somewhat rarely; they usually participated in the lawsuit as partners of their representative (guardian). Consequently they could make statements during the trial independently of their guardian. When a conflict of interests emerged between a *sālār* and a widow that resulted in the giving of contradictory statements, another *sālār* had to be appointed and the new *sālār* was bound by the widow's statement.[28] When the deceased had no descendants his widow could participate in the lawsuit even without a guardian as co-plaintiff against a third person.[29]

A woman could not appear in her own right as plaintiff in a dispute related to ownership.[30] Children were always represented by their guardian in a lawsuit. If a male child came of age before the suit came to an end the guardian could not continue it, and if he did so he was qualified as of bad intention (*wadkhāh*) and a judgment was passed against him.[31]

The date of the proceedings was set by the judge (*dādwar*),[32] at which the parties were obliged to appear at court. When both parties appeared at court, this was registered (*kār rāyēnēd*: continues the lawsuit). If one of the parties failed to appear the fact of absence (*nē āmad*: did not come) had to be recorded in the protocol.[33] Absence from the hearing was called *azishmānd*, a complex and somewhat puzzling judicial term designating, among others, misconduct during a trial. Three successive *azishmānds* resulted in the loss of the lawsuit.[34] A proceeding started in the morning and the judge was to pronounce his judgment on the same day.[35]

---

27 Perry 1978: 205–15.
28 MHD 16. 14–17.
29 MHD 15. 8–9.
30 MHD 16. 5–10.
31 MHDA 32. 9–13
32 MHDA 25. 16–17.
33 MHD 73. 13–74. 5.
34 MHD 10. 16.11.7.
35 MHDA 13. 17.14. 1; Macuch 1981: 16; 155.

When both parties appeared at court the lawsuit could begin. It was the task of the proceeding judge to identify the parties, their age (literally the blackness and whiteness of the hair), their gender, name, seal and their reliability.[36] The hearing then continued with the statements of the parties, standing at a distance of three steps from the judge. The plaintiff's (*pēshēmār*) statement was followed by that of the defendant (*pasēmār*). The designation of the parties reflects the order of the statements to be made (*pēshēmār*: the one who speaks first; *pasēmār*: the one who speaks later).[37]

As a rule the parties were bound by their statements and it was not possible to make subsequent modifications. In exceptional cases, however, both parties had the right to alter their former statements. Both defendants and plaintiffs were entitled to make their statements 'more credible' at any time.[38] In addition plaintiffs had the right to modify their action provided the modification affected the title of the claim.[39] If the defendant modified their statement (*washtag sakhwanīh*) to a less credible version, a judgment had to be passed against them, at least according to the majority opinion.[40] The defendant lost the suit if he modified a statement qualified as sure earlier.[41] It was the plaintiff who had to notice that the defendant had modified his previous statement. If the plaintiff signed the protocol, he could no longer refer to *washtag sakhwanīh* and no judgment was to be passed against the defendant because of it.[42]

Not every modification was considered *washtag sakhwanīh*, only those which related to the essential facts – for instance the time and title of possession or the person of the legal predecessor in a lawsuit on ownership.[43] When the defendant first denied and later acknowledged the statements of the plaintiff, it was qualified as *washtag sakhwanīh*.[44]

Protocols (*sakhwan nāmag*) were produced during the hearings to record the statements of the plaintiff and the defendant, which had to be sealed by both parties. If the defendant's seal was missing, the protocol was invalid.[45] By contrast, if the plaintiff's seal was missing the judge was entitled to continue the lawsuit ex officio, but this issue was disputed among Persian legal scholars.[46] To cover the costs of the proceedings a fee was to be paid, the sum of which was established

36 MHDA 25. 15–26. 11.
37 Macuch 1981: 160.
38 MHD 102. 9–11.
39 MHD 102. 9–11.
40 MHD 9. 1–4.
41 MHD 77. 9–10.
42 MHD 9. 6–8.
43 MHD 9. 14–10. 7
44 MHD 10. 7–9, 9–11.
45 MHD 90. 4–6.; MHDA 28. 7–11.
46 MHDA 28. 7–11.

by *kardag*. Accordingly, it was between 22 and 30 per cent of the value of the disputed object – but never more than 2 or 3 drachmas.[47]

When both parties had made their statements the proceeding entered into its next phase. Now the judge had to decide on whom the burden of proof rested because there was no law regulating this issue in general. In other words, Sasanian law did not know the maxim that the burden of proof rested on the plaintiff. In fact, in a considerable number of cases known (mostly in lawsuits on ownership and property) it was the duty of the defendant to prove that the plaintiff's claim was not true (*nē ēdōnīh*).[48] The decisive factor in selecting which party bore the burden of proof was what kind of formulae the parties used in their contract because different wording or syntax (e.g. active/passive) resulted in different legal consequences.

Statements could be proven by witnesses, documents[49] or material proof.[50] It is important to note that during a lawsuit the testimony of a single witness was acceptable.[51] By contrast, three witnesses were required to certify a private document outside the court (e.g. in the case of an oral testament).[52] It was the witness's obligation to testify; it is not known whether or not sanctions were applied against reluctant witnesses, but post-Sasanian sources clearly refer to strong moral condemnation.[53]

When no witnesses, documents or any other material proof were at hand the issue was settled by ordeals or oaths. Statements that were unusual or difficult to believe had to be confirmed by oath, too (e.g. if the debtor stated that his debt was annulled by the creditor).[54] In such cases the proceeding was suspended in the court, to be continued only after an ordeal or taking of an oath had taken place, usually in a different location. According to the Dēnkard[55] 33 oaths were known but only four of them are mentioned in the MHD+A: the *war ī dēnīg*, *war ī pāy nishān*, *war ī pad sōgand* and *war ī pad nāmag passāz*.

The *war ī dēnīg* (oath on faith) was to confirm whether a statement of a party was positive (*ēdōnīh*) or negative (*nē ēdōnīh*). Thus this kind of oath served to confirm material truth. The meaning of *war ī pāy nishān* becomes clear in the light of later sources.[56] This form of oath was not used to confirm material truth but to

47 MHDA 15.17–16.5.

48 MHD 6.2–6,15. 12–14, 14–16, 108.6–8; MHDA 30.17–31.3.

49 MHD 83.17–84.5.

50 MHD 7.3–4.

51 MHD 107.9–12, 12–14.

52 Macuch 1981: 137.

53 Dēnkard 715.18–19 (in Macuch 1981: 194) considers the sin of a witness denying to make a testimony equal with the crime of a judge intentionally passing an unjust (*drōg wizīr*) judgment.

54 MHD 8. 15–16.

55 Dēnkard 644.14ff. in Macuch 1993: 135.

56 According to Perikhanian during this oath the feet of the person taking the oath were surrounded by a sacred belt while he was saying the words of the oath; Macuch 1993:

prove the integrity of the person taking the oath. It does not prove that a statement is actually true but confirms only that the testifying person is of integrity The force of such an oath was obviously weaker than that of the *war ī dēnīg*. According to widely accepted scholarly wisdom the *war ī pad sōgand* was a special kind of oath, during which the person involved drank sulphur water. If he had given a false oath he would burn to death because of the sulphur in his body, as it was believed.[57] This widespread explanation is now subject to criticism by Martin Schwartz.[58] Nothing is known about the content of *war ī pad nāmag passāz* (oath used at taking records) besides what the term itself means. It seems that a legal representative could also take the two latter types of oaths.[59]

It is important to note that it was not necessarily the person charged with the burden of proof who testified under oath. By contrast, it was the person called *wehdādestāntar* who was given the opportunity to swear – that is, whose oath could be trusted more. Unfortunately, the conditions by which such a person was selected from the parties are unknown, but moral and religious considerations certainly were among them. It often happened that it was the defendant and not the plaintiff who qualified as *wehdādestāntar*; therefore he had to give his oath on the plaintiff's statement which was made against him. In such a case the defendant's oath was aimed at denial (*nē ēdōnīh*).[60] Co-plaintiffs had to give their oath jointly, otherwise the oath was invalid.[61]

Taking an oath was considered an advantage in the lawsuit because the party swearing the oath could influence the outcome of the lawsuit. This is clear from the judgment divesting the defendant of his right to give an oath in case he committed an act of *azishmānd*, and the privilege of taking an oath was transferred to the plaintiff qualified earlier as less worthy.[62]

Oath-giving did not take place in the law court but in the *khwārastān* under the supervision of the *war-sālār*.[63] This official conducted the entire procedure up to sealing the *yazishn nāmag*, the protocol of the oath-taking.[64] This protocol did not certify the content of the statement but merely the fact that the oath was taken properly. Oaths were taken on a certain day of the month: on the third day of the month according to the čāshtag, and on the sixth day of the month according to

---

135 referring to Perikhanian.

57 Boyce 1975: 35.

58 Schwartz 1989: 293–5.

59 MHD 78.15–17.

60 MHD 6.2–6, 13.6–13, 13.16–14.2, 14.2–5, 5–7.

61 MHD 13.6–13.

62 MHD 14.12-17.

63 MHD 8.15–16, 8.16–9.1, 57.3–12; the term was discussed at length by Bartholomae 1922: 39–42.

64 MHDA 27.7–9.

the *kardag*.[65] When a person obliged to take an oath did not perform his task he committed an act of *azishmānd* and was condemned by an interim judgment.[66]

Ordeals had similar functions to oaths, therefore the word *war* also meant 'ordeal'. It is remarkable that in private litigation reference to ordeals is rather unusual, while in cases of capital crimes it was more frequent. Perhaps disputes of private individuals about material goods were considered not worth invoking God by ordeals and therefore oaths were sufficient to decide such cases. By contrast, to decide on crimes (which could be sanctioned with capital punishment) was looked at as important enough to make use of ordeal, too. This might explain why the MHD+A, mostly dealing with issues of private law, hardly refers to ordeals.

The division of ordeals into hot and cold goes back to ancient tradition. Walking on hot embers, pouring molten metal on the chest or dipping the hand into boiling oil belonged to the hot ordeals. Consuming huge quantities of food or cutting the limbs with a knife were particular forms of cold ordeal. Ordeals were also held in a place set aside for this purpose, in the presence of priests and witnesses, while sacred texts were recited.[67]

When the oath was properly taken and administered the suit continued in the court room. The judge, now with all evidence at his disposal, was able to pronounce judgment. Until this time the plaintiff had the right to ask for a suspension of the procedure, but the defendant's consent to this was required.[68] If the plaintiff intentionally hindered the procedure the defendant could demand compensation.[69] Until the judgment was passed the parties could also conclude an agreement outside litigation. Such an agreement resulted in the termination of the lawsuit which, however, did not prevent the parties starting new litigation later. In such a case the protocol taken earlier was regarded as null and void and a new *sakhwan nāmag* had to be taken.[70]

The conclusion of an agreement outside the lawsuit proved to be advantageous to the defendant under certain circumstances – even if the content of the agreement did not fully reflect his interests – because as long as he was a defendant in a lawsuit he could not start a lawsuit against the same plaintiff on another issue.[71] In such a situation the defendant could free himself from his defendant's position with the help of a disadvantageous agreement, which allowed him to take another action to the law court. Later on, when the case was settled, he could start a lawsuit against the former plaintiff for correction of the agreement reached outside the lawsuit which was disadvantageous to him. It is not known for certain that such

65 MHDA 13.7–8; Macuch 1981: 151.
66 MHD 13.13–16.
67 Dhalla 1922: 106.
68 MHD 90.6–8.
69 MHD 77.15–78.2.
70 MHD 74.9–12.
71 MHDA 32.7–8.

practices have in fact taken place but at least in theory procedural law did not hinder the use of such techniques.

If the lawsuit was not suspended or the parties came to no agreement outside litigation the judge pronounced the judgment. The verdict was committed to writing (in all probability by the clerks) and a copy of it was kept in the archives.[72] If the judgment was at variance with the rules of procedure it had to be considered as 'not good' (*ne pad khūb dāshtan*);[73] if it was *contra legem* of norms of substantial law it was considered a 'lie judgment' (*drōg wizīr*).[74]

When the judgment was announced the parties could decide whether to accept it or appeal against it. After their statement of acceptance the parties could not change their mind.[75] Presumably those who violated the rule of *res iudicata* were punished; at least this may be inferred from one judgment.[76]

If both parties (or one of them) appealed against the judgment the procedure continued at a second or third instance court, depending on which court previously started the lawsuit.[77] This court informed the appellate court about the facts of the case.[78] Lacking any sources concerning trials at appellate courts, it is impossible to say more about such procedures.

A particular form of legal remedy took place in the royal court during two major festivals of Zoroastrianism, *Nawrūz* and *Mihragān*. According to the Kitāb al-tāj of al-Jaḥiẓ, during these occasions complaints against the king and his officials could be presented by anyone who was dissatisfied with previous judicial procedures for whatever reasons. The *mōbedān mōbed* in person guaranteed, with the help of soldiers, that entry should not be denied to anyone. The procedure started with the complaint of those who complained against the king being grouped around the imperial chief scribe. Next the king would kneel down before the high priest in a rather ceremonial manner and swear that no matter how he decided he would accept the high priest's decision. In case justice was given to the complainant the king had to redress the complaint, otherwise the complainants were punished for high treason. After the cases of people complaining against the king were dealt with the rest of the cases were discussed. This custom is said to have been in practice for centuries until Yazdagerd I. abolished it. Obviously, the text of al-Jaḥiẓ, produced centuries later, contains an idealized state of affairs highlighting the importance of the chief priest, a kind of Zoroastrian priestly propaganda not

72 MHDA 26.6.

73 MHDA 14.5–6.

74 Macuch 1981: 194.

75 MHD 3.1–3.

76 MHD 3. 3–5; Macuch 1993: 62.

77 MHD 3. 6–8

78 MHD 110. 13–15.

necessarily identical to historical reality. Nevertheless, other sources also attest to the existence of such a practice.[79]

Criminal Procedural Law[80]

As seen above, private procedural law is relatively well documented in the MHD+A. By contrast, some important issues of criminal procedure remain in the dark because the MHD+A contains only sporadic references to criminal procedure. Therefore, to reconstruct Zoroastrian criminal procedural law one must rely on a variety of sources, such as the Syriac Acts of Martyrs, religious and secular literary works, and sometimes even pamphlets of dubious historical reliability (e.g. the so-called 'Letter of Tansar'). None of these sources belong to legal literature since they focus on different topics (the martyrdom of Christians, the praise of Persian kings etc.) but contain some data on criminal procedure. Therefore, the only way to study criminal procedure is to consult these sources and interpret them very carefully. What complicates the matter is that the majority of the available texts focus on substantial criminal law or, more precisely, on punishments, but they have very little to say about criminal procedure. We are, therefore, relatively well informed about capital crimes (apostasy, treason, robbery) but know next to nothing about other crimes.

It is not known whether criminal procedure started on the accusation of the injured party or on that of an 'attorney general'. Perhaps lesser crimes were in the hands of the injured party but conclusive proof is lacking. Serious crimes committed against the king and the official religion (i.e. Zoroastrianism) were ex officio prosecuted. Therefore the procedure was not initiated by a private individual but directly by the king or the Zoroastrian clergy.

Officials called *frēzwān* and *zēndānbān* were authorities who took part in the criminal procedure. The *frēzwān* rendered assistance to the judge in conducting the lawsuit. It was his task to collect evidence and present it at the proceedings; identify the parties; arrest the accused; and to take him away after the proceeding.[81] The *zēndānbān* was a prison inspector (or warden); his competency was not precisely delineated but perhaps he had tasks similar to those of the *frēzwān*.[82] The *zēndānbān* kept records relating to prisoners and was responsible for the safekeeping of convicts.[83]

79 Perry 1978: 204. According to al-Ṭabarī, too, the custom of royal audience was abolished by Yazdagerd I. The Syriac Acts of Martyrs, however, know it differently: accordingly public hearings were held in the first week of every month, when nobles had the opportunity to refer cases of misconduct and oppression to the king; see Braun 1915: 179.

80 This section is based on my article devoted to criminal law; see Jany 2007.

81 MHDA 27.10–12; Macuch 1981: 202–3.

82 MHDA 28.11–16.

83 MHDA 28.17–29.6.

Studying the Syriac Acts of Martyrs, Gernot Wiessner distinguishes between two types of procedures: the one in which the king was personally involved, the other in which only his officials took part. In cases of political significance when dignitaries and leading officials were charged, the king actively took part in the hearings, but in cases of no political interest he left the case to his commissars. The judgment, however, was passed even in these cases by the Persian king.[84] In criminal procedures against Christians the commissars were called the king's representatives (*sharrīra de malkā* in the Syrian text),[85] who proceeded in their own right without consulting the *frēzwān* (the official responsible for investigations) and were various dignitaries of the Zoroastrian priesthood.[86]

Investigation started when the accused was made acquainted with the charges against them and could defend themself against the accusations. The charges and the plea were made orally, sometimes in the presence of the monarch. Protocols were produced during the hearings which contained the accusation; the questions put to the accused and their answers to those questions; denial or confession. Protocols recorded during a criminal procedure were called *pursishn-nāmag* (book of questions),[87] which was, somewhat astonishingly, more than protocols because they not only contained the oral declarations of the parties but also functioned as indictment – and even the judgment had to be recorded in it at the end of the procedure.[88] Thus, all relevant information was ultimately recorded in a single document. Such protocols were not produced, however, in every criminal procedure. It was compulsory only when a capital crime was committed (the perpetrators of such crimes were called *margarzān*, 'worthy of death'); in cases of minor importance producing a *pursishn-nāmag* was left to the discretion of the judge.[89]

When one hearing was sufficient to decide the case, judgment was pronounced at the end of it, otherwise more hearings were necessary. There was no rule whatsoever concerning intervals between hearings. Between hearings the accused was kept in custody either in jail or on house arrest,[90] sometimes for a long period, during which torture was common (at least in investigations against Christians) which resulted in serious corporal mutilation (the tongue of the accused was cut out, his teeth were knocked out, his bones were broken).[91]

---

84 Wiessner, G. (1967): Zur Märtyrerüberlieferung aus der Christenverfolgung Schapurs II. Göttingen: Vandenhoeck and Ruprecht.

1967: 167–8.

85 Perhaps it is the equivalent of Middle Persian ōstīgān; see Macuch 1993: 632–3.

86 Wiessner 1967: 169–78.

87 Braun 1915: 203; MHD 78.4.

88 MHDA 34.8–9.

89 MHDA 34.6.

90 Braun 1915: 208.

91 Braun 1915: 2–3.

As attested by both the Acts of Martyrs and the Letter of Tansar, apostates were put in jail before the judgment was pronounced. According to the latter apostates were jailed for one year in order to let them change their mind and return to Zoroastrianism, during which torture was common but was called with some pathos 'advice and persuasion'.[92] Such captivity, however, did not necessarily last a full year because there is evidence of some accused who spent only a couple of weeks or several months in jail, as well as three years.[93] While in custody, the accused was:

> put among robbers and assassins;
> fettered by heavy chains;[94]
> interrogated and harmed repeatedly during the day;[95]
> left without food and drink for long spells of time;[96]
> whipped with thorny pomegranate branches;[97]
> and it was prohibited to visit the captives, or supply them with food, drink and clothes.[98]

Almost nothing is known about the prison conditions of the day. Reference has already been made to keeping the captives in chains and torturing them, but treatment was left to the discretion of the officials. A reference found in the Syriac Acts of Martyrs to fellow prisoners going out to the city to beg for food for those who were prohibited to do so suggests that more freedom was ensured for certain captives, though the cooperation of the jail wardens (*zēndānbān*) was also necessary.[99] The practice of corrupting jail wardens is suggested by several texts. According to the chronicle of al-Ṭabarī, King Kawād – jailed by his opponents – was freed from prison by his sister promising the warden that he could satisfy his love for her. Although he was tricked at the end, the king nevertheless was freed.[100] Needless to say, what al-Ṭabarī recorded is not history but folklore, yet at the same time such stories reflect the corruptness of Persian officials. Contemporary reality was also recorded in the Syriac Acts of Martyrs, according to which a rich Christian woman could enter a prison to treat the wounds of captives caused by

92 *naṣīhat konand wa edalle wa (barāhīn) barū ʿarẓ dārand*: Ibn Isfandiyār 1942: 22 – 'advise him and lay arguments'. Boyce 1968: 42, who correctly claims, referring to Darmesteter, that this 'seems to be the earliest record of an inquisition'.

93 Braun 1915: 123; Hoffmann 1880: 35.

94 Braun 1915: 145.

95 Braun 1915: 94.

96 Braun 1915: 101.

97 Braun 1915: 120.

98 Braun 1915: 122.

99 Braun 1915: 122.

100 Nöldeke 1879: 144.

torture by bribing the warden with a considerable sum of money.[101] Bribery was a risky business because jail wardens risked a lot since they were responsible for safeguarding the prison. If a prisoner escaped the *zēndānbān* was punished, sometimes with capital punishment.[102]

Prisoners could escape captivity by lawful means, too. According to Sasanian law a prisoner could be released on bail (although there was no legal term for it); at least this can be inferred from a single case. Narse, a jailed Christian repeatedly tortured, was released on request of local residents who paid a large sum as bail and acted as guarantors for his appearance in the subsequent hearings. Thereupon a written accord was drawn up naming the person responsible for his supervision. As a result Narse regained his freedom and was at the disposal of the authorities for continuing the procedure against him.[103]

The supervision of jails was within the king's competency. We can find wise counsel of Buzurgmihr in the chronicle of al-Masᶜūdī, which recommends that the king visit the detainees frequently in order to release the innocent and select the culprits.[104] As other counsels of Buzurgmihr contain rather realistic proposals (honouring and controlling clerks and officials, keeping arms ready, checking weights used in markets etc.) there is no reason to doubt that the advice quoted here reflects the real prison conditions of the Sasanian period. It is reasonable to think, therefore, that a large number of innocent people were also detained in prison and that prisons could be overcrowded from time to time. This is indirectly supported by a royal edict preserved in the Acts of Martyrs. Accordingly, the king ordered the local governor (*marzbān*: border marquis) to execute those who deserved death, to punish those who deserved corporal punishment and to set the rest free.[105]

When the last hearing ended, judgment followed it immediately. The judgment of capital punishment usually contained the crime the person was accused of, the sanction and the type of execution, giving a detailed description of how it was to be done. Execution was postponed until delivery if the convict was a pregnant woman because the unborn child was regarded as innocent and could not be condemned to death.[106] Most frequently capital punishment was decapitation by sword carried, out by an executioner.[107] Occasionally, decapitation was made even more severe: in such cases the executioner first cut off the fingers, next the hands and feet and only then decapitated the convict.[108] A single executioner, however,

101 Braun 1915: 128.

102 MHDA 13.10–12.

103 Braun 1915: 145–146; Hoffmann 1880: 37–8.

104 al-Masᶜūdī 1989: 232.

105 Braun 1915: 146.

106 Nyberg 1964: 10.

107 Braun 1915: 34; 55; 81; 95; 99; 104; 105; 148; 169; Hoffmann 1880: 16.

108 Braun 1915: 153; 176.

was insufficient when large numbers of convicts were to be executed, therefore on such occasions jailed assassins were ordered to carry out the executions.[109]

Crucifixion was another way convicts were put to death, and occasionally the condemned was crucified head first.[110] Crucifixion was the punishment of robbers and witches.[111] Sometimes culprits were cut in two at the waist[112] or were burnt alive after having been smeared with naphtha.[113] There was also a precedent of gouging the condemned's eyes with a hot needle and then leaving him to die[114] or of burying him in earth to half his height and then shooting a shower of arrows at him;[115] or vinegar and mustard were squeezed into his eyes, mouth and nose.[116] Stoning was a rarely applied mode of execution. A particularly cruel variant of punishment was when the inhabitants of the village and members of the Christian congregation were forced to participate in the execution of their fellows.[117] Occasionally elephants were also used in executions, mostly against Christians, robbers and murderers.[118] Revolts were also suppressed by elephants, as shown by the decision of Šābuhr II, who had the inhabitants of the city of Šūš trampled on by 100 elephants after a failed uprising. The Letter of Tansar mentions two more tools of execution, the 'cow' and the 'donkey': the former was a cauldron filled with lead and the condemned was squeezed into it; while the donkey was an iron tripod on which the condemned was hanged until they died.[119]

Executions took place in a public place where sometimes a crowd was gathered around, therefore order was guaranteed by soldiers whose task was to guard the corpses, too. Sometimes, however, soldiers were unable to keep order, particularly in mass executions when some people who were not accused and condemned were also executed. Once, when a favourite servant of the king was also among those executed, the monarch learned about the chaos experienced during the executions. As a result he issued an edict that the personal data of the condemned should be

---

109 Braun 1915: 84.

110 Braun 1915: 185; 187; 268. The request by Mār Gīwargīs to be crucified head first was refused by the soldier saying that the order was not about that and if doing otherwise the king would be upset. At the same time Tahm Yazdagerd, a martyred *mōbed*, was crucified head first. It seems, therefore, that any arbitrary execution was prohibited; capital punishment had to be executed as it was put in the judgment and could not be made graver even if the condemned asked for it.

111 Ibn Isfandiyār 1942: 26.

112 Braun 1915: 4; 92; Hoffmann 1880: 33.

113 Braun 1915: 183.

114 Braun 1915: 4.

115 Braun 1915: 4.

116 Braun 1915: 185; Hoffmann 1880: 56.

117 Braun 1915: 3, 136.

118 Braun 1915: 182. The Letter of Tansar confirms that elephants were favoured against heretics; see Ibn Isfandiyār 1942: 26.

119 Ibn Isfandiyār 1942: 26.

put in writing (their name, the names of their mother and father, place of birth, domicile, religion and their responses to the accusations), and that only those who possessed such a written document could be executed. The Acts of Martyrs, hardly sympathetic towards Persian rulers, acknowledge that after issuing this edict some order was manifest in the executions.[120]

Corpses were left hanging on the cross for three days and were removed only afterwards.[121] The burial of the executed, however, was a starting point of further conflict. As Christians did not want to bury their dead according to Zoroastrian custom they turned to extra-legal means: they stole the corpses at the dark of night or, more commonly, bribed the guard and carried the corpses away to bury them.[122] When a prominent person was put to death and the king personally wanted to learn that the convicted was dead such means were ineffective since the head of the corpse was cut off and presented to the ruler.[123]

Judicial Procedure in Jewish Law

Organs of Procedure

As seen previously the judiciary witnessed significant changes during the course of centuries. In the Second Temple period the *Sanhedrīn* became the most important judicial forum, therefore this section starts with problems related to it.

Rabbinic sources see the *Sanhedrīn* as an organ of the administration of justice having legislative functions, too. The *Sanhedrīn* consisted of the leading legal scholars and was governed by the 'pairs' (*zugōt*). By contrast, according to Greek sources it was a decision-making body, the leader of which was the king or the high priest. As a result of such contradictions some scholars suggested that there were two *Sanhedrīn*s, one for the administration of justice and another for political decisions. This theory was represented, among others, by Büchler, according to whom the great *Sanhedrīn* and the *bēt dīn ha-gādōl* ('grand court'), both operating in Jerusalem, were two different institutions. The *bēt dīn ha-gādōl* was primarily a religious institution, the leaders of which were the Pharisees headed by the 'pairs': the *nāśī* and the *'ab bēt dīn* who, as chairman and deputy, acted as heads of the religious judiciary. The great *Sanhedrīn*, on the other hand, was primarily a political institution and a criminal court which was governed by the priesthood. This institution was under Roman influence and, therefore, disappeared with changing Roman policy and with the destruction of the Temple. Greenwald, Lauterbach and Aptowitzer agreed.[124]

120 Braun 1915: 85–7.

121 Braun 1915: 272; Hoffmann 1880: 112.

122 Braun 1915: 4, 81, 125, 137, 162, 177.

123 Braun 1915: 3.

124 The different views are surveyed by Mantel 1965: 60–64.

By contrast, scholars such as Schürer, Hoffmann and Chwolson do not believe in two *Sanhedrīn*s and dissolve the obvious contradictions of the sources historically. According to their argumentation the *Sanhedrīn* had different functions in different historical periods and, therefore, its leaders were different, too. The Greek and rabbinic sources, these scholars believe, differ from each other because they refer to different historical periods. According to Hoffmann the Pharisees were the leaders (the *nāśī* and the *'ab bēt dīn*) of the *Sanhedrīn* who were repeatedly squeezed out of leadership as a result of the changing political situation. Herod limited the authority of the *Sanhedrīn* to religious issues, and its authority was further decreased during the leadership of the Roman procurators. Segal holds that two institutions were called by the same name because leading legal scholars were present in both. Their decision was of a legal or political nature depending on whether the gathering was to decide upon some details of the *halakah* or to investigate other cases.[125]

In addition to these views there is also the suggestion that there had been three *Sanhedrīn*s, each having 23 members. According to Geiger one court was made up of the priests, the second of the Levites and the third of the Israelites. If a decision had to be made on an issue of general interest the three judicial councils had a joint session, thus forming the Great *Sanhedrīn* – which was then headed by the high priest.[126]

What complicates matter is that the term *Sanhedrīn* denoted not only this high-ranking judiciary and political body but also local courts. As a result the *Sanhedrīn* and the *bēt dīn* became synonyms by which local courts were also called. Thus smaller courts, consisting of 23 members (*bēt dīn*) were also called *Sanhedrīn* in the sources (M Sanh 1:5–6). Now it is understandable why the *Sanhedrīn* of Jerusalem was called the Great *Sanhedrīn* which denoted, according to Mantel, an organ of the administration of justice and not a political institution. In Mantel's view the legal and the political forums of the same name should be distinguished from the lesser courts operating in the countryside which were also called *Sanhedrīn* (*bēt dīn*). The Great *Sanhedrīn* operated independently of these local *Sanhedrīn*s but was not an appellate court.[127]

Now, coming to the legal competencies of the court, these consisted of legislation, legal interpretation and some administrative functions. The court as a legislative body issued ordinances (*takkanah*) in various fields of law, including agricultural law, civil law and laws on ritual purity.[128] The law defined by this court was binding on everybody.[129] As a supreme court the Great *Sanhedrīn* was entitled also to give legal advice to lower-level courts when they requested it, being in

125 Mantel 1965: 55–8; Segal 1996: 129.

126 For Geiger's theory and its followers, see Mantel 1965: 58–60.

127 Mantel 1965: 92–6.

128 Mantel 1965: 84.

129 Cohn 1974: 562.

doubt on any legal issues. This opinion of the court, however, was binding.[130] Among the court's administrative functions perhaps the most important in legal practice was the appointment of the smaller courts of 23, while decisions such as the declaration of war and making additions to the city of Jerusalem and to the courtyards of the Temple[131] became more and more irrelevant in the course of history.

The court as a judicial body made judgments in important issues which were not to be decided on by any other court. These issues were considered important because of the persons involved or because of their subject-matter. Thus, the high priest, a false prophet[132] and the head of a tribe[133] could be judged by this court only; a king was exempt according to Mishnah 2:2, but this rule was subject to dispute in Talmudic times.[134] A rebellious elder (*zāqēn mamre*)[135] was also judged by the court of 71[136] together with certain crimes punishable by death (such as the judgment of a rebellious son, a false witness and one who leads a town to apostasy or who leads people away to idol worship): in these cases the judgment of other courts would be confirmed by the Great *Sanhedrīn* before execution was implemented.[137]

Rabbinic sources claim that the *Sanhedrīn* was headed by the *nāśī*, a term of long history and multiple meaning. Prior to the early biblical period a tribal chief or the head of a larger family unit was called *nāśī*, as were the leaders of the people in the wilderness (Ex. 16:2; 34:31), but the term lost its significance for some time with the establishment of the monarchy. Jewish rulers called themselves *nāśī* in the Second Temple period in order to avoid being called 'king'. Bar Kokba' also called himself *nāśī* on a coin.[138] Rabbinic tradition interprets this title narrower and understands it as the head of the *Sanhedrīn*. According to present knowledge it is impossible to say who first filled the office of the Pharisee *nāśī*. Some scholars think that this office emerged before the Maccabees; others accept the tradition that the first Pharisee *nāśī* was Hillel (first century BCE); and a third group of scholars accept R. Yūdah (second century CE) as the first authentic person.[139] The office was eliminated in 425 by Theodosian (Codex Theodosianus XVI: 8.22).

The most important task of the *nāśī* was to chair the *bēt dīn ha-gādōl*. The order of the session was set to underline the leading role of the *nāśī*: members of

130 Cohn 1974: 562; Mantel 1965: 96, 223–4.

131 M Sanh 1:5.

132 M Sanh 1:5.

133 Sanh 16a.

134 Sanh 19a; see also Tos Sanh 4:2.

135 A legal scholar refusing to accept the decision of the majority of legal scholars in matters of law and continuing to implement his own doctrine.

136 M Sanh 11:2; Tos Sanh 3:4.

137 Tos Sanh 11:6.

138 Nasi in *Encyclopedia Judaica* vol. 12, 834–5 (G. J. Blidstein).

139 Mantel 1965: 2–7.

the *Sanhedrīn* were seated in a semicircle so as to see each other's face, the *nāśī* sitting in the middle, flanked by the leading legal scholars.[140] When the *nāśī* entered the room all had to rise and could only sit down when he gave them permission.[141] He enjoyed such prestige due to his mastery in law and jurisprudence and not only because of his office alone. Outstanding *nāśīs* of scholarly reputation were Hillel, R. Gamalī'el II and R. Yūdah, who is said to be the compiler of the Mishnah. In the generations following R. Yūdah, however, one may find a decreasing number of legal scholars among the *nāśīs* who primarily had administrative and political functions. Characteristically the last *nāśī*, Gamalī'el VI, was a well-known physician.[142]

The functions of the *nāśī* can be grouped into four categories:

1. religious functions
2. administrative functions
3. political functions
4. functions in the administration of justice.

The *religious* functions of the *nāśī* included the fixing of the calendar, intercalation, determining the leap year and the proclamation of national fast days – these with the support of a court of three.[143] The *nāśī*, together with the *'āb bēt dīn*, led the prayer for rain.[144]

The aim of the *administrative* functions of the *nāśī* was to lead the Jewish community of the Roman Empire. This leadership consisted of legal guidance by answering questions put to him and sent back through his emissaries who visited communities in the Diaspora with his authorization. The emissaries of the *nāśī* were respected legal scholars who performed several religious functions and took part in the administration of justice, chaired the local courts and passed judgments. In addition, they had the right to remove any religious or lay official from office if they did not respect the principles or rules of law. The high social prestige of the emissaries is indicated by the fact that R. ᶜAqībah, one of the most outstanding legal scholars of his age, did not find it below his rank to visit various communities as the *nāśī*'s emissary. The right to extend hospitality to an emissary was considered an honour. In addition to adjudication the emissaries founded schools and collected money for the *nāśī* to enable him to perform the tasks of his office, and for helping legal scholars and maintaining schools. Though the ratio of the contribution was not specified, it was customary to donate 2 per cent of the income. The emissaries, however, sometimes interfered deeply in the life of a community, as shown by the Jews of Antioch who called a legal scholar acting in the name of the *nāśī* a

140 Tos Sanh 8:1.

141 Tos Sanh 7:8.

142 Mantel 1965: 178, 253.

143 Sanh 11a; Mantel 1965: 179-88.

144 Mantel 1965: 188.

tyrant. Besides the emissaries the *nāśī* also appointed the inspector of markets, who controlled weights and measures, and even set prices if necessary. This office was regarded as the most important in the country[145] and greatly resembles the office of the Byzantine *agoranomos* and that of the *muḥtasib* in Islamic law. Thus, the *nāśī* could govern rather effectively even remote communities.

The *nāśī* started to exercise his *political* function after 70 CE. The Romans acknowledged the *nāśī* as a political leader despite the fact that he did not govern a certain territory, but rather the dispersed Jewish communities. The political and social prestige of the *nāśī* in the Roman Empire is proven by the Codex Theodosianus (XVI: 8.11), according to which his public oral abuse was punishable. This rule was implemented by the Romans even against their own consul when Hilarius was removed from office because of such an act. Emissaries of the *nāśī* enjoyed privileges in the Roman state (Cod. Theod. XVI: 8.15.); the office of the *nāśī* enjoyed the highest acknowledgement since it was titled *honoraria praefectura*, while the *nāśī* himself was a person belonging to the *spectabiles*. As the *nāśī* was the political representative of the Jews, Hellenistic customs otherwise prohibited to any Jew were permitted to him. Thus he could learn Greek, have a hairstyle like the pagans and could even use a mirror. The *nāśī* participated in political activities and negotiated with representatives of the Roman state.[146] In brief, the *nāśī* was treated as if he were a king, though according to Jewish law he did not qualify as such. He did not enjoy the privileges of a monarch; therefore, in theory, he could be sentenced to flogging, a punishment a king was exempt from.[147] Yet, by stressing their descent from the House of David by the female line, the *nāśī*s clearly referred to their claim to be rulers. Morbid as it is, they could achieve this status only at their death because they had to be buried with royal honours.[148]

Concerning the *administration of justice*, the *nāśī* had a separate court which included eminent legal scholars, too. This court, however, was not an appellate court as other prominent legal scholars also had their courts and the *nāśī*'s court was no higher in the hierarchy than these courts. The Mishnah clearly states that there was no appellate court in the modern sense of the term when it says that the judgment of a court can only be altered by a court larger in size and higher in wisdom. Thus, the *nāśī*'s court was of equal standing and had no more authority

145 Mantel 1965: 188–203.

146 Mantel 1965: 235–43. R. Gamalī'el, for instance, negotiated with the governor of Syria and for this purpose he even travelled to the governor's headquarters: Sanh 11a.

147 The Mishnah regulates the legal position of the king in detail: he could not be charged at a law court; he does not give testimony and no one can give testimony about him; he does not enter into a levirate marriage and no one enters levirate marriage with his wife; no one can stop him while he is on his way; no one can ride his horse or sit on his throne; no one can see him naked, or in the bath or while his hair is being cut; further, he has to keep the Torāh scroll with him at all times and to study it (M Sanh 2: 2–3: 1); but these rights did not extend to the *nāśī*. Mantel 1965: 243.

148 Tos Sanh 4:3; Mantel 1965: 243–4.

than other courts of other eminent legal scholars. But the *nāśī*'s court played an important role in legislation, too, proven by the numbers of *takkanah*s and *gezerah*s issued by either the *nāśī* alone or attributed to the *nāśī*'s court.[149] The *nāśī* alone, later together with his court, was entitled to ordain a scholar. We will return to the somewhat complicated problem of ordination later; suffice it to say now that ordination meant in the long run an appointment to the position of judge. Ordination was of importance since ordained scholars enjoyed immunity from liability when pronouncing erroneous judgments.[150]

Finally, excommunication pronounced by the *nāśī* should be mentioned in relation to the *nāśī*'s authority. The right to excommunicate is the terrain of legal scholars, but it is open to any Jewish person, too, when he observes a violation of a religious rule by one of his fellows. Excommunication pronounced by the *nāśī*, however, was particular because it was obligatory for all. Excommunication could be for a short time (one week, 30 days) or indefinite when the person involved did not meet his obligations even after two warnings (*ḥērem).* A person could be excommunicated not only because of the violation of a religious rule but also for disrespectful behaviour towards legal scholars, for disregarding court decisions or for not repaying debts. The particular right of the *nāśī* concerning excommunication is discernible in his power to invalidate an excommunication that was supposed to be irretrievable (for instance the excommunication was stated by a legal scholar who died with the passage of time).[151]

Jews living in Babylonia (called *gōlāh*) in the Parthian Empire – and after its fall (224) in the Sasanian Empire – also enjoyed legal autonomy, though its extent underwent changes due to the changing policy of the Persian rulers. The principle of *dīna demalkūta' dīna* ('the law of the kingdom is law'), worded by the famous *amora* Shamū'el, reflects the acceptance of the Persian government by the Jews. Though the interpretation of this principle caused several problems, even for medieval legal scholars, it nevertheless pronounced the rightfulness of taxes collected by the Persian authorities.[152] (Jewish legal scholars considered taxes collected by the Romans as unjust and hence robbery.)[153] The large number of Persian loan words in the Babylonian Talmūd, including a number of legal terms, shows that Babylonian Jewish legal scholars were familiar with Zoroastrian law and legal practice. Babylonian Jews had their own leader whose standing was similar to that of the *nāśī*, though with minor differences in detail. The leader of the Babylonian Jews, the *rēsh galūta'*, just like the *nāśī*, claimed descent from David – and that from the male line. The *rēsh galūta'* was usually addressed by the Mesopotamian Jews as *rabbana'* (our Lord) or *mār*. Similarly to the *nāśī*, the

149 For a detailed discussion of the legislative functions of the *nāśī*'s court, see Mantel 1965: 227–35.

150 Sanh 5a; Mantel 1965: 210–12; Falk 1972: 90.

151 Mantel 1965: 225–7.

152 Shilo 1974: 710–14.

153 Segal 1996: 105.

rēsh galūta' appointed the inspector of markets[154] and judges proceeding in private cases.[155]

Legal scholars made every effort to monopolize jurisdiction, though there were other forums, too, which were free from their influence. One of them was the courts composed of non-professionals (*hedyoṭōt*) which, similarly to the earlier courts operating at the city gates, did not consist of legal scholars but of local leading personalities ('elders'). Days of judgment were Mondays and Thursdays according to a rule attributed to Ezra. Non-professional courts had to proceed in a college of three in each case, otherwise their ruling was invalid. By contrast, the judgment of a legal scholar had to be considered valid even if he acted alone unless the parties raised any objection to it. A further sign of negative attitude towards lay courts was a rule produced in later rabbinic tradition, according to which a lay judge was financially responsible for a wrong decision, while a legal scholar or a legal expert skilled in law (*mumḥeh le-bēt dīn*) was exempt of responsibility. Despite rabbinic efforts, however, the court of non-professionals was not to be eliminated.[156]

Arbitrary courts, too, played an important role in ensuring the implementation of Jewish law during times when Jewish legal autonomy was narrowed down.[157] By contrast, Roman courts, open to Jews in civilian cases, were considered a more dangerous rival because they did not implement Jewish law and threatened, therefore, Jewish legal autonomy and social cohesion. This is the reason why the scholar R. 'Elīᶜezer Ben Hyrcanus prohibited the Jews from turning to Roman law courts.[158]

The Competency of the Courts

The competency of the courts was determined by the importance of the cases they dealt with. Thus, cases of minor importance were decided by smaller courts, while more important cases were dealt with by larger courts and the whole system was headed by the 71-member Great *Sanhedrīn* seated in Jerusalem. It is important to note that this system does not constitute a judicial hierarchy since there were no appellate courts and, therefore, instances were unknown. Therefore a larger court was not a higher forum than a smaller court, even if occasionally it could alter the judgment of a smaller one. This right, however, did not follow from a hierarchy in the judiciary but from the principle that the judgment of a smaller court could be altered only by a court incorporating more members and greater wisdom.

Setting up a court was a community obligation. The members of the courts depended on the number of residents: in a settlement of fewer than 120 residents

154 Mantel 1965: 202, 240–43.

155 Tos Sanh 5a.

156 M Sanh 5a, 33a; Falk 1972: 92; Mantel 1965: 208.

157 Mantel 1965: 223, referring to the results of Allon.

158 Rabello 1996: 148.

it was enough to establish a three-member court, but in a city of more inhabitants a court of 23 members had to operate. Membership was set at the minimum of three judges and no smaller court was allowed to operate. This was because of the principle that only God can decide alone, and in order to assert the majority principle a court always had to have an odd number of members. Consequently, the membership of a court could not be less than three. Only the validity of a judgment passed by a legal scholar alone was accepted but that too only in civil cases and when both parties agreed to it. Such decision making was, however, condemned morally (with reference to God's tribunal).[159] Some scholars were of the opinion that the majority should be of three persons and therefore the court should consist of at least five members. This view, however, was ridiculed by R. Abbahū as *reductio ad absurdum*, saying that when applying this idea the Great *Sanhedrīn* would also have to have a minimum of 141 members, which was impossible and against the law.[160]

The competencies of the three-member courts consisted of:

1. theft and damages
2. compensation
3. lawsuits on rape
4. intercalation
5. procedures relating to the removal of shoes (breaking off levirate).[161]

This court also had the authority to judge in issues relating to divorce; criminal cases punishable by fines and by flogging;[162] lawsuits deriving from not releasing a slave after the completion of the sixth year; and pushing a thief unable to pay compensation into slavery.[163] In addition the three-member court was also needed for certain ritual acts: oath-taking; sacrifice of a heifer because of an unknown corpse etc.).[164] Serious crimes punishable by capital punishment belonged to the competency of the court of 23 members, together with procedures related to sexual crimes; animals accused of manslaughter (lions, panthers, bears, leopards, snakes); and to condemn a goring ox, and occasionally its master.[165]

The membership of the Great *Sanhedrīn* of 71 persons was based on the tradition according to which Moses had appointed 70 respected men to help him decide on legal disputes (Num. 11.17). As Moses should be added to those 70 people, this is how the 71 members were set (at any rate, the court must have an odd number of members). In theory, the Great *Sanhedrīn* was competent in

159 Sanh 2b, 5a, 33a; Cohn 1974: 563.

160 Sanh 3b.

161 M Sanh 1:1–1:3; Tos Sanh 2:1.

162 Sanh 2a; Gittin 5b.

163 Cohn 1974: 561.

164 Sanh 2a; Cohn 1974: 561; Deut. 21.1–9.

165 M Sanh 1:4; Sanh 2a.

every case, but there were cases in which it had exclusive competency. As we have seen above, it was in its power to judge on false prophets, the high priest, a tribe and its leader, a *zāqēn mamre*, and in certain cases it had to approve the capital punishment of another court before the judgment was implemented.[166]

Finally, some words about the competency of arbitrators are in order. According to Menachem Elon, arbitration emerged during the reign of Emperor Hadrian when the Roman authorities restricted the legal autonomy of Jews even in private legal cases (*dīney mamōnōt*). As a large majority of Jews wished to live according to their own law legal disputes were settled by arbiters not acknowledged officially as courts. Therefore, it is not by way of accident that legal disputes about arbitration emerged in that period among Jewish legal scholars (R. Me'īr and his contemporaries). By contrast, among the Babylonian Jews, where the Parthians ensured a far broader autonomy, arbitration did not play a significant role. Consequently arbitrators decided primarily on private cases, either in relation to an already existing dispute or to smooth over an emerging conflict.[167] It is not by chance either that the *Tōsefta'* produced in that period stresses that arbitration was a religious obligation.[168]

The principle that the decision-making body had to have at least three members was also asserted in arbitration. One member was chosen by the defendant and one by the plaintiff, but it was disputed who elected the third member. According to R. Me'īr the parties had to agree upon the third arbiter, but according to the majority of legal scholars the two already elected arbiters had the right to do so.[169] Finally, *halakah* specified that the parties had to give their consent to the third member selected by the arbiters, particularly if the arbiters were not authorized to pass judgment but were supposed to elaborate a compromise between the parties. Contrary to the practice of regular courts, the arbiters were not obliged to justify their decision in writing, even if this was requested by the parties. Arbiters received a fee for their work independently of the outcome. The arbiters' fee had to be paid by the party who had chosen them. To avoid corruption, later a proposal was announced that arbiters should be paid out of a special community fund set up for this purpose, but it was not adopted. In every other respect, however, the arbiters were of equal standing to the judges (*dayyānīm*).[170] If, however, the judicial procedure ended with judgment there was no further possibility for arbitration.[171]

166 M Sanh 1:5–1:6; Sanh 2a; Tos Sanh 11:7.

167 Elon 1974a: 565–6.

168 Tos Sanh 1:3.

169 M Sanh 3:1.

170 Elon 1974a: 567–9.

171 Tos Sanh 1:2.

The Procedure

The beginning of the history of procedural law is subject to dispute. According to Cohn procedural law preceded the development of substantive law and, therefore, Jewish law belongs to those legal cultures in which the rules of substantive law ultimately grew out of procedure.[172] By contrast, Falk considers it a rather late development. He demonstrates that self-help was acknowledged for a very long time in Jewish law and later it continued to be tolerated in cases for which there was judicial remedy, too – for example, in monetary matters.[173]

Procedural law, particularly criminal procedure, was a matter of dispute between the Pharisees and the Sadduceans. According to Daube, the story of Susanna is a literary work of the Pharisees in which they call attention to the untenability of the interpretation of the Sadduceans in criminal procedure and underline the eminence of their interpretation of law, wishing to realize a legal reform particularly of the rules pertaining to witnesses.[174] Be that as it may, the rules laid down in the Mishnah already mirror an elaborated system of procedure which basically shows the Pharisee interpretation (including the hearing of witnesses separately and the examination of their statements fixed already as a norm).

Private Procedural Law

A lawsuit started with the plaintiff's action.[175] Any person, either man or woman, could be a litigant (except minors and mute, deaf and mentally ill persons). Guaranteeing the right of litigation for women is particularly important because women usually did not appear in public; they could not be witnesses or judges. This is why the exceptional rule was made that a female defendant, if she did not wish to appear in court personally, could make her statement in her home, which was recorded by a judicial clerk sent out. This was the only exception to the rule that litigants were obliged to appear in court in person to make their statements. A guardian acted on behalf of minors, deaf, mute and mentally ill persons, but to avoid any possible conflict of interests the consent of the court was required. Thus

---

172 Cohn 1974: 561.

173 Falk 1972: 93–8.

174 Daube 1986: 412–19. In the story of Susanna two elderly men want to initiate sexual intercourse with the young heroine, but she refuses. The men then accuse her of adultery and the court condemns the woman to death on the basis of their false testimony. They are already walking towards the place of execution when Providence intervenes in the form of a young man with his proposal that the witnesses should be questioned separately and their statements examined. As a result, the woman was acquitted and the false witnesses were condemned to death. Daube is of the view that the message of the story composed by the Pharisees is that witnesses should be heard separately in order to realise the contradictions in their testimony and so prevent judgments based on false testimonies.

175 Tos Sanh 6:3.

representation by a guardian was accepted within limits, while representation by an attorney was regarded with serious resentment as the legal scholars of Babylon considered them as robbers.[176]

The province of the proceeding court was determined by the defendant's domicile. The plaintiff's claim was recorded on receipt by the clerks. The parties were warranted for the lawsuit by the court. The court warned the defendant that his appearance was compulsory and his absence could be justified only by a serious reason. Such an accepted reason was travel, among others, but the excuse had to be properly justified even in this case. No hearing could be carried on if the defendant was absent,[177] except in some obvious cases when the defendant had already acknowledged the plaintiff's claim in writing and testified through witnesses. Another exception was if the defendant was away on a journey lasting for more than 30 days. According to Maimonides the reason for this rule was so that no one could take out a loan and then move away somewhere in order to hinder the creditor asserting his demand. The court proceeded in the order of the arrival of actions – that is, the case that came in first was dealt with first, but exceptional rules were laid down out of consideration or keeping social status in view. Thus priority was accorded to cases of widows and orphaned children; similarly, scholars were given preference so that they would not be away from their studies for long. Any case involving women also had to be accorded priority so that they should not have to wait for long.[178]

Hearings started early in the morning and went on without a break up to mealtime (for about six hours), which originally could not be broken off even by prayers. The trial had to be completed by sunset and the final decision announced on the same day as the trial itself.[179] It was prohibited to hold court on the *Shabbāt* and on holidays.[180] At the beginning of the trial the members of the court walked in and the parties had to stand up.[181] The parties and the witnesses could sit down expressly with the permission of the court.[182] Due to the principle of impartiality, however, it had to be ensured that both parties be seated – no partial permission could be given. It was asserted even in cases when the social status of the parties was not equal (as in the case of a scholar who enjoyed great esteem). The equality of the parties was to be expressed even by their garments, therefore a conspicuously richly dressed party was called to dress similarly to the other party (and he was not allowed to speak until this was done).[183] As equal treatment of the parties was derived from biblical commandments (Lev. 19.15; Ex. 23.3; Deut. 1.17) a series of

176 Falk 1972: 100–101; Cohn 1974a: 573–5;
177 Sanh 7b.
178 Falk 1972: 102–3; Cohn 1974a: 575–6.
179 M Sanh 4:1; Cohn 1974a: 574.
180 M Sanh 4:1.
181 Tos Sanh 7:8.
182 Tos Sanh 7:8.
183 Tos Sanh 6:2.

sub-rules were produced to reach this goal. The most important among them were that no party could be questioned in the absence of the other party,[184] and that both parties had to be granted an equal length of time to present their case. Moreover, it was particularly stressed that the judge was prohibited from passing a judgment to the advantage of a poor man out of sympathy.[185]

The trial was oral. The parties made their statements orally and were not recorded in protocols because these were used only for recording the words of the judges. First the plaintiff presented his claim, to which the defendant had to respond, but the court could accord him sufficient time to think and prepare himself. The court was not allowed to assist either party, instruct them about their rights or help in wording their argumentation, not even by showing any argumentation in the form of a hypothetical case. The parties had to support their statements by evidence, that is, through witnesses and written documents. In theory evidence had to be available by the day of the trial, but the court could give an additional 30 days to the parties to present their evidence.[186] If either of the parties stated at court that neither witnesses nor documents were available then any evidence presented by them later was not accepted for it was thought to be produced by forgery (otherwise the party would not have made a statement of denial previously). If, however, either of the parties stated that evidence was available but was unable to present it, the court called for the presentation of the evidence by anyone able to do so. This was done in the form of a public proclamation, threatening with *ḥērem* (who retained any evidence), but no witness was ex officio summoned to court.[187] The parties were entitled to present further witnesses and evidence until the trial was completed, but not afterwards.[188] Contrary to criminal procedure, where the confession of the accused was void, the acknowledgement of either party (that is, acknowledging the demand of the counter-interested party) was acceptable, for the acknowledgement of a litigant party '*was equivalent to a hundred witnesses*.'[189]

After hearing the parties and the witnesses the court discussed what was heard and seen. The discussion of the court was held in a closed session so that the parties could not learn how the judges argued and voted. The disciples of the legal scholars, however, could participate in the closed session and could even join in the discussion. During the course of the discussion any of the judges could alter his previously expressed views until the decision was made. Decision making began with the argumentation of the oldest presiding judge, though there were efforts to let the youngest member speak first (similar to criminal procedure) in order for him not to be influenced by the opinion of the older and respected members. The proceeding judges had the right to state in the decision-making phase that they

184 Sanh 7b.

185 Cohn 1974a: 576–7.

186 M Sanh 3:8.

187 Falk 1972: 103–4; 122; Cohn 1974a: 577–8.

188 Tos Sanh 6:4.

189 Falk 1972: 128.

were unable to take any stand. In this case the court was supplemented by two further members and discussion of the case started anew. If the court was unable to pass judgment a decision was taken to the advantage of the defendant, based on the principle that the plaintiff was unable to persuade the court about the rightness of his claim.[190]

Judgments were made either on consensus or on majority vote. In issues of private law a majority of one judge was enough to guarantee a sufficient majority.[191] The decision had to be made on the day of the trial as any delay was considered a violation of the biblical commandment of a just decision (Lev. 19.15). After the decision was made, the court called the parties back to learn the verdict while standing.[192] The chairman of the court only announced the judgment but did not mention whether it was reached by consensus or by majority vote, and he did not disclose the stand of the individual judges. The judgment was presented orally and committed to writing only if the parties requested it. The reasons for the decision were made public upon the parties' request, too. The judgment was not committed to writing on the same day the decision was taken and there was no deadline whatsoever for the court to do so.[193]

The judgment came into effect immediately but it was possible to alter a judgment if new evidence unknown at the time of the decision making came to light. Obviously, any new evidence was presented by one of the parties, save if he was not entitled to do so (because he had stated previously that no evidence was available; see above). To pronounce a new judgment was the right of the court which proceeded in the case previously. A new judgment could also be made because of a mistake in law. It was not an easy task however to determine what a legal mistake was because, due to legal pluralism, several competing doctrines existed until the *halakah* was established. Therefore a mistake in law was ultimately limited to the rules of the Mishnah, while in those cases for which the *halakah* was not fixed the judgment could not be altered because the judge had the right to make his choice from legal doctrines.[194] As will be shown in the next chapter, this feature of Jewish law is identical to Islamic law where the judge could also make his choice from competing doctrines, even within his own school.

---

190 M Sanh 3:6, 4:1, 4:2; Sanh 36a; Cohn 1974a: 578–9.

191 M Sanh 4:1.

192 Tos Sanh 6:2.

193 Cohn 1974a: 579.

194 Cohn 1974a: 578–9. But if a legal scholar did not follow the interpretation accepted by the majority he was held responsible, despite the fact that the *halakah* was not yet formally fixed: T Sanh 33a.

Criminal Procedural Law

Since rules of criminal procedure are similar in many respects to private litigation the following section will discuss only the differences.

Criminal procedure, too, had to be conducted during the day and terminated at sunset. A judgment resulting in the acquittal of the accused had to be announced on the day of the trial, but a decision finding the accused guilty could only be declared the following day, thus giving any judge a chance to reconsider his decision during the night and to change his mind.[195] Obviously, no trial could be held on the *Shabbāt* or on a holiday (not even on the previous day), keeping in view the possibility of a continuation the next day were the announcement of the judgment to fall either on the *Shabbāt* or on a holiday.[196]

In criminal cases it was the 23-member court or the Great *Sanhedrīn* that proceeded. Here the judges sat in a semicircle in order to see each other's faces, the chairman sitting in the middle. The clerks of the law court recording what was said were located left and right of him. One clerk recorded the arguments pleading guilty and the other one recorded the arguments for innocence. The disciples of legal scholars were also present, sitting in rows expressing their erudition in jurisprudence – that is, the most distinguished sat in the first row. If the number of the court dropped below the compulsory number the disciple sitting in the first place of the first row took up the vacant place.[197] The room would already be filled with disciples and the public before the court entered. They were obliged to rise when the judges entered and were allowed to sit down only if the chairman entering last gave them permission to do so.[198]

Only a single criminal case could be discussed on the same day and this rule was interpreted very strictly. If the perpetrators of the same crime were to be punished differently (for instance in the case of fornication the man was to be strangled and the woman was to be burnt to death if she was a priest's daughter) their case had to be discussed on two separate days. Thus this rule was not adjusted to the case but to the person accused. Hence the exceptional rule is understandable, according to which several judgments could be made on the same day only when more than one accused received equal punishment.[199]

In cases of homicide the procedure was launched upon request of the blood-avenger, who acted as prosecutor and was also entitled to execute the judgment[200] (a rule perfectly in accordance with the rules of Islamic law). From this Cohn infers by way of analogy that in cases other than homicide it was the victim who could initiate the procedure and who acted as prosecutor. If a crime which required

195 M Sanh 5:5.

196 M Sanh 4:1.

197 M Sanh 4:3–4; Tos Sanh 8:1.

198 Tos Sanh 7:8.

199 Tos Sanh 7:2; Sanh 46a.

200 Sanh 45b. If there was no blood-avenger the court appointed one: Sanh 45b.

'public accusation' was committed the court launched the procedure ex officio on the basis of the testimony of witnesses. At any rate, no criminal procedure could be launched if the accused was not present.[201]

The trial continued with the hearing of witnesses. First the court warned the witnesses about the consequences of giving false testimony; next their testimony was investigated.[202] This was taken rather seriously because every difference or contradiction in the testimonies could result in their rejection (see the above comments on Susanna's story). The accused had to be present during the examination of the witnesses. According to biblical law at least two witnesses are required to prove the accusation (Deut. 17:6) but rabbinic tradition – in keeping with its accused-centred approach – further narrowed the possibility of conviction by the rule that the witnesses did not only have to prove that the act was committed by the accused but also that they had warned him/her before committing the act that it would be a criminal act. The accused could only be condemned if he was aware of this and acted despite the warning.[203] R. Yūdah went even a step further when claiming that the witnesses did not only have to warn the accused about the legal consequences but also about the manner of execution of capital punishment, for if he was not told he could not be executed. Based on R. Yōsē's view, however, scholars did not have to be warned (because they knew the law).[204] In accordance with rabbinic efforts to help the accused, any of those present in the court room, but particularly the disciples of legal scholars, were entitled to speak in the interest of the accused and, what is more, they were even encouraged to do so. A disciple speaking in the interest of the accused was seated among the judges, where he remained for the entire day.[205]

Moreover, a judge and the accused person were allowed to say something in favour of acquittal when the judgment was pronounced and the convicted was on his way to the place of execution. In such a case the accused was brought back to court and the person speaking on his behalf was listened to when there was substance in his utterance. If afterwards the accused was found innocent he was dismissed, otherwise he was returned to the place of execution. For the same reason when proceeding to the place of execution a herald would go ahead of the accused proclaiming his name and the crime committed, together with the names

201 Cohn 1974a: 581. Any next of kin who was entitled to inherit the deceased's estate was regarded as a blood-avenger, a rule perfectly in accordance with Islamic law. In Jewish jurisprudence, however, the task of a blood-avenger was disputed: according to one opinion he only initiated the proceedings, while others thought he participated in the trial as a prosecutor; according to a third view the blood-avenger enjoyed the right and privilege to execute the death penalty: Cohn 1974b: 530.

202 M Sanh 4:5.

203 Sanh 9b; Tos Sanh 11:1–3.

204 Sanh 8b.

205 M Sanh 5:4.

of the witnesses, and call for anyone who knew something on the behalf of the convicted to speak in their favour.[206]

The convicted could be returned to court repeatedly on his own words.[207] In order, however, to prevent abuse of this right after the second return to the court two legal scholars were sent with the accused who, after listening to him/her, decided whether the words were relevant to the case or not.[208] At the same time the accused was not allowed to say anything against themself; were they to do so, they were silenced and called on to behave properly.[209]

The prohibition of confession originates from the Talmudic period since examples of it can be found in the Bible (2 Sam. 1.16). Rabbinic tradition, however, argued against it on the basis of Deuteronomy, according to which at least two witnesses were needed to pronounce guilt (Deut. 17.6) – which excludes the possibility of considering other evidence. A further argument supported by theological consideration was added, according to which no one could give up their life because life – in contrast to property – was a matter for God exclusively. Moreover, since the accused could not be a witness at the same time his confession could not be taken into consideration. Consequently, the rule emerged that no one could accuse themself of having committed a crime.[210] It is a very important point because it led to the rejection of torture, for if voluntary confession could not be considered then it would be absurd to force anyone to confess. As will be seen, Muslim legal scholars came to a similar opinion, though by a different argumentation, while torture was not alien to Zoroastrian legal practice.

After hearing the witnesses and the accused the deliberations of the court began. First it was decided whether the witness testimonies were in concert or not. If the testimonies were contradictory or inconsistent a judgment of acquittal had to be passed. If the witness testimonies were accepted by the court the discussion began. At the beginning arguments in favour of the accused were pronounced, then the opinion of those who were for condemnation was heard. If a judge spoke for the acquittal of the accused he could not change his mind later. By contrast, if he held the accused guilty at first and later changed his mind he could join those who were for the innocence of the accused.[211] It was the task of the court to weigh up the evidence if it was accepted previously. But the court also had to decide on legal questions, in particular whether the act that seemed to be proved was a crime or not. In order not to be influenced by judges of higher authority it was always the youngest member who spoke first[212] (as seen above, attempts were made later to apply this rule to private litigation, too). The judges made their decision on the

206 M Sanh 5: 4, 6:1.

207 M Sanh 5:4, 6:1.

208 Sanh 43a

209 Tos Sanh 9:4.

210 Sanh 9b; Cohn 1974a: 614.

211 M Sanh 5:5.

212 Tos Sanh 7:2.

basis of their own assessment, knowledge and conviction, therefore the conference of the court had outstanding significance.

If a majority could be obtained for innocence the judgment of acquittal was announced on the same day. If not, the passing of the judgment had to be postponed until the next day. In this case the judges spent the night discussing the case, disputing it in pairs. During the night they could eat only a little and could not consume alcoholic beverages at all.[213] Next morning the clerks of the law court once again counted the votes, which could only change in favour of acquittal (see above). It should be noted that a one vote majority was sufficient for acquittal, whereas a majority of at least two was required to declare someone guilty.[214]

Voting was possible only in an adequately spacious room.[215] In a judgment pronouncing the accused guilty the mode of execution had to be specified, but the reasons were not expected to be made public. If the court declared the accused guilty of a capital crime he was regarded as dead and, therefore, anyone could kill him without being guilty of homicide[216] (even a medieval authority such as Maimonides refers to this rule)[217] – an argument resembling that of the Muslim legal scholars (see notes 335–336 and related text).

Usually the person condemned to death was executed immediately after the judgment was pronounced. In order to make his suffering lighter and to sedate him the condemned was given wine sprinkled with frankincense seeds. Usually it was offered by the women of Jerusalem, but if they failed to do so it had to be provided by the community.[218]

Before the execution the condemned had to confess to his crime so that he could have a share in the world to come.[219] Repentance had a set formula and if the condemned did not know what to say the court taught him the text to be said. There was a separate formula if the condemned knew that he was to be executed on false testimonies. By that kind of repentance the condemned could state his opinion for the last time.[220] The court, hearing it, 'broke out in tears' on learning that they had condemned an innocent man to death, but the judgment could not be altered. In such cases the court stated that the blood of the executed innocent person rested on the conscience of the witnesses.[221] Thus the court, once it accepted the witness testimonies, was bound to them even if later on the very

213 M Sanh 5:5.

214 M Sanh 4:1. Legal scholars established this rule by way of analogy. Since one could be found guilty on the testimony of at least two witnesses, consequently at least two majority votes were needed for a judgment pronouncing guilt: Tos Sanh 3:7.

215 Tos Sanh 7:2.

216 Sanh 71b; Cohn 1974a: 583.

217 Maimonides 1981: 115.

218 Sanh 43a. Cf. also the evidence of the New Testament.

219 M Sanh 6:2.

220 M Sanh 6:2 has the formulas to be said.

221 M Sanh 6:2; Sanh 44b; Tos Sanh 9:5.

same court became convinced of the opposite; in this sense the court depended fully on the witnesses.[222] Recall here the case of the son of the famous legal scholar Shimᶜeōn b. Shetaḥ. As the legal scholar had 80 'witches' of Ashkalon executed,[223] the relatives of the women took revenge on him by falsely accusing his son of a crime. The court condemned him to death but the witnesses were alarmed by their deed before the execution and confessed to the falsehood of their testimony. But the court could not withdraw its judgment and the unfortunate man was executed, though by then everyone had known that he was innocent. This ruling was made on the basis that no one could be a witness twice; they could not withdraw their first testimony and replace it with another one; and the court could not alter its judgment.[224] It is worth noting the remarkable similarity between Jewish and Islamic legal thinking in this respect, too. Muslim lawyers expressed the judges' dependence on witnesses by saying that the judge was a 'captive of witness' (*asīr al-shāhid*).

In the biblical period execution by a state authority was unknown, so it was realized with the participation of the witnesses and, at times, of the entire population.[225] Stoning was carried out with the participation of the entire population, when members of the community kept on throwing stones until the condemned died. Stoning had to be started by the witnesses and if that resulted in death no one else had to throw more stones[226] (similar to Islamic law where the judge had to be present, too). The accused was taken to a place which was twice their height.[227] Here their clothes were removed but their body was partially covered. It was prohibited, however, to stone women naked.[228] A fornicating, betrothed maiden had to be stoned at the entrance to her father's house.[229]

Hanging was rather meant to humiliate the corpse and not as a punishment because it was the corpse of the executed that had to be hung out on a tree but had to be removed before night set in (Deut. 21.22–3). Talmudic law restricted these post-mortem hangings to those convicted of blasphemy and idolatry only.[230]

Talmudic law extended the biblical rules of execution and introduced execution by sword (decapitation) and strangulation beside stoning and burning. The aim of

---

222 Falk 1972: 116.

223 M Sanh 6:4.

224 Sanh 44b; Falk 1972: 108–9.

225 Daube 1986: 408.

226 M Sanh 6:4. This was interpreted by some scholars rather rigorously. According to Samuel, when the hands of the witnesses had been cut off (between giving evidence and execution) the verdict could not be implemented and the condemned had to be released: Sanh 45b.

227 M Sanh 6:4; Tos Sanh 9:6.

228 Tos Sanh 9:6. Not everybody, however, agreed with this: according to R. Yūdah there was no distinction between the sexes in this respect, see Sanh 45a.

229 Tos Sanh 10:10.

230 Cohn 1974c: 529.

this reform was to introduce more humane ways of execution and to avoid the body being mutilated because when God takes away someone's life (they die naturally) their body is not mutilated. Death by the sword was introduced to be suffered by murderers.[231] Strangulation was regarded as the most humane punishment, of least mutilation, and was executed by two witnesses who had to strangle the person with a shawl fixed round the condemned's neck while the two ends were pulled in opposite directions.[232] Legal scholars regarded strangulation as the least painful manner of execution.[233]

Talmudic law did not only introduce new modes of execution but also reinterpreted earlier methods. Burning had to be performed by pushing a burning wick down the throat of the condemned so that he burnt from inside.[234] It should be noted, however, that there is no evidence suggesting that anyone was executed in this way. There are, however, references to surrounding the condemned with twigs and executing them by burning. The rabbinic texts note in this case that the judgment was perhaps of a court of the Sadducees.[235] Talmudic legal scholars reinterpreted stoning by saying that it was not to be carried out by throwing stones but rather by pushing the person from a high place. Therefore the condemned was pushed from a place high enough to ensure death.[236]

Perpetrators of sexual crimes, people found guilty of blasphemy, idolatry and violation of the *Shabbāt* had to be condemned to stoning, together with rebellious sons and sorcerers.[237] A person who had simultaneous sexual relations with a mother and her daughter should be burned and so too a fornicating daughter of the high priest.[238] Murderers and residents of an apostate city had to suffer execution by the sword.[239] Persons hitting their parents (Ex. 21.15), stealing an Israelite (Ex. 21.16), legal scholars who defied a court's decision, false prophets and persons prophesying in the name of an idol, persons fornicating with a priest's daughter and persons falsely accusing such a girl of fornication were condemned to strangulation.[240] No condemned, however, could be executed by arrow or spear[241] (contrary to Sasanian law). Tools necessary for the execution had to be provided by the community because no one could be obliged to make their own possessions available.[242]

231 M Sanh 7:3; Cohn 1974c: 527–8.

232 M Sanh 7:3.

233 Tos Sanh 12:5.

234 M Sanh 7:2.

235 Sanh 52b; Cohn 1974c: 528.

236 Cohn 1974c: 526–9.

237 M Sanh 7:4–8:5.

238 M Sanh 9:1.

239 M Sanh 9:1. In the case of execution by sword it was always the edge of the sword that had to be used: Tos Sanh 14:6.

240 M Sanh 11:1

241 Tos Sanh 14:6.

242 Sanh 43a.

When the condemned met their death their corpse could not be taken to the family tomb, but an official grave was allocated for burial: one for the beheaded and strangled, and another for those who were executed by burning and stoning. Later the corpses could be removed from these graves and the bones could be buried in the family tomb, but no public mourning was permitted. The relatives of the condemned had to visit the witnesses and the judges to express that they did not harbour anger against them because they were just in their judgment.[243]

Evidence

It was evidence by witnesses which had the most important role in a procedure; documents were only of secondary importance. When no other means of evidence were available, the missing proof was supplemented by oath.

Different rules pertained to private and to criminal cases because in criminal procedures far more rigorous rules had to be followed. While in criminal law a little uncertainty or doubt in the proof of the accusation led to the acquittal of the accused, the implementation of these rigorous rules of evidence would have led to making commercial activities impossible. Therefore attempts were made to moderate the burden of proof and its legal consequences in disputes of private law. To achieve this goal a series of presumptions were developed, such as no one pays a debt before expiration; no one accepts faulty goods; no one purchases goods without looking at them; no one spends their time and money without good reason; no one can be expected to remember things they were not personally involved with.[244]

The rule of a minimum two witnesses is one of the basic tenets of biblical law (Deut. 17:6, 19:15) and no exception was made in criminal cases. Occasionally a single witness was enough in private cases; for instance the court permitted a woman to remarry if her husband's death was testified at least by one witness. The joint use of a document and a single witness was regarded as the realization of the rule of two witnesses. A distinction was made between whether witnesses authenticated a transaction or testified to a fact and event at court. Authenticating witnesses were present when a legal transaction was concluded and they authenticated the document, which was invalid otherwise. A document proved by two witnesses and approved by the court was good enough in private cases and was regarded as equivalent to the oral statement of two witnesses made in the law court. A distinction between the two kinds of witnesses was also important because the rules of exclusion (see below) pertained only to witnesses testifying to facts and events.[245] (This distinction of witnesses can be found in Islamic law, too; see Chapter 4).

---

243 M Sanh 6:5.

244 On the details of the various presumptions, see Cohn 1974c: 600–604. According to the presumption of Rēsh Laqish witnesses do not sign a document about which they know that the vendor has not come of age: Sanh 29b.

245 Cohn 1974c: 605.

Rabbinic law excluded certain individuals from among those eligible as witnesses. Generally speaking women were excluded, but this conclusion was reached merely by interpretation because no such text was available.[246] One argument was that the Bible used the word 'witness' in the masculine form, but this argument was not fully accepted for the entire text was written in the masculine, therefore it was not sufficient to exclude women. According to other arguments women could not act as witnesses because their place was in the home and not in the law court. Yet their acting as witnesses was acknowledged in a particular sphere: in 'female issues' about which men knew nothing, matters concerning purity etc. (this rule could be found in Islamic law, too). Slaves and non-Jews were also excluded, though the statement of the latter could be accepted by the court if its members saw no reason to doubt their objectivity. Minors (persons below the age of 13) were also excluded[247] and 'young persons' could only act as witnesses in a narrow sphere: they could not act as witnesses between the age of 13 and 20 in a case pertaining to property.[248]

Further, the blind, the deaf and the mute could not act as witnesses; neither could mentally ill and mentally disturbed persons. Persons considered 'guilty' or 'corrupt' were also excluded on the basis of the biblical commandment (Ex. 23:1), but later rabbinic law identified further categories within this restriction, such as: criminals, crooks, false witnesses, spies and illiterates. Anyone who had committed a serious crime or a misdeed punishable by flogging was also excluded from those who could give testimony. Robbers, herdsmen, usurers and those who were suspect in money matters were disqualified under all circumstances,[249] together with gamblers, players of cards and dice,[250] and those who raced pigeons.[251]

246 Daube 1986: 415–17.

247 Tos Sanh 9:11. R. 'Elīᶜezer bar Ñādoq informed other legal scholars about the execution by burning of the high priest's daughter because of fornication, which he had seen in childhood. According to him dry twigs were placed around her and she was burned that way. The report was significant because it was disputed at this time how burning was to be executed. At any rate, the report of R. 'Elīᶜezer was rejected by his colleagues, saying that when he made that observation he was a child whose evidence was invalid.

248 Cohn 1974d: 606.

249 M Sanh 3:3; Tos Sanh 5:5.

250 Toys made of wood or of the seeds of pomegranate: Tos Sanh 5:2. The reason for the exclusion of people partaking in gambling led to disputes in Talmudic times and finally an agreement was reached that the reason for prohibition was that those partaking in such games did not contribute to the public good and general welfare: Sanh 24b. Interestingly, Maimonides also mentions Persian games such as *nard* and čatranj (chess) when commenting on this rule, whereas it is not included in the original texts. Maimonides 1981:33.

251 M Sanh 3:3. It is worth noting that pigeon trainers were also excluded from among the witnesses in Islamic law, not because they were committing a crime but because they were stupid enough to spend their time on unnecessary things. The exclusion of pigeon trainers in Jewish law was extended by interpretation to all those who trained any sort of animal: Tos Sanh 5:2.

Vagabonds were excluded on the presumption that such persons committed criminal acts through their way of life. Tax collectors were also excluded because they were considered to collect more than what was lawful and hence they qualified as freaks. Illiterates were also excluded on the presumption that they did not meet basic requirements of civilization, hence they were loafers. This presumption, however, could be refuted if it was proved that the behaviour of the person was impeccable despite being illiterate, hence they were suited to being a witness. Obviously, persons intentionally violating the law and rites (such as heretics) were excluded. Informers, being more despised than criminals, were excluded from among the witnesses. Those who misbehaved by disregarding social conventions but without having committed any crime were also excluded (eating in the street, publicly accepting alms from a non-Jew etc.).[252]

Relatives and persons interested in the outcome of the trial were also excluded because of conflicts of interest. This could be regarded as a typical example of a norm produced by rabbinic legal understanding. The Bible says nothing about this issue, but Deuteronomy 24:16 states that 'Fathers shall not to be put to death for their children, nor children put to death for their fathers; each is to die for his own sin.'[253] This rule, clearly pronouncing the principle of individual liability was, however, interpreted by legal scholars to exclude close relatives from giving evidence, saying that neither the father nor the son can be condemned on the basis of evidence given by a son or a father. This argument gave way not only to the rule that father and son were ineligible as witnesses, but it was transformed by way of generalization to exclude close relatives from being witnesses in general.[254] Closed relatives are: father, brother, paternal and maternal uncles, brother-in-law, father-in-law, husband of the wife's sister.[255]

In order to prevent witnesses finding a way out of the obligation to give evidence, no one could accuse themself and thus be disqualified from attesting or testifying.[256] Therefore, it was the counter-interested party that had to prove during the procedure that a witness was excluded from testifying. At the same time no one was permitted intentionally to testify with a person they knew could not be accepted for some reason. This was because when only a single witness was among the witnesses whose testimony was unacceptable it would make the testimony of the other witnesses *ipso iure* invalid. To avoid such a situation the person testifying rightfully had to deny giving joint testimony with a person not

252 Cohn 1974d: 607. According to R Naḥman those accepting alms from non-Jews were excluded only when they accepted alms publicly although they had the opportunity to do so privately: Sanh 26b.

253 Scripture taken from the HOLY BIBLE, NEW INTERNATIONAL VERSION® NIV® Copyright © 1973, 1978, 1984, 2011 by Biblica, Inc.™ Used by permission. All rights reserved worldwide.

254 M Sanh 3:3; Sanh 27b; Cohn 1974d: 606–7.

255 M Sanh 3:4.

256 Sanh 9b.

competent to do so. It was one's duty to testify; only the king and the high priest enjoyed exemption from giving evidence.[257]

Witnesses were heard one by one, then all the witnesses were called back and they had to repeat their testimony in the presence of the others.[258] Witness testimonies were investigated.[259] A witness could withdraw their testimony up to the time of the investigation but not afterwards.[260] As a rule a witness could testify only about what they had personally seen, heard or experienced, and could not communicate secondary information – even if their source proved to be fully reliable persons. Witnesses could not express personal views, for their task was limited to the presentation of what they had experienced. Any witness who started to say more than required was immediately silenced.[261] No indirect evidence was accepted from the witnesses. According to the example of the *Tōsefta'* even if witnesses stated in concert that they had seen the victim run into a shop to flee his pursuer and next they saw him dead and blood was dripping from the knife in the hands of his pursuer, this statement was not accepted[262] (because they did not see the act itself).

The testimonies of the witnesses were investigated in three separate phases. The first phase was *ḥaqīrah* (inquiry), which pertained to the circumstances of the case (when and where the act took place). Contradictions experienced were taken seriously: for instance, if a witness said that the act took place on the second day of the month but the other witness said that it was on the third day, it was disregarded because no one was obliged to be familiar with intercalation (one may make a mistake about one day); but if the act took place on the third day according to one witness but on the fifth according to the other their testimonies were deemed invalid.[263]

Derīshah (examination) pertained to the essential elements of the act: who committed it; was the perpetrator of the crime warned in advance; how they did it etc. The *bedīqah* (interrogation) was a cross-examination of the statements of the witnesses. This was regarded as the most important element because the possibility of giving false evidence could be excluded best in this way. The extent of *bedīqah* was left to the discretion of the proceeding court, but judges were encouraged to implement this technique as far as possible. By contrast, the validity of a judgment without *bedīqah* was not challenged. The *bedīqah* came to the foreground particularly when the proceeding court became suspicious about the credibility of the witnesses due to some circumstance: for instance if the witnesses described the act and its circumstances in identical words it suggested a testimony

257 Cohn 1974c: 606–9.

258 Tos Sanh 6:3.

259 M Sanh 3:6.

260 Tos Sanh 6:4.

261 M Sanh 5:4.

262 Tos Sanh 8:3.

263 M Sanh 5:3.

composed and learned in advance. If the judge could not prove that a statement was false but his doubts remained he could not pass judgment and had to transfer his seat to another judge to carry on with the case. When the witness testimonies of the two sides contradicted each other in relevant issues the state of affairs could not be identified on the principle that it could not be established without doubt which of the parties was telling the truth and which was not. The contradiction, however, could hold only for essential points and contradictions in inessential circumstances could not lead to the same result. If contradictions manifested only in the witness testimonies of one party but those of the other party were consistent the decision had to be to the advantage of the latter party.[264]

A contradiction in the testimony was not sufficient reason to accuse someone of giving false testimony. In order to find a witness guilty of giving false testimony two more witnesses were needed who unanimously testified that the witness was not present at the given place and time where the action he was testifying to took place. The punishment of a false witness was regulated by the Bible (Deut. 19.18–21), but interpretation of the text became a matter of dispute between the Sadducees and the Pharisees. The Bible says:

> The judges must make a thorough investigation, and if the witness proves to be a liar, giving false testimony against his brother, [19] then do to him as he intended to do to his brother. You must purge the evil from among you. [20] The rest of the people will hear of this and be afraid, and never again will such an evil thing be done among you. [21] Show no pity: life for life, eye for eye, tooth for tooth, hand for hand, foot for foot.[265]

The Sadducees interpreted the text literally and thought that the false witness could not be executed until the person accused by him was executed; in other words they took verse 21 as their basis of argumentation. By contrast the Pharisees, whose interpretation ultimately led to the rules of the *halakah*, took verse 19 as their point of reference. Therefore they interpreted the text in a way that the false witness was responsible only if the accused was not condemned – in other words, if the false testimony did not produce any result. This interpretation has led some researchers to interpret the conflict between the Sadducees and the Pharisees differently. Finkelstein has reached the conclusion that it was the Sadducees who insisted on the original meaning of the law, whereas the Pharisees extended the rule by their interpretation of the law. Daube, however, refuted this argument, showing

264 Cohn 1974c: 610–611. According to an anecdote about Ben Zakk'ay he questioned the witness even about the characteristics of the fig tree under which the presumed crime was committed, that is, he considered such accompanying circumstances also as important: Sanh 9b.

265 Scripture taken from the HOLY BIBLE, NEW INTERNATIONAL VERSION® NIV® Copyright © 1973, 1978, 1984, 2011 by Biblica, Inc.™. Used by permission. All rights reserved worldwide.

that the Pharisees did not punish the witness when the result was achieved, but only in the case of a miscarried attempt. The story of Susanna, already referred to, also testifies to this because the two old men were condemned to death for giving false testimony since they wanted to achieve the death sentence of Susanna (the punishment of a fornicating woman is death), but they could not accomplish their aim.[266]

In Talmudic times this argument caused some headache, arguing that if someone deserved death due to their mere intention (attempt), how much more capital punishment was due if the result was achieved – that is, the accused was executed on false testimony. This counter-argument, however, was rejected with reference to the principle that no criminal deed can be assumed by analogy (Sanh 74a, 76a). When a false witness's testimony led to the corporal punishment of the accused, the witness received the same punishment according to the biblical passage quoted above. If false testimony was given in private litigation and one party suffered material disadvantage, the false witness had to compensate the loss *in toto*. If the loss could not be compensated in this way (for instance the priest was removed from his office), the punishment of the false witness was flogging. A single witness could not be condemned for giving false testimony, only both of them – though heated debates emerged around this rule. At any rate, names of false witnesses were announced in public to obey the rule of the Bible (Deut. 19:20) and to exclude them from those eligible to give testimony in the future.[267]

Already biblical law knew the oath when ruling that if a depository took over any object for safekeeping but was unable to return it to the owner, he had to swear an oath that he had not stolen it and was not guilty in the disappearance of that item. The owner had to accept the oath without claiming anything.[268] If, however, it turned out later that he took a false oath, he had to restore the property, pay compensation and make a sacrifice for his crime committed.[269]

Talmudic law accepted oaths exclusively in private cases but not in criminal procedures, and then only if no other evidence whatsoever was available. Several kinds of oaths were known, the most important distinction being between the oath of the plaintiff and that of the defendant. The oath had to be taken standing in the name of God, the hand being put on the Torāh scroll. If the defendant did not take the oath despite being obliged to do so, he immediately lost the case. If he refused to take the non-biblical oath he could be punished by *ḥērem* and even by flogging, but he did not lose the case *ipso iure*. While legal scholars regarded oath as a necessary tool, wisdom literature discourages every form of oath, condemning it as completely wrong and incitement to commit sins.[270] The teaching of Jesus against taking oaths fits well into this intellectual atmosphere.

266 Daube 1986: 412–15.

267 Tos Sanh 6:6; Cohn 1974e: 517.

268 Ex. 22.7, 10.

269 Lev. 5:21–6.

270 For details on oath see Cohn 1974f: 616–20.

Judicial Procedure in Islamic law

Two types of procedure can be distinguished in Islamic law: a process regulated by the rules of the *sharīʿa* and a procedure outside its domain. Procedure and the administration of justice conducted by officials appointed by the Caliph or the governor were not covered by the rules of the *sharīʿa*, therefore they missed the procedural guarantees of the *sharīʿa*; at the same time they were easier and, in many cases, more effective, too.

Procedure According to the Sharīʿa

Procedure regulated by Islamic law put the parties' behaviour under extremely formal and rigid rules. This had two consequences: on the one hand legal guarantees covered the process from beginning to end in order to establish a fair and impartial procedure. On the other hand, the dogmatic insistence on these legal formalities resulted in a process being out of touch with contemporary social reality which resulted, therefore, in unsuitable and unjust judgments, being subject to criticism by the parties and legal scholars alike.

Another general feature of Islamic procedural law is that civil and criminal procedures are not strictly separated from each other. This is because criminal cases were usually conducted within the framework of an accusatory procedure; that is, criminal cases were launched by demand of the plaintiff. A procedure based on the principle of investigation was only an exception, when the judge himself became acquainted (*ʿilm al-qāḍī*) with an act running counter to the law and started a trial ex officio.[271]

The accusatory nature of the process is also reflected in terms denoting the parties involved: the plaintiff is *muddaʿī* ('claimer') while the defendant is *muddaʿā ʿalayhi* ('claimed against').[272] At the beginning of the procedure the judge studied the claim (*daʿwā*), and if he found it not his court's business he rejected it without setting the date of any trial.[273] Otherwise he fixed the date of the trial and it was his responsibility to ensure that the defendant turned up, at least according to the Ḥanafite school, which supported ex officio warranty. The defendant was obliged to appear on the warrant save he was ill or was a woman who did not usually leave her home. In such cases it was the appointed representative of the defendant who acted in their stead. If the defendant did not appear at court in due time the judge gave a document and his seal to the plaintiff in order to persuade the defendant to change his mind. Should he still resist the call of the judge, this was recorded and testified to by two witnesses, and the judge obtained the assistance of the governor, who arranged for the defendant's presence with the help of the police (*shurṭa*). The unwilling defendant could be jailed by the judge for a duration not specified

271 Hallaq 2009: 344–5; Müller 1999: 142.

272 Coulson 1964: 124.

273 Müller 1999: 143.

by law. In fact the custody lasted until the judge was convinced that from then on the defendant would be at the court's disposal. If the defendant hid in his own house to dodge the police the plaintiff could ask for the sealing of the house after two witnesses had proved that the defendant was present in the house. If this did not produce any result the judge was supposed to follow the strategy suggested by Abū Yūsuf: an appointed person, accompanied by two witnesses, should be sent three times to call upon the defendant to appear at the law court by shouting. If all three attempts failed, the judge should appoint a representative for the defendant (despite the latter's will), thus making the beginning of the hearing possible. If the judge became personally convinced that the defendant was in their own house he could issue an order to break down the door by force and take the defendant to court. It is clear from the above that the Ḥanafite legal scholars considered every possibility and had proper legal solutions even for the more difficult cases, although this strategy was subject to debate.[274]

Things were different, however, when the defendant lived far from the place where the suit started. Since travel was a heavy burden in medieval times, the custom of having recourse to the assistance of the *qāḍī* working next to the defendant's residence developed in these cases. This was done through written communication between judges called *kitāb al-qāḍī ilā al-qāḍī*, but this technique was subject to debate and not every school accepted it.[275]

The day of the hearing was established by the judge in advance. After hearing the plaintiff's claim and the defendant's counter-argument (*midfaʿ*) the parties had to prove their claims by giving evidence. Priority was accorded to the testimonies of witnesses but occasionally written documents were also accepted, though according to classical *fiqh* only the testimony of witnesses (*bayyina*) and acknowledgement (*iqrār*) were regarded as proof.[276] The burden of proof rested with the plaintiff, but this could change during the trial. For instance in a trial about a loan, if the defendant denied the plaintiff's claim, saying he had already repaid the sum, he had to prove it.[277] Since procedural presumptions were in favour of the party who denied the claim it was important to clarify who had to prove their case, a decision determining also the outcome of the litigation because should the plaintiff fail to prove his claim the other party would win the procedure without much effort.[278]

In short, after the counter-argument of the defendant the judge determined what claims the parties had to prove. If the plaintiff succeeded in proving his claim according to the strict rules of the *sharīʿa* the judge decided to his benefit.[279]

274 Ziadeh 1996: 309–12.

275 Hallaq 2009: 346-7. For more on the debate of Muslim legal scholars about *kitāb al-qāḍī ilā al-qāḍī* see Hallaq 2001a: 208–13.

276 Müller 1999: 143.

277 Coulson 1964: 124–5.

278 Schacht 1964: 191.

279 Müller 1999: 143.

If he failed to do so but the judge thought that the statements of the plaintiff were not without foundation he could oblige the defendant to deny the charges against him by oath.[280] If the defendant did so the judgment was to his benefit. If the defendant refused to take an oath (*nukūl*) the judgment was worded in keeping with the plaintiff's claim, provided he gave the oath expected of him. In this respect, however, there was no agreement among legal scholars: according to the Ḥanafites the plaintiff's oath was not needed because in cases of financial claims the defendant's refusal resulted *ipso facto* in the plaintiff winning the trial, while according to Mālik and al-Shāfiʿī the refusal in itself was insufficient for the plaintiff to win.[281]

During the trial court assistants helped the judge carry on the procedure properly. The doorkeeper (*bawwāb*) guided the parties into the room and kept them at a distance from the judge. He informed the judge about the identity and rank of the arriving witnesses so that the judge could greet them properly. The minion (*aʿwān*) helped the judge ensure the defendant's presence, though the police could also be used for this purpose. The judge's most important assistant, however, was the scribe (*kātib*), who was expected to be well versed in official language and in the art of drawing up documents. He had to have good handwriting and be able to draft protocols and judgments. Detailed knowledge of the law was not a precondition but was considered a major advantage. In addition to professional qualifications high moral standards were also required to prevent corruption, since those wishing to corrupt the judge had access to him through his scribe. Interpreters also worked at the court, particularly in the peripheral areas where a large part of the population spoke no Arabic, in the Maghreb and in the Iranian regions. This was necessary because Arab judges were appointed for those provinces as well. Further, interpreters were needed in cases when one of the parties was an Arab and the other party was not.[282] The judge's ruling was recorded and deposited in the court archives (*dīwān*). Upon request of the parties copies were made of the judgment.

Evidence

Testimony of witnesses and confession were evidence accepted by *fiqh* as tools of proof, while a claim could be proven by documents only in exceptional cases. If no other evidence was available, oath was used in order to establish the facts and to enable the judge to pronounce judgment, but this kind of evidence was surrounded by scepticism and, therefore, Muslim legal scholars called the oath the weakest proof.[283] Despite this in some particular cases the oath alone determined the outcome of the lawsuit. A most obvious proof of this is the procedure to

280 Serrano 2000: 195.

281 Ibn Rushd 1996: 563–4.

282 Schneider 1990: 40–49.

283 Ibn Rushd 1996: 569.

be followed in the case of *liʿān*. *Liʿān* was a particular form of divorce when a husband accused his wife of adultery but could not prove his allegation, while his wife denied committing any crime. If the wife swore that her husband was lying she could not be condemned for adultery, yet at the same time her husband was also exempt from punishment for false accusation. While it is obvious that one of the parties was not telling the truth it was not the judge's task to discover it. His task was restricted to supervising the order of procedure and to pronounce the divorce at the end of the lawsuit as an expression of the parties' mutual will.[284]

Due to the accusatorial nature of procedure Muslim legal scholars rejected every form of torture with the exception of the Mālikites. A forced confession was null and void, and a judge ordering torture and pronouncing a judgment based on such 'evidence' should be sanctioned – the reason being that the judge had violated the principles of procedure, abused his authority and challenged the entire administration of justice. Disagreement appeared only on how to punish such a judge. According to the Ḥanafites the rules of *talio* (*lex talionis*) should be implemented, while others were of the view that he should be condemned to death. On the other hand, Muslim lawyers regarded the oral statements of the parties and the testimony of witnesses sceptically, and did not think that these statements necessarily contained the material truth. Accordingly, a judge was unable to establish the actual truth with certainty because he was exposed to the statements of the parties and witnesses and had to decide on the basis of facts about which he had never acquired first-hand information – save the judgment rested on his own knowledge (*ʿilm al-qāḍī*), which was accepted as a type of proof.[285]

Bearing all this in mind it is not difficult to understand the rules pertaining to witnesses either. As the system was based on oral communication in general and on witness testimonies in particular, credibility and reliability of witnesses was of utmost importance. Since the logic of the system did not focus on facts but on persons presenting them, to select eligible persons was vital to prevent the system collapsing. In doing so, Muslim lawyers were assuming that the testimony of an honest and decent person was acceptable whereas the testimony of a person who did not meet the standards was to be rejected. According to Coulson, this feature of the procedure is clear evidence of the idealist, academic nature of Islamic law and of its ineligibility for practical implementation. In his view the reason was that Islamic law did not develop out of daily practice but as a result of the work of legal scholars aiming at the elaboration of an ideal law.[286] Coulson's opinion, however, can be challenged on the basis of comparative legal history, since Islam was not the only legal system focusing on persons rather than facts. As seen previously, this approach could be discerned in Jewish law and also in Roman law, which could hardly be regarded as a system expressing abstract idealism. According to Emperor Hadrian (117–38), a judge proceeding properly would believe in the

284 Johansen 2002: 172.

285 Johansen 2002: 170–71.

286 Coulson 1964: 126.

witness and not in his statement (*testibus se, non testimoniis creditur*). The Roman legal scholar Callistratus also holds that the person, the social rank and the hostile or friendly emotions of the witness in respect of the parties should be examined together with his financial position.[287]

It is small wonder, therefore, that only honest persons (*ᶜudūl*) were eligible to testify as witnesses. The letter of Caliph ᶜUmar addressed to Abū Mūsā al-Ashᶜarī established the circle of honest men rather broadly since, accordingly, the testimony of every Muslim can be accepted save the relatives and those who had suffered *ḥadd* punishment (100 strokes or one year in jail) or given false testimony previously.[288] Abū Ḥanīfa was of the same opinion. According to his view all Muslims were to be considered honest until their debauchery was disclosed. In criminal cases, however, the judge had to examine the person of the witnesses. His disciples, Abū Yūsuf and al-Shaybānī, were more cautious because according to them the judge had to be convinced of the honesty of the witnesses in every lawsuit. The judge could identify the witnesses' character with the help of the *muzakkī*, an official acting on behalf of the court for this purpose. According to al-Khaṣṣāf's *adab al-qāḍī* the judge gave the *muzakkī* the name, address and personal description of the witness to be examined in secret; he then started his activity by interrogating the witness's neighbours. Meanwhile the judge could also appoint others for the same purpose who would act independently of the first *muzakkī*. Next the judge called the plaintiff to name persons who could publicly testify to the honesty of the witness in the presence of the defendant. If the witness succeeded in these investigations his statement could be accepted by the judge. In the next phase of the procedure, if the defendant denied the testimony of the witness he could challenge the witness's honesty rather than the facts presented by him since the defendant was entitled to prove the dishonesty of the witness even after his acceptance by the judge. If the court became convinced of the dishonesty of the witness his testimony had to be regarded as null and void.[289] This was the only possible way for the defendant because it was not possible to cross-examine the witnesses on facts,[290] a practice at variance with Jewish legal thinking and tradition.

Obviously, there were persons who could not be accepted at all because they were devoid of the required honesty. This group included robbers, highwaymen, fornicators, wine drinkers, homosexuals, hired mourners, those who played chess as gambling, trainers of pigeons and other birds (for competitions), usurers and singers. Although the reason for the majority included in this list is obvious (such as robbers), some require explanation. This was felt by al-Jaṣṣāṣ, the commentator on al-Khaṣṣāf's work, who claims that trainers of birds did not lose their honesty

287 *Digesta* 22, 5, 3, 3.

288 Serjeant 1991: 67.

289 The work of al-Khaṣṣāf is quoted in Ziadeh 1990: 80.

290 Coulson 1964: 125–6.

due to their occupation but because they were simply fools spending their time on useless things.[291]

Needless to say, this system encapsulated subjective rather than objective criteria and considerations. The report of the *muzakkī* already contained subjective judgments of the interrogated persons and the assessment of these reports was the responsibility of the judge, whose decision was also subjective. Examples of subjectivity abound. What follows mentions only some of the well-known cases: a judge did not accept the testimony of a witness because he was said to have treated his previously divorced wife improperly. In another case the very same judge did not accept the testimony of a northern Arab (*muḍarī*) against a southern one (*yamanī*) and vice versa. Another judge did not accept the confession of a poet because he had disrespectfully depicted women as belonging to the local social elite in one of his poems.[292] There was even an example of a judge not accepting the testimony of the ruler who had originally appointed him. Such a high rate of subjectivity drew the procedure to the brink of operability, while mapping the character of the witnesses took up a lot of time and energy. The judge's subjective assessment of the witnesses had fundamentally endangered the rights of the litigants. In order to eliminate these difficulties the parties turned to witnesses who had already been acknowledged as honest by the court. Obviously, such witnesses assisted in legal transactions at the conclusion of various contracts. At the end of this development a circle of professional witnesses (*ᶜudūl*) emerged who operated alongside the courts and authenticated documents for legal transactions. This, however, placed tremendous power in the hands of the official witnesses, who could abuse it in the interest of their own benefit, as some actually did. Yet the contracts authenticated by professional witnesses had such great prestige that even a Jewish court proceeding between Jewish parties accepted only contracts which were confirmed by professional witnesses, as proven by the documents of the Cairo *Genizah*.[293]

The majority of legal scholars rejected both the office of the *qāḍī* and that of the professional witnesses. But there were some who were not so consistent in their principles and who clung to the rather lucrative job of the witnesses. If they could not secure the job some were ready to pay significant sums, convinced that their 'investment' would soon be profitable. The lucrative nature of the job of witness was known by the judges too, therefore there were judges who removed all professional witnesses only to reappoint them after receiving remuneration. The professional witnesses themselves regarded their job both as an economic (*ṣināᶜa*) and a scholarly (*ᶜilm*) activity. It was thought to be a scholarly activity because they were required to know all the means of drawing up official documents and have skills in calligraphy.[294]

291 Ziadeh 1990: 81–2; see also Hallaq 2009: 348–9.

292 Ziadeh 1990: 83 with further references.

293 Ziadeh 1990: 81–4.

294 Makdisi 1981: 202.

Professional witnesses were only present at legal transactions. Therefore, witnesses testifying to facts (*shuhūd*) played an important role, too, since documents were accepted only in rather exceptional cases. Thus, a significant part of the facts had to be proven with their help.[295]

Besides honesty (*ᶜadāla*), adulthood, free personal status and Islam as religion were additional requirements for witnesses to testify. The testimony of non-Muslims was not acceptable save last wills made during travel. The testimony of minors was invalid, but the Mālikite school considered it circumstantial evidence.[296] Family members were not allowed to testify for each other. Thus, a father and mother's favourable testimony regarding their child was invalid and vice versa. The testimony of married couples about each other was, however, a matter of dispute among legal scholars. Abū Ḥanīfa and Mālik rejected such testimonies, while al-Shāfiᶜī did not. In a similar vein, Abū Ḥanīfa accepted the testimony of foes and enemies against each other, while Mālik and al-Shāfiᶜī did not.[297]

As a rule, identical testimonies of two witnesses were required to prove a claim, but there were exceptions. In the case of *zinā* (fornication) four male witnesses were needed. According to Ḥasan al-Baṣrī four witnesses were needed not only in the case of *zinā* but also when any right had to be justified, but this was not accepted by the other schools. In commercial transactions the testimony of a male and two female witnesses was also permitted. By contrast, in cases of *ḥadd* the testimony of women given separately or jointly with men could not be accepted. The separate testimony of females could be considered only in cases for which the relevant facts were not accessible to males, such as birth, suckling and other 'female issues'. There was once again dispute about how many female witnesses were needed to justify the necessary facts: according to Mālik two were enough, but according to al-Shāfiᶜī four were needed.[298]

In exceptional cases the testimony of a single witness could be sufficient, provided his words were confirmed by the plaintiff by oath. This was the opinion of Mālik, Ibn Ḥanbal and al-Shāfiᶜī, but was refuted by Abū Ḥanīfa. The oath consisted of the invocation of the name of Allāh and of the acknowledgement that he was the one and only God, but the specific text of the oath varied by school. The place to take an oath was subject to dispute among legal scholars; only its time was specified in the case of *liᶜān,* when the oath had to be taken after the afternoon prayer.[299] In non-criminal cases experts could also be heard. They did not take an oath or give a witness testimony, yet their statements, based on their knowledge, could be accepted despite the fact that whatever they said was not confirmed by a second person.[300]

295 Schneider 1990: 47.

296 Ibn Rushd 1996: 556–7.

297 Ibn Rushd 1996: 558.

298 Ibn Rushd 1996: 559–60.

299 This, according to Mālik; see Ibn Rushd 1994: 488–505; 1996: 560–63.

300 Johansen 2002: 174–5.

It was the judge's duty to greet the witnesses properly in keeping with their ranks and social status. Witnesses could not wear black turbans and garments like the judge wore. Usually they had to take their seat to the right of the judge because the scribe sat to his left. Both judge and scribe had to see and hear the witnesses during the procedure. It was possible to hear the witnesses simultaneously, but the *adab al-qāḍī* literature advises that they should be heard one by one, separately. The witnesses were not called to the trial by the judge but the parties proposed their hearing and asked for permission from the judge for this purpose. If the judge granted it the parties had to arrange for the appearance of the witnesses.[301] In Andalusia it was common practice to keep the identity of a witness secret (*al-shāhid al-muktafī*) so that when the witness gave his testimony about what he had seen or heard he could not be seen by anyone. This was needed when it would have been impossible to persuade the witness to give his testimony in the usual mode of the procedure.[302]

As time went on demand for the acceptance of written documents emerged in Islamic legal procedure. In judicial practice they were accepted, despite the objection of legal scholars.[303] Occasionally circumstantial evidence was also accepted, even in criminal procedure, but this issue provoked heated debate. According to the majority of the legal schools the mere fact that an unmarried woman was pregnant was sufficient proof that she had had a prohibited sexual relationship and, therefore, she could be condemned for fornication even if other proof was lacking. Only the Ḥanbalite school protested against this, saying that pregnancy could just as well be the consequence of rape, hence one circumstance or fact in itself was insufficient proof if it was not supported by something else.[304] The procedural principles and formalism of the classical law was vigorously attacked by the neo-Ḥanbalites, first of all by Ibn Taymiyya and his disciple al-Jawziyya saying that the requirements set by lawyers were alien to life and did not correspond to the practice of the first generation of Muslims. Therefore one should return to the practice of the early Muslims, and the formalism and scholasticism of legal scholars by which they diverted Islamic law from its true interpretation should be disregarded. Therefore, besides oral testimonies of witnesses other proof should also be accepted because this is what corresponds to common sense and experience. Circumstantial evidence and other facts should also be accepted as proof: for instance, that someone could precisely describe an item he said he had lost earlier should be regarded as proof of his ownership. Similarly, a brand on an animal could also testify to ownership. It is the judge's task to accept all these signs and to learn to read them. This, however, required the judge to give up his earlier comfortable and neutral position and to take up an active role in the procedure. As a result, a much broader range of proof would become available

301 Schneider 1990: 127–9.

302 Serrano 2000: 195.

303 Serrano 2000: 195.

304 Johansen 2002: 174–5.

and the judge would also be relieved of his exposure to the parties. On the other hand, however, supporters of this new approach developed a parallel and rigid system similar to the formal procedure they attacked. Accordingly, as social status was an important circumstance from which one could also 'read', a category of suspects was elaborated – including Bedouins, Kurds, peasants, deserters, the urban poor and prostitutes. In this way, social considerations were incorporated in legal procedure. It resulted in more serious consequences than the dysfunctions of the rigid system which they had rightly. For example, a person of lower rank accusing another of good reputation and higher status was condemned without any investigation of his claim because he had violated the reputation of a high-ranking person. Thus social position could be interpreted as the assumption of innocence, at least in the case of people of higher social status. Besides social position an important role was attributed to physiognomic features. This consideration led to the acceptance of torture, which, according to the neo-Ḥanbalites, was a lawful method. In this newly defined procedure, being part of the programme announced under the term *siyāsa sharʿiyya*, suspicious elements could be prosecuted, incarcerated and flogged on the basis of mere suspicion, or could be forced to confess.[305]

Legal Remedy

The subsequent revision of a judgment in Islamic law is subject to debate in modern scholarship. There was no appeal against the decision of the *qāḍī* and, therefore, no appellate court was established. It is the view of Joseph Schacht,[306] Noel Coulson,[307] Bernard Weiss,[308] Asaf Fyzee[309] and Lawrence Rosen,[310] just to mention some scholars of repute. By contrast, Emil Tyan,[311] David Powers,[312] Baber Johansen[313] and Hashim Kamali[314] refuted this, together with Christian Müller[315] and Delfina Serrano,[316] the latter two on the basis of Andalusian examples. According to the latest results of these scholars subsequent modification of a judgment was possible not only because of a legal mistake but a factual error could also lead to the same

305 Johansen 2002: 179–93.
306 Schacht 1964: 189.
307 Coulson 1959: 21.
308 Weiss 1978: 205.
309 Fyzee 1974: 328.
310 Rosen 1989: 48.
311 Tyan 1962: 81–90.
312 Powers 1992: 320–24; 1993: 102–5.
313 Johansen 1993: 34.
314 Kamali 1993: 49–83.
315 Müller 1999: 155–60.
316 Serrano 2000: 214–20.

result. That is, the lack of an appellate court does not rule out the possibility of legal remedy, though this was achieved by other methods.

According to the testimony of chronicles the Caliph Hārūn al-Rashīd established the office of the *qāḍī al-quḍāt* ('the judge of judges'), thus creating a central judiciary seated in Baghdad, and appointed a well-known scholar of the Ḥanafite school of the day, *Abū Yūsuf*, to head it. This is reported in al-Jāḥiẓ's (160/776–255/868) Kitāb al-tāj, Ibn Saᶜd's (168/784–230/845) Ṭabāqāt and Wāqidī's (130–207) Futūḥ Al-ᶜAjam as well, each of them stating that this office corresponded to the office of the *mōbedān mōbed* of the Sasanian Persian Empire.[317] The *qāḍī al-quḍāt* had some rights in respect of the courts since in theory no judge could be appointed or removed without consulting him. At the same time it is also true that the *qāḍī al-quḍāt* was primarily the judge of the capital and no historical data support that one should see an imperial appellate court in this office. As shown in a recent paper dedicated to this issue, the claim that the office of the *qāḍī al-quḍāt* was modelled on previous Iranian judicial structure in general and the *mōbedān mōbed* in particular is also without foundation and should be refuted.[318]

What complicates matters is that the ᶜAbbāsid Caliphs established the *maẓālim* courts (*dīwān al-maẓālim*) to control the excesses of the officials. At the beginning the Caliph participated personally in these cases to find out the truth regarding his officials and hence be able to better control state governance. The growth of the number of cases, however, forced the Caliph to give up his personal involvement and to appoint a judge to head the *dīwān al-maẓālim*. Though the *dīwān al-maẓālim* was mainly a court of public administration (judging disputes between citizens and the state) the fact that one could turn to this court against the *qāḍī's* ruling made it functionally a peculiar appellate court. This court, headed by the *ṣāḥib al-maẓālim*, had general competency for it accepted complaints from the entire empire. The *dīwān al-maẓālim* survived even after the fall of the ᶜAbbāsid Caliphate, particularly in Egypt under the Mamlūks where it acquired considerable power. In social practice, however, people turned to the monarch with their complaints, asking for justice; thus the procedure was less formalized and rather ad hoc in nature[319] (for more on *maẓālim* courts see later in this chapter). Thus there was a way by which the revision of a judgment could be achieved, but it can hardly be called an appellate system as known from continental or common law. This model was introduced in Islamic countries only in the modern period following the European pattern.[320]

The lack of an appellate court may perhaps be surprising to a Western reader but it is in harmony with the principles and practice of Islamic law. Since according to the classical theory a judge had to be qualified to exercise *ijtihād* – that is, independent legal opinion – his decision could be challenged only when it

317 Tyan 1960: 128–30.

318 Jany 2008: 149–68.

319 Kamali 1993: 62–3; Coulson 1964: 122, 128; Schneider 1990: 242.

320 Rosen 1989: 48.

was unlawful. The power of the judge to interpret legal doctrines was guaranteed by the legal pluralism accepted by all. Since legal opinions pronounced with the help of the legal methods established by *uṣūl al-fiqh* (Islamic legal theory) were regarded as equal to each other – one *ijtihād* being as probable as another – there was neither reason nor need to consider one decision superior to another one. Thus the equivalent epistemological value of opinions and decisions hindered the emergence of the idea that a judge may alter the ruling of another judge.[321] The lack of any ecclesiastic organization and hierarchy in Sunnī Islam was another factor which contributed to the situation that no hierarchically organized judicial structure emerged. In short, the lack of appellate courts was not a system deficiency or organizational torso, but a phenomenon deriving logically from the basic position of law.

Ijtihād, however, is a very complex mental activity where the possibility of legal mistake could not be ruled out. Therefore, Muslim legal scholars were in agreement that a judgment being obviously contrary to the rules of the Qur'ān, the *sunna* and *ijmāᶜ* (*al-ḥukm al-mukhālif lil-naṣṣ wa'l-ijmā*) should be revised. Although *naṣṣ* texts contain the revelation in one way or another, at the same time some legal scholars noted that the need for revision pertains only to texts that are clear and do not require interpretation, since an interpretation is already *ijtihād* – and no *ijtihād* is superior to another *ijtihād*, as the accepted principle has it. Therefore, according to Abū Ḥanīfa and Mālik the rules based on *ijmāᶜ* are more important because they incorporate the legal scholars' consensus and this is a more solid basis of law than the *naṣṣ* texts subject to several interpretations. Thus, a decision made against rules on *ijmāᶜ* needs revision by all means.[322]

A judgment pronounced regarding parties for whom the judge could not figure as witness should also be revised. To put it simply, this is the rule to prevent conflict of interest: since a person could not be a witness in favour of his close relatives (father, son etc.), he could not be a judge in their cases either. This was an objective criterion; therefore the judgment had to be revised even if it was correct. Thus the mere fact of family relationship was sufficient for legal revision. There are some further reasons resulting in revision:

1. Serious shortcomings and injustice emerged during trials. For example decisions rested on a fact which was not proven or which did not exist at all; the accepted witness did not meet the requirements set for witnesses.
2. New facts came to light after the judgment was pronounced.
3. The judiciary exceeded its authority and passed judgment in a case where it was not entitled to do so.
4. The judgment may have violated the rights of a third person not involved in the lawsuit.

321 Hallaq 1997: 155–6.
322 Kamali 1993: 72–3.

5. The judgment was not properly supported; in other words if legal argumentation and proof were missing.
6. The judgment was clearly unjust and the judge was prejudiced against one of the parties or the decision was the result of bribery.[323]
7. Revision was also possible if the judge diverted from the doctrine of the school he belonged to.[324]

These are clear words, but it was less obvious where to turn for the revision of a judgment one was dissatisfied with. It was open to the parties to turn directly to the monarch, as in medieval Egypt or in Andalusia. This was rather an ad hoc correction for which the assistance of the political authority was needed.[325] In medieval Morocco a court of review emerged, but further research is needed to say more about this issue.[326]

Since a large number of judgments were based on the opinion of a consulting body (*shūrā*) or of a *muftī*, it was possible for the losing party to consult another *muftī*. In al-Wansharīsī's collection there is a case in which a judge fined a Jew and ordered him to be flogged because he had not sold *kosher* meat to a Muslim. The case, however, was presented to the *muftī* of Cordoba, who called the advising *muftī* 'weak minded' and someone who should not give legal advice in issues he could not understand. According to him both the legal adviser and the judge were responsible for the wrong judgment – and the latter even deserved punishment.[327]

In the majority of cases a judgment was reviewed by a new judge, successor to a former one in his office. A revision could be launched ex officio, but usually the procedure started upon the complaint of a party. In some cases a *fatwā*, written by a *muftī* who had not participated in the previous procedure, could help the new judge discover the legal mistake in the judgment. If the new judge realized that legal mistakes were made not only in individual cases but that the entire activity of his predecessor was against the law, all previous judgments were subject to revision. Judgments considered correct by the new judge remained in force but others were regarded as null and void. Revisions by the successor in office were the exception not the rule. General revisions were made rarely. A revision of an individual case happened only if it was a case of importance or if laws of procedure were violated considerably. A revision of an earlier judgment could also take place if the official successor found the witnesses guilty (*fāsiq*) and consequently not suitable to act as witnesses. Chances for subsequent revisions, however, were reduced in many places – notably in Andalusia, where dynasties of *qāḍīs* developed whose members were not interested in legal revision.[328] Since some kind of 'professional

323 Kamali 1993: 72–80.

324 Johansen 1993: 34.

325 Schneider 1990: 242; Serrano 2000: 215–16.

326 Powers 1993: 105.

327 The case is presented in Powers 1993: 104–5.

328 Müller 1999: 156–9; Powers 1993: 103–4; Rebstock 1999: 15–16, 21–3.

consciousness' and a corporatist attitude emerged among legal scholars and judges, this obviously hindered revision.[329] A judgment relating to *ḥaqq allāh*, however, had to be reviewed ex officio if it was contrary to a clear text of the Qur'ān, a prophetic *sunna*, or consensus.[330]

The proceeding judge also had the right to correct a mistake he noticed subsequently and to withdraw his ruling (*rujūᶜ ᶜan qaḍā'*). This right of the judge was based on Caliph ᶜUmar's letter to Abū Mūsā al-Ashᶜarī encouraging the addressee to correct subsequently his earlier mistake discovered by him, for returning to justice was still better than insisting on something that was null and void.[331] A similar opinion was formulated by al-Shāfiᶜī. According to him, if a judge realized that his decision contradicted the Qur'ān or the *sunna* he had to revise his former judgment. If he made a mistake only in the applied analogy – that is, if he later discovered a better analogy (*ratio legis* could be better applied) – he could compose a new judgment but was not obliged to revise his earlier judgment.[332]

Execution

There is no general rule in Islamic law concerning the execution of judgments. In criminal law the execution of judgments relating to cases of *ḥudūd* was different from that of homicide and bodily injuries (*jināyāt*). Since *ḥudūd* consisted of violating divine law, execution was definitely the responsibility of the community, but in cases of *jināyāt* the victim and his relatives could also play a role.

In the case of fornication execution of the punishment was the right of the *imām*, the head of the Muslim community, because it was a crime committed against God. During stoning the physical condition of the culprits, illness or external conditions (cold, heat) were not considered for the aim of the punishment was definitely to achieve death. However, punishment could not be executed on a pregnant woman until delivery (and so long as a proper wet-nurse was found for the child) or, if such a person was missing, until the baby could be weaned from the mother. Stoning had to be done in an uninhabited place outside the settlement. It was prohibited to carry out stoning in a mosque. A ditch up to the breast had to be dug for women so that their decency could be respected (excepting the view of Mālik and Abū Ḥanīfa). According to the Ḥanafites the first stones had to be thrown by the witnesses, but other schools disagreed on this. The inhabitants of the settlement participated in stoning standing in a queue, headed by the judge who had pronounced the judgment. After death had set in the body was washed in keeping with ritual regulations, enveloped in a shroud and prayers were said over the corpse. By contrast, in the case of flogging, the physical condition of the

329 Serrano 2000: 217.

330 Powers 1992: 323.

331 Müller 1999: 144 with further references.

332 Rebstock 1999: 11.

culprit and the external circumstances were taken into account. If the condemned suffered from a disease which did not allow for execution of the punishment it had to be postponed until the culprit recovered. It was also prohibited to execute the punishment in particularly hot or cold weather. The whip should be neither new nor overused and, in order to avoid danger to life, it was also prohibited to add a knot or anything else (nails, iron etc.) to the whip. Men and women were flogged in different ways. Men were flogged standing, undressed to their pants, whereas women were seated and only their outerwear was removed. No hits were allowed on vital parts of the body such as the head and genitals, and it was also prohibited to hit the same point or part of the body for the whole 100 (or 50) lashes. Commentaries stress that the hits should be distributed evenly on the body in order to avoid danger to life. Flogging and stoning together could not be meted out for any condemned person, though this was a rather disputed issue.[333]

In the case of *jināyāt* the victim and their relatives (*walī al-dam*) could participate in the execution if they chose to take revenge (*qiṣāṣ*). In theory a *walī al-dam* was entitled to execute the judgment, but legal scholars disputed how to do it. For example, some argued, it could be justly assumed that the victim's heir would have such hostile sentiments towards the culprit that they would not execute the culprit properly – that is, they would cause more harm than was done by the culprit previously and would commit excesses. In other words, the problem of proportionality emerged, an important issue in a framework of thought based on *lex talionis*. As a result, legal scholars disputed the modes of execution in general. According to Mālik and al-Shāfiʿī it should be done in the same way as the crime was committed (someone who killed by drowning had to be drowned), but according to the Ḥanafites the culprit should be decapitated by the sword irrespective of the manner in which he had committed the crime. The execution could be carried out only when the Caliph or his representative was present. If the entitled person was unable to carry out the execution for some reason (e.g. he did not have sufficient physical strength) the task was to be done by another person appointed by the ruler. If several entitled persons insisted on participating in the execution the actual executioner had to be selected by drawing lots.[334] If the entitled person took his vengeance before the Caliph's approval it did not qualify as homicide because, according to the arguments of Muslim legal scholars, he had only exercised the right that was his by any means, but he had to answer for disregarding the Caliph's authority.[335] This line of argument again resembles the legal reasoning of Jewish legal scholars.[336]

333 Ibn Rushd 1996: 527–8; al-Māwardī: 278–81; al-Miṣrī 1994: 611.

334 Ibn Rushd 1996: 489–90; al-Miṣrī 1994: 586–7.

335 al-Māwardī: 293.

336 See p. 91.

Procedures outside the Sharīʿa

As seen earlier, the *sharīʿa* does not embrace every social condition but leaves a significant part of them untouched. In order to avoid these being left unregulated, the right of the Caliph (state) to pass laws was acknowledged (*qānūn*). As a result, new norms outside the *sharīʿa* were produced which were implemented by state officials other than the *qāḍī* and governed by procedural laws outside the scope of the *sharīʿa.*

The formalism of the *qāḍī* adjudication was another reason leading to the emergence of extra-*sharīʿa* procedures. Since the criteria of proof were impossible to meet in some cases an office headed by the *ṣāḥib al-radd* evolved, which investigated cases in which the parties were unable to meet the rigorous requirements of proof set by the *sharīʿa*. In criminal law, too, there are procedures not governed by *sharīʿa* law. In these procedures officials heard not only the *ʿudūl* witnesses but anyone, irrespective of their ethical assessment. The testimonies of the witnesses, however, were checked and witnesses confronted each other. Moreover, circumstantial evidence was taken into account, too. In addition to procedural law substantive criminal law was also the prerogative of the Caliph, provided those rules did not contradict *sharīʿa* law. As a result, the Caliph was able to define crimes and their punishments outside Islamic law in his own right. The punishment for these crimes was called deterrence (*taʿzīr*) because the aim was to deter people from committing them. *Taʿzīr* was, however, subject to disputes among legal scholars. Some were of the view that *taʿzīr* punishments could not exceed the measure of the respective *ḥadd* punishments – that is, 100 strokes or one year in jail. The Mālikites, however, insisted on the logic of proportionality, saying that the punishment had to be in proportion to the crime and held, therefore, that *taʿzīr* could include even capital punishment.[337] Prison terms were strictly limited by both the Shāfiʿīte and the Ḥanafite schools. According to the former, prison terms usually lasted for half a year but were never to be more than a complete year. The Ḥanafites, however, also took social standing into account: while the elite, including legal scholars (*ashrāf al-ashrāf*), were exempt from corporal punishment and imprisonment, merchants could be jailed; and the common people could be jailed as well as having to endure corporal punishment. The Mālikites, by contrast, did not restrict prison terms for according to them a prison sentence could last from one day to a lifetime.[338] The discretional nature of *taʿzīr* punishment is proven by the fact that a person could be jailed even on mere suspicion, without committing any crime, by suggestions that their presence had a detrimental effect on society. Such discretionary procedures belonged to the province of both the political authorities and the *qāḍīs*.[339]

---

337 Coulson 1964: 127–33.

338 Schneider 1995: 163–4.

339 Johansen 2002: 176.

Among officials other than the *qāḍī* the market inspector (*muḥtasib*) was very important in the everyday life of Muslim societies. According to al-Māwardī cheating, abuses in the markets (manipulating measures and prices) and refusal to repay debts were the most important wrongdoings falling into the competency of the *muḥtasib*. The procedure of the *muḥtasib* differs in two important aspects from that of the *qāḍī*. First, he could launch a procedure ex officio, without a plaintiff or a victim. Second, since the aim of this procedure was deterrence, any violence applied during the procedure could be regarded neither as a violation of law nor as exceeding his competency. The market inspector could employ informers and spies, and investigate to discover misdemeanours. In addition to abuses in the markets it was his task to control participation in public prayers and to take measures against people who intentionally and notoriously kept themselves away from prayers. The *muḥtasib* had to strengthen and maintain the city walls at the treasury's expense; he had to arrange the city's water supply and also support transiting passengers; he had to supervise public morals and punish those who possessed alcoholic beverages in public spaces. According to al-Shāfiᶜī the market inspector could also destroy the drink, but this view was challenged by Abū Ḥanīfa, according to whom the possession of alcoholic beverages was not to be condemned in itself – therefore the *muḥtasib* could not destroy it otherwise he would violate the right to ownership. The *muḥtasib* could destroy prohibited musical instruments used by musicians but only to an extent that the pieces could still be used for another purpose. Men wishing to make themselves attractive to women by dyeing their white hair black did not escape the rigour of the *muḥtasib*s either. The market inspector also had to arrange for the proper segregation of genders, particularly in boats during voyages. The *muḥtasib* also engaged in disputes of private persons but only if they asked him to do so. In this regard he was not empowered to start a procedure ex officio. He also settled labour disputes between employer and employee, upon their request, when the former retained the rightful pay of the worker or the latter did not do the work specified in the contract. The market inspector also had some tasks in maintaining public order: among others he could prevent an overloaded boat from setting out of port, or a regularly loaded boat leaving port in stormy weather. Guaranteeing the safety of cemeteries was also part of his competencies, in order to safeguard the peaceful rest of the dead. The *muḥtasib* supervised the observance of the duties of the *dhimmī*s, namely that they should not build higher buildings than their Muslim neighbours had; they should wear distinct garments; and they should not speak in public about Jesus and Ezra. At the same time it was also the duty of the *muḥtasib* to protect the *dhimmī*s from harassment by Muslims.[340]

In the Muslim West – notably in Andalusia governed by the Umayyads – the market inspector was called *ṣāḥib al-sūq*, which was changed to *muḥtasib* only in the eleventh century. The *ṣāḥib al-sūq* was seated in the central market and was accompanied by armed policemen in the market while he was inspecting measures

340 al-Māwardī: 299–322.

and the quality of goods. Acting in this competency he could set fines; destroy goods that proved to be adulterated; carry out corporal punishment on a merchant, expel him from the market and even destroy his shop. The market inspector was assisted by simpler law books which summarized the norms of his competency and procedure. Part of the competency of the *muḥtasib* was exercised by the *praefectus urbi*, the *ṣāḥib al-madīna* who was directly answerable to the ruler. In addition to defending the walls of the city he occasionally functioned as a military leader, and executed capital punishment if the ruler was absent.[341]

The *maẓālim* court, established already at the time of Caliph al-Mahdī, was another institution for extra-*sharīʿa* procedures. Contrary to the *sharīʿa* courts, however, the terrain and power of this court remained elastic and varied according to time and place. Although, as we have seen, occasionally legal remedy could be obtained from this court against *qāḍī* judgments, to designate it a court of appeal would be misleading because it was not organized as a court of appeal, an idea alien to Islamic legal thinking. By contrast, *maẓālim* courts were designed to oversee and remedy injustice done by state officials, sometimes *qāḍīs*, leading to 'oppression' (*ẓulm*), hence its name. The supervision of the *maẓālim* courts was the responsibility of the Caliph or his deputies, such as the viziers and governors or their deputies. It was suggested already by al-Māwardī that the precedent of the *maẓālim* could be found in Sasanian Persia, but it is unlikely. As seen earlier, the public hearing, led by the king and the *mōbedān mōbed* was abolished already during the fifth century and it is difficult to see how the idea survived to the early ᶜAbbāsids. Despite this, the aim of the institution is similar to the Persian public hearings – to control the officials personally by the ruler or by one of his leading dignitaries.

The jurisdiction of the *maẓālim* courts was very wide and included, among others, petitions against abuse of power, legal remedy against *qāḍī* judgments and confiscation of *iqṭās*.[342] It was al-Māwardī again who elaborated a theory concerning *maẓālim*. According to him there were ten classes of competencies attached to this court:

1. complaints against oppression and maltreatment of the public by government officials;
2. complaints against tax collectors claiming more rates than lawful;
3. monitoring the secretariat of government departments;
4. complaints against inadequacy of pensions, delay in paying salaries;
5. restoration of usurped property;
6. monitoring of endowments – concerning private endowments this was to be done only on request, but concerning public endowments it was a duty ex officio;

341 Müller 1999: 106–41.

342 Nielsen 1991: 933–4.

7. implementation of the *qāḍī's* judgment if the judge was unable to do so because of the party's social standing;
8. investigation of matters of public welfare and morals;
9. ascertaining public acts of worship and military duty;
10. settlement of quarrels and disputes.[343]

As it is clear from the above, *maẓālim* courts were not courts in a sense the *sharīʿa* courts were, but could be regarded as an executive organ dealing with various cases. It is small wonder, therefore, that *maẓālim* courts were headed by top governmental officials and not by *qāḍīs*, although in fact sometimes *qāḍīs* are also found among their members.

It is not only the area of competencies but also the law of procedure which makes *maẓālim* courts very different from *sharīʿa* courts. It was again al-Māwardī who listed the differences between these two judicial institutions. Accordingly, a *maẓālim* court:

1. had more authority to stop quarrels by litigants;
2. had more freedom of actions;
3. in order to find out material truth could rely on evidence on which a *qāḍī* could not, e.g. circumstantial evidence;
4. could discipline whoever was guilty of injustice;
5. had more time to handle a case and postpone his decision, a licence no *qāḍī* had;
6. could dismiss the parties in order to reach a compromise;
7. could also hear unqualified witnesses a *qāḍī* could not;
8. could force witnesses to take an oath;
9. could call for witnesses on its own initiative to testify in order to clarify the circumstances of a case, whereas in a procedure before a *qāḍī* the parties provided witnesses.[344]

Now it is evident that *maẓālim* courts were not bound by strict *sharīʿa* rules, which gave them more freedom to weigh evidence, find out the material truth and free themselves from the rigid, ritualistic procedure of the *sharīʿa* courts. Yet at the same time this negligence of the rigid procedural law could open the way for arbitrary judgments and subjective adjudication which could lead to *ẓulm* (injustice), which they were designed to fight against. It is also worth noting that by and large *maẓālim* courts put in practice what Ḥanbalī jurists called for under the umbrella of *siyāsa sharʿiyya* later.[345]

Notwithstanding this, *maẓālim* courts existed for centuries both in the Muslim East and West, since these courts were also established in al-Andalus, although

343 al-Māwardī: 100ff.

344 al-Māwardī: 105–6.

345 Nielsen 1991: 934–5.

only later, during the tenth century. Here, too, *maẓālim* courts operated along the same pattern, that is, were parallel to the *sharīʿa* courts: cases were dealt with by high-ranking officials of the rulers and not by the *ʿulamāʾ* and they were not appellate courts.[346]

Legal scholars looked down on these offices with considerable aversion. Since some of them refused the office of the *qāḍī* they were more unwilling to take up the task of offices outside the realm of the *sharīʿa*. They considered these officials as unjust, realizing oppression (*ẓulm*), and as not leading pious lives pleasing God but acting in the interests of material wealth and state authority. The sharp distinction between the respectable life of legal scholars and the immoral life of officials in the service of the ruler, dotted with excesses, was perhaps best worded in al-Mawrūrī's biography. Al-Mawrūrī is said to have dedicated his life to the study of *ḥadīth* and jurisprudence, but later on took up office and sank into worldly pleasures. In seeking power he even served in the job of military commander and urban leader, thus participating in the oppression of the people.[347] To emphasize the disillusionment in a former companion, turning his back on jurisprudence and on his colleagues could not be worded any better than that he took up office in the service of the ruler.

Muslim legal scholars were disturbed by this parallel forum of adjudication, representing the interest of the state and threatening their influence and power. The aversion towards state offices, stressed time and again in biographies, is only one sign of it. Another is that they tried to neglect them, omitting them almost totally in their works on jurisprudence, notwithstanding the fact that *maẓālim* courts were very important rivals to the *qāḍī* courts.[348] When there happened to be a just judge in the *maẓālim* court people turned to him and neglected the *qāḍī* court, as happened in Egypt during the ninth century.[349] Thus, it was not only procedural law that mattered but also the personality of the presiding judge. Were he known as a just judge he could succeed in overcoming the *qāḍī* court, notwithstanding the fact that in the latter strict procedural law was designed to prevent abuses – at least in theory. In short, it was possible for a qualified judge to pronounce just judgments in a system which gave him more freedom and, therefore, more freedom to misuse his power, while strict rules in themselves were ineffective to prevent the injustice of corrupt judges.

Extra-Procedural Competencies of the Courts

Besides litigation Islamic, Jewish and Zoroastrian courts had a variety of administrative and social functions. Muslim courts were the busiest of them.

346 Müller 1999: 128–31.

347 The biography is in Müller 1999: 115–16.

348 Schneider 1993: 152–5.

349 Shahar 2008: 127.

Islamic Courts

Concerning Islamic law al-Māwardī lists the non-procedural tasks of the judges as follows:

1. to exercise guardianship over persons who have no power to act on their own behalf, such as minors and the insane;
2. to exercise supervision over *waqf*s (charitable foundations) so that their wealth should be used legally and in keeping with the founder's intentions. The judge could accomplish these duties in two ways: either indirectly, by checking the activities of the head of the *waqf*, or by direct management;
3. to dispose of legacies in keeping with the deceased's last will and testament;
4. to arrange proper marriages for widows and divorcees if they had no guardian (save the Ḥanafite school, according to which divorcees and widows could marry of their own will);
5. to end street disturbances and usurpation in streets and public places;
6. to supervise and control his deputies, scribes and witnesses, who should be removed immediately if the slightest proof of their corruption emerged.[350]

A further task of judges was the supervision of jails and care of the prisoners. A newly appointed judge was obliged to investigate the case of all prisoners, and if their incarceration was unjustified or the plaintiff (victim) did not keep up his complaint they had to be released. The *adab al-qāḍī* literature strongly underlines the protection of prisoners; it prohibits their torture and stresses their proper handling, which presumably also served as a distorting mirror for the practice of the day.[351]

With the supervision of *waqf*s and the guardianship over women and insane persons, a considerable part of Muslim society was placed under judicial control. *Waqf*s can be regarded as one of the most important private law institutions of Islamic law. A huge number of *waqf*s came into being during the centuries, accumulating enormous wealth (mostly land), which financed, among others, religious schools, hospitals and the maintenance of the poor. *Waqf*s were managed by private persons (*mutawallī*) authorized to do so. Should such a person fail for whatever reasons, management of the *waqf* was taken over by the court to guarantee its permanent and lawful activity. The guardianship over orphans and widows was meant to improve their situation, but this was subject to debate. The Mālikites acknowledged the court's power to guardianship over minor girls, while the Shāfiʿītes did not. The Ḥanafites developed an intermediary position: they did acknowledge the guardianship of the court, but at the same time guaranteed a woman's right to terminate her marriage contract when she came of age if it was concluded when she was a minor.[352]

---

350 al-Māwardī: 89–91.

351 Schneider 1995: 167–8.

352 Bakhtiar 1996: 427.

Zoroastrian Courts

Zoroastrian law also empowered the courts with non-procedural competencies during the Sasanian period. It is interesting to note that these competencies relate to fields which were identical to the most important non-procedural tasks of the Muslim courts, that is, the supervision of endowments and guardianship over women and insane persons. Sasanian Fire-temple endowments resembling English trusts[353] were not supervised by the secular courts but by the *rad*s, who had to control their documents and activities. In order to control effectively these 'Fire-temple trusts' an archive was established (*dīwān ī kardagān*) which contained all the relevant documents.[354]

By contrast, concerning marriages in general and guardianship in particular, the role of the Sasanian courts was more significant than that of their Muslim counterparts. Zoroastrian law knew a particular form of marriage (čagar), similar to levirate but different in detail, which could be obligatory for persons defined by law (*stūr*). If a *stūr* was missing in the family for whatever reasons, it was the task of the court to appoint a *stūr*, who was obliged to enter into a marriage. Children produced in such a union were considered heirs of the deceased.[355] Thus, Sasanian courts not only arranged a proper marriage for widows and orphans as Muslim courts did but also acted on behalf of a person who died without a male offspring. In doing so the court came to the assistance of the deceased man since it prevented his being nameless (*abē-nām*) and at the same time helped his family in keeping its wealth compact, which was an important issue for the nobility.[356]

Jewish Courts

By and large Jewish courts had similar non-procedural competencies to their Islamic and Zoroastrian counterparts. Jewish courts functioned as guardians of the property of widows, orphans, the deaf and other impaired persons, or appointed a guardian for the management of the property of such persons. The court also supervised the activities of such appointed guardians.[357] In subsequent centuries the administration of such estates was put in the hands of laymen called 'trustees of the court', proven by the Cairo *Genizah* documents. This separation of power relieved the court of non-procedural obligations and at the same contributed to the fact that Jewish courts were the least corrupt of the three legal systems compared here.[358]

---

353 For details see Jany 2004.

354 MHDA 27:2, 37:5; Macuch 1981: 200.

355 For details of *stūr* and čagar marriages see Carlsen 1984: 103–14.

356 Macuch 1993: 151–66.

357 The Babylonian Talmūd contains several cases in relation to these problems which are analysed in Neusner 1969: 214–17.

358 Goitein 1999: 319.

Chapter 4
The Judge and the Litigants

Relations with the Parties during the Trial

Zoroastrian Law

The relationship between the court and the parties during the trial is difficult to discern because available sources are meagre in this regard. Generally speaking, while the equality of the parties was an important principle to be followed in private litigations, in criminal procedures legal guarantees were not available for the accused person.

In private litigation *azishmānd*, a somewhat puzzling and complex legal term, seems to be of importance. At least this can be inferred from the Mādigān ī Hazār Dādestān (MHD+A) since its editor dedicated a separate chapter to this issue. At the present stage of knowledge it is impossible to say with certainty what was understood by *azishmānd* by Persian lawyers in the Sasanian period since a variety of minor misdeeds came to be designated with this term. On the other hand, it is clear from the MHD+A that acts hindering the conduct of lawsuits properly by the parties were qualified as *azishmānd.*

When a judge realized that any of the parties had committed *azishmānd* he noted it in a separate judgment. Such notices cannot be considered simply as orders to conduct the trial because they could affect the final judgment, too. If notices were made three times regarding the same litigant, they lost the lawsuit.[1] If it was the plaintiff who hindered litigation, they also had to give a pledge as security, at least according to Zurwāndād.[2] When co-litigants participated on one side in the lawsuit each of their *azishmānd*s affected all the other co-litigants, therefore co-litigants had to face the legal consequences, too.[3] This rule itself shows that the function of *azishmānd* was not to establish liability but to ensure rapid and smooth conduct of the trial and to hinder procedural tricks. The sum of any fine and the pledge had to be deposited at the court. If the party lost the case because of their third *azishmānd* the sum of the fine and the pledge were received by the other party.[4] A party committing *azishmānd* lost their right to take an oath.[5] There was no appeal against notices passed in *azishmānd* cases. According to the judgments

1 MHD 10. 12–11. 7.
2 MHD 10. 12–11. 7.
3 MHD 11. 8–13.
4 MHD 11. 8–11, 11–13.
5 MHD 14. 12–17.

found in the MHD+A refusal to take an oath[6] and contradictory statements of more legal representatives in the lawsuit[7] qualified as *azishmānd.*

During private litigation the parties had to stand three steps away from the judge to deliver their statements in order to show respect towards him,[8] but nothing is known about etiquette the judge had to follow in respect of the parties. By contrast, in criminal procedure no etiquette seems to have been followed by the court since, as seen previously, interrogated persons could be beaten during hearings, tortured between hearings and had neither the right nor the opportunity to defend themselves against physical onslaughts.

Islamic Law

Islamic legal thinking in general and the *adab al-qāḍī* literature in particular puts emphasis on the correct behaviour of the judges and their neutrality towards the parties. In their effort to draw a picture of a somewhat ideal type of a judge, works of the *adab al-qāḍī* literature regulate the interactions of the judge with the parties from the beginning till the end of the procedure, going into hair-splitting details. Although the aim was obviously to create a situation in the court room in which the impartiality of the judge was discernible even in his gestures and other symbolic acts, the result was a very ritualistic etiquette which was unlikely to be followed completely in every case of litigation.

Impartiality was considered of vital importance even before works on the *adab al-qāḍī* came into being. An early text such as Caliph ᶜUmar's letter referred to already highlights: (1) the impartiality of the judge in any trial, making it compulsory even towards noblemen (*sharīf*); (2) the permissibility, and what is more, preference of peaceful agreements; and (3) the rapid settlement of the disputes of foreigners so that they could go home as soon as possible.[9] The requirement of impartiality is defined as a prohibition of siding with persons of superior power due to their economic and social status, an issue which can be regarded as a topos of the later *adab al-qāḍī* literature. It is also important to note the preference for compromise against the judgment of the court, a pre-Islamic tradition going back centuries with the wise *ḥākam* as a central figure in these arbitrations.

At the beginning, there were no permanent buildings for law courts. Therefore, the venue of adjudication became subject to dispute among legal schools. The Shāfiᶜītes expressly prohibited adjudication in mosques, but other schools made no objection against such a practice. According to the Shāfiᶜītes it would de-sacralize the mosque if parties in dispute were shouting at each other where other people wished to focus their thoughts on God. By contrast, Abū Ḥanīfa argued that the

6 MHD 13. 13–15.

7 MHD 75. 9–12.

8 MHDA 26. 3–4.

9 Serjeant 1991: 66–7.

execution of *ḥadd* punishments had a force of deterrence which could be more effective if done in a mosque. Instead of the mosque the Shāfiʿītes recommended a 'proper place' for adjudication which was comfortable enough with no disturbing circumstances hindering the judge in adjudication. Such a place could be anywhere in the city provided there was a sufficient quantity of food and water, it was not dark and was protected against cold and heat. These conditions were important because otherwise the judge could lose patience and would not proceed properly. The judge's own house could also be a proper place, which was indeed common practice in the early period. Mosques were particularly favoured by the Ḥanafites, while the Mālikites instead built separate buildings for the judiciary. These buildings did not exist necessarily for long because if a new, non-Mālikite judge was appointed he had it pulled down immediately so that the next Mālikite judge could restore it.[10]

Authors of the *adab al-qāḍī* literature particularly stress that the judge had to make his ruling free of all detrimental physical circumstances. He could not be hungry, thirsty, lacking sleep, ill or angry. Moreover, to be able to preserve his reserve and objectivity in respect of women even his sexual desires should be satisfied before the trial.[11] The aim of these preconditions was that the judge should pay attention exclusively to his important office and no other issues should burden his attention.

No matter where the trial was held, the judge had a separate carpet which kept him at a distance from the parties, both physically and symbolically. The cushions on the carpet served exclusively the judge's comfort. On the day of the trial the judge had to appear in a clean and particularly nice garment, with shawl and turban, the latter supplemented with a cap exclusively preserved for judges (*qalansuwa*). Further, he was expected to be groomed (hair combed, nails clean) and to make himself suitable for an appearance in public with a perfume of 'non-disturbing' fragrance. The judge had to take his seat facing the entrance so that he could see all who entered.[12] When someone entered the court room the judge had to remain seated, just nodding his head so that he would show nobody any favour by a greeting. According to an anecdote, reflecting rather an ideal and not necessarily a real situation, Caliph al-Mahdī got involved in a lawsuit with one of his governors and turned to a court. When he entered the room the judge bowed his head but remained seated, but at the end of the proceeding he stood up and politely greeted him. The Caliph told him that he would have immediately dismissed him from his office had he greeted him thus upon entry and would have done the same had the judge not greeted him at the end of the trial.[13]

---

10 Schneider 1990: 50–60.

11 Schneider 1990: 61–8. Ibn Rushd also stresses the importance of the judge being free of detrimental physical conditions, but if a proper judgment was pronounced under such conditions it had to be executed; see Ibn Rushd 1996: 571.

12 Schneider 1990: 123–4.

13 This anecdote is quoted in Schneider 1990: 77.

The parties had to be seated in front of the judge on their own carpet as it was required by respect shown towards the *qāḍī*. Men had to kneel, but women had to be seated cross-legged. The seriousness of the ceremonial attitude is indicated by the fact that authors of the *adab al-qāḍī* literature discussed the question of whether a judge greeted only by one of the entering parties should reciprocate only in the direction of the person honouring him or greet both parties. Obviously, during the sometimes heated debates not everyone cared for the observance of the court etiquette with minute precision. It is shown by the fact that a litigant disturbing the order of procedure and cursing his adversary could be warned orally; condemned to beating either with a stick or a shoe; or, in more serious cases, locked up in jail. Such measures were made by the judge at his own discretion, depending on the seriousness of the act and in keeping with the social status of the parties. As the freedom of the judge was not limited in this respect, reports on actual lawsuits show that beating by stick could last even as long as blood started to flow. As a curious example a case is known where one of the parties died because of such measures. Now it is understandable why authors of the *adab al-qāḍī* works often stress that a judge should not be angry or lose his temper during a procedure.[14]

Though in principle both men and women could participate in the trial at the same time, judges were rather advised to mark a day of hearing of men and women separately. The trial opened with the statement of the parties, but it was up to them which of them presented their request first. If the parties could not agree on the order of presentation it was decided by drawing lots, or the judge sent them away until they could agree in this issue.[15]

The personal observations of the anthropologist Lawrence Rosen made during his field work in Morocco prove that this traditional way of the procedure has not changed significantly even up to the end of the twentieth century. The parties are let into the room by a uniformed guard, who also functions as interpreter for Berbers not speaking Arabic. The parties greet the judge but there is not much time for formalities because the guard rapidly guides them to their place. At the judge's first question the parties start shouting, everyone wanting to tell their own version first, while there is no patience for listening to the other party. Sometimes the judge lets them shout freely so that he can continue the procedure after the overheated emotions are let out. If this is not productive court assistants rush in and hold the shouting people fast, who, after being divested of the possibility of indispensable gesticulation, keep quiet. In this respect there is no difference between men and women because both genders speak out about what they want to say with equal vehemence. The court scribe takes notes of the parties' statements amid these somewhat chaotic conditions and draws up the protocols. Despite these somewhat turbulent circumstances the judge has full control over the situation and

14 Schneider 1990: 79–85.

15 Schneider 1990: 131–5.

is capable of closing down the case with spectacular rapidity, quite often passing more than ten judgments within a single forenoon.[16]

What the field work of an anthropologist could prove for a scholar dealing with contemporary societies, literary tradition could do the same for students of the past. Therefore, studying the Qābūs-nāme, a mirror for princes written in classical Persian, is in order. In this work the author, an educated member of a north Iranian ruling family, instructs a young prince with advice in the art of good governance. The topics of the work cover broad areas containing, for example, the art of warfare, entertainment, sciences and the administration of justice. In the chapter about justice is a humorous story which aims to draw attention to the hardship of making judgments and at the same time proves that the passive position of the judge is not sufficient to arrive at a just judgment. The story can be summarized as follows. There were two friends living in a small village. One of them fell in love with a slave girl and wanted to buy her but lacked the money to do so. Therefore, he asked his friend to help him. In order to discuss the matter in private they went to a park, outside the town. Here, under a tree, they settled everything and his friend lent him the necessary sum. Having the money, the man could buy the girl for himself, but failed to pay the debt back in due time. After repeating his request for repayment in vain the creditor went to the court, asking the judge to help him. The debtor, however, denied everything and the creditor was unable to prove his claim. The judge, convinced that the plaintiff was indeed telling the truth, decided to find out the truth with a trick. He ordered the plaintiff to go to the park and ask the tree to come to the court to testify. The plaintiff, shocked by such an order, nevertheless went to the park and read the judge's order to the tree which, obviously, did not move. In the meantime the judge repeatedly asked the defendant whether the plaintiff had arrived. As the defendant answered negatively, saying that the place was far away, the judge continued the process of other litigants. When finally the plaintiff came back and testified that the tree had not moved, the judge pronounced the judgment in which he ruled – based on the testimony of the tree – that the plaintiff was right and that the defendant had to repay the debt. Hearing this, the defendant complained that no tree had testified in the matter and that it was indeed absurd to require a tree to testify in a legal dispute. The judge, in turn, answered that the defendant was wrong. Had he not asked for money under the tree, as the plaintiff claimed, he could not have known which tree was mentioned and, therefore, he could not have known either that the park was far away from the court. As a result, the plaintiff was deemed right and the defendant had to pay the money back.[17]

The aim of this short story was to draw the young prince's attention to the fact that one cannot always decide on what was learned from books only. At the same time it provides an alternative interpretation of the judge's role in a trial, differing from mainstream Islamic legal understanding. Accordingly, the judge is not only a

16 Rosen 1989: 6–7.

17 Qābūs-nāme: 115–17.

neutral person in the dispute of the parties but should also participate actively – if necessary, one-sidedly – to discover the truth. All this confirms a rather sceptical approach to the parties and their claims during trials.

Jewish Law

Although there is no literary genre similar to the *adab al-qāḍī* literature in Jewish legal culture, problems discussed there by Muslim scholars were equally important to their Jewish colleagues. Biblical references were treated as a basis from which a variety of rules were deduced, both symbolic and procedural. The demand for equal treatment of the parties, for example, was deduced from verse 19:15 of Leviticus commanding impartiality.

Obviously, no trial could be held on the *Shabbāt,* and Jewish custom selected two days, Monday and Thursday, for litigation. Trials started early in the morning, when judges put on their special garments. When entering, the parties and the witnesses had to stand up and remain standing until the court allowed them to sit down. Not even the monarch was exempted from this rule, as proved by the case of Alexander Jannaeus (first century BCE). The leading legal scholar of his age, Shimᶜeōn ben Shetaḥ, called on him to stand up when he appeared at the law court because he was actually not facing the court but the tribunal of God. The king, however, rejected the demand and no one dared to repeatedly order him to stand up.[18]

This court etiquette did not change during the Talmudic period since the parties had to respect the court by standing. The parties, the witnesses and other interested persons were already present in the room when members of the court arrived. The entry of the court had its own choreography, as it was the chairman of the court who entered last. Only the chairman of the court could give permission for people in the room to sit down. Such permission, however, could only be given to both parties; in other words no preference could be given to either of the parties by this gesture.[19] Maimonides, however, living in the post-Talmudic period, laments that these old rules were rarely implemented in his age, as the court automatically gave permission to the parties and the witnesses to sit down.[20]

In practice, however, legal scholars did enjoy a privileged position if one of the litigants came from among them, irrespective of the formal and ceremonial equality of the parties. This privilege was also shared by rabbinic students. It was not only that they were relieved of appearing before the court and giving testimony whenever possible, but also that judgments were expressly and deliberately in their favour. A saying, attributed to Rava', clearly expresses this attitude: 'I did not lay my head on the pillow before I saw points in his favour.'[21] Ordinary people,

18 Piattelli–Jackson 1996: 43.

19 Tos Sanh 6:2, 7:8.

20 Cohn 1974a: 576.

21 Quoted in Neusner 1969: 313. The Babylonian Talmūd (BT) contains several cases in which prejudice for rabbis is discernible; these are analysed in Neusner 1969: 313ff.

who were in no position to oppose such judgments, accepted rabbinic decisions even if they were contrary to their own interests and in the Rabbis' favour.[22]

There is little information about the garments of the parties from the biblical period. One remark of Josephus Flavius, however, indicates that in criminal cases the accused appeared in black garments, with their hair loose and behaving humbly and reserved. The reason was not that there were rules regarding this issue, but that the accused should raise sympathy in their judge.[23] As a rule judges appeared in a white or gold-trimmed cloak, as this was the usual attire of the Rabbis.[24] Some Babylonian Rabbis were Iranicized in their garments because towards the end of the Parthian period they started to wear a *kamar* (belt), part of the *mōbed*s' garments expressing rank. They also wore the tall pointed cap (*kulaf*), a headgear of the Iranian peoples (Sakas, Parthians) originating from Siberia (*bashlyk*).[25] The implements of the judges were the rod, the lash, the horn and the sandals.[26]

There was no general rule about the garments of the parties in the Talmudic period but no party was allowed to express their social or economic superiority by garments. Consequently, a party appearing in a provocative or rich garment was obliged to put on a garment similar to that of the other party. Until he did do so he was not allowed to make a statement in court. The parties had to be given an equal duration of time for speeches and neither party could make a statement in the absence of the other one. Usually the parties made oral statements, but it was also possible to make written statements by dictating them to the court scribe (as in the case of women not wishing to come to court) or by filling in documents of set form. The court regarded the parties with suspicion, saying that everyone was capable of keeping the truth secret in order to strengthen their own position in a lawsuit. This realistic scepticism was certainly the result of a long practice at courts, being similar to the experience of their Muslim colleagues (see also the lessons of the Persian story quoted above).[27]

Great emphasis was put on peaceful settlements because a compromise between the parties was regarded as superior to the judgments of the courts, again a similarity to the Islamic legal thinking (see earlier in this chapter). Therefore, at the beginning of the procedure the court asked the parties whether they insisted on the lawsuit or would prefer to settle their conflict by agreement.[28] Even if the parties did not show any inclination to agree on the conditions of a compromise, the court did not start the procedure immediately but asked the parties whether they wanted to authorize the court to elaborate the framework and conditions of a possible compromise. If the parties rejected this, the court started the legal

22 Neusner 1969: 135.

23 Josephus 1963: XIV, 171–3.

24 Neusner 1969: 135; Mantel 1965: 214.

25 Neusner 1965: 75, 96, 108.

26 Sanh 7b.

27 Sanh 7b; Cohn 1974a: 577.

28 Sanh 6b.

procedure per se. The dominant understanding, however, was that the court had to do everything in order to persuade the parties to compromise and to dissuade them from insisting on a legal procedure. If, however, the parties insisted on continuing the lawsuit, the court was not entitled to instruct either of the parties about their rights and opportunities. The court was not allowed to advise either of the parties on how to argue effectively in their case; neither could it be done by references to analogous or hypothetical cases.[29] Until the judgment was pronounced the opportunity to reach a compromise with the cooperation of the court was still left open to the parties. But if the court had announced the judgment the possibility of compromise waned.[30]

The lawsuit was regarded as a struggle between the parties where 'the stronger should prevail'. Behind this principle was the assumption that the one who was right would better and more effectively struggle to prove his rightfulness and present more convincing proof than the other party who was wrong.[31] Here again the approach of Jewish and Islamic law is rather similar. In both legal cultures private procedure is regarded as a struggle between the parties in which the court's task is restricted to supervising observance of the rules of this struggle and finally to announcing the winner.

In the post-Talmudic period and the following centuries the relationship between the court and the parties underwent some changes, though essentially it remained the same. The Jewish court, operating free of charge, offered an attractive alternative to the parties, who, as a result, did not turn to the far more costly Muslim court – though they had the right to do so. Evidently, the aim of this was to prevent the parties going to the Muslim court and to preserve the observance of Jewish law, an effort whose success varied by time and place.[32]

In this period a peculiar institution of medieval Jewish law, the right to interrupt public prayer, was already known. Accordingly, a person who felt that he was unjustly treated in a court procedure could make the gathering listen to his complaint by interrupting community prayer or hindering its beginning. A case is known of someone who, by hindering the reading of the Torāh scroll, occupying the reader's post and making his complaints public, could make his defendant be taken to court.[33]

This was not the only way of taking one's adversary to court. Threatening to turn to a Muslim court usually proved sufficient (because in that case ultimately

29 Cohn 1974a: 576–7.

30 Sanh 6a–b; Tos Sanh 1:2–3.

31 Cohen 1991: 133–4.

32 The competition between rabbinic and *sharīʿa* courts remained for centuries. We know that in sixteenth-century Jerusalem Jews often preferred the Muslim courts and neglected the rabbinic ones; see Shahar 2008: 124. The situation is similar to that under Roman rule when Jewish courts had to face the possibility that the parties could turn to the – sometimes favourable – Roman courts.

33 Goitein 1999: 323–4.

the Muslim state arranged for the defendant's appearance). The practice of compromise at courts survived, though it was permissible only in disputes concerning issues of private law. By contrast, rigorous observance of the rules of law was made in the field of family law (levirate) and inheritance. This is the reason why many complaints were directed against judges, saying that they were too hard and rigorous in their judgments. By contrast, complaints against corruption were formulated rather rarely. In fact the courts did a great deal to preserve their good fame and honour, at the same time preventing the parties from losing face, too, particularly if the party involved was rich or had high social prestige. In such cases the court, before passing its judgment, called the losing party to satisfy his opponent's claim so that he might by all means avoid the shame of losing the case. The court decided to the detriment of the party only when this offer was rejected. If, however, he continued to refuse the court's decision, a final solution – that is, excommunication – was announced, which had rather serious consequences according to Jewish law.[34]

The Judge's Liability towards the Parties

Both Jewish and Islamic law has something to say about the liability of a judge towards the parties when pronouncing a wrong judgment and causing harm to one or both parties.

It is not known whether or not **Zoroastrian law** made judges responsible for their wrong judgments because there are no sources available. An erroneous judgment was called in the Dēnkard *drōg wizīr* ('Lügenurteil')[35] but its legal consequences remain in the dark since there are no hints to them in the MHD+A. By contrast, in Iranian apocalyptic writing such as the Arda Wirāz Nāmag can be found moral and religious condemnation of corrupt judges who received bribes and pronounced unjust judgments. Accordingly, the souls of these judges suffered in Hell by iron nails being driven into their heads. Alternatively, in a different locus of the same text, such a judge was killing his own child and eating his brains.[36]

In **Jewish law** the liability of the judge depends on the one hand on the proceeding judge's personal status and on the other on whether he committed a mistake during the trial. As already seen, laymen – being community leaders and elders – could also be judges in a three-member court beside legal scholars and professional judges.

These lay judges preserved their influence in the Second Temple period and in the subsequent centuries since they mainly adjudicated in 'private law' cases. Legal scholars started to discriminate against lay judges at the time when the Pharisees gained strength by establishing some rules detrimental to their operation. Thus a

34 Goitein 1999: 318–19, 328, 342.

35 Macuch 1993: 63.

36 Vahman 1986: 214–16.

lay judge could not accept money for his activity, otherwise his ruling qualified as invalid. As a next step the Rabbis made lay judges financially responsible for mistakes committed by them. A lay judge had to pay compensation out of his own wealth for a wrong judgment, whereas R. ᶜAqībah relieved the non-lay judge from this obligation. According to the view of Ze'ev Falk the reason for this distinction was that the Rabbis tried to push lay adjudication into the background because they believed it could not meet the required professional standard and, therefore, adjudication should be the privilege of the legal scholars – that is, the Rabbis. The financial responsibility of lay judges also served to discourage people from participating in this kind of adjudication. Were this in fact their aim they could not accomplish it for lay adjudication continued for a long time and tenaciously defended itself against rabbinic discrimination.[37] When both parties accepted a single judge he had no financial responsibility towards them, otherwise the judge had to make restitution out of his own resources.[38]

A judge appointed by the head of the Babylonian Jews, the *rēsh galūta'*, or an ordained person was exempt from liability and its consequences. Therefore, Rab and Shamū'el agreed that if someone wanted to be exempt from liability he had to ask for authorization from the *rēsh galūta'*.[39] It does not necessarily mean that he was acknowledged at the same time as a Rabbi because the *nāśī* and the *rēsh galūta'* could appoint (*rēshūta'*) someone to decide about monetary issues. Such a person was called *mumḥeh* ('expert') and could proceed alone and pronounce judgments but was not authorized to impose fines. Without *rēshūta'*, however, even a legal scholar had financial liability, save his liability was excluded by the agreement of the parties.[40]

Factual and legal wrongs were considered mistakes. Due to the prevalent and accepted legal pluralism, to ascertain a legal mistake was a complicated issue. Therefore the Talmūd has it that if the judge did not observe the rules of the Mishnah his judgment was faulty and required revision. The reason is that the Mishnah – in contrast to the Talmūd, containing different legal opinions – can rather be regarded as a work in which law was recorded unambiguously, therefore disrespect of its contents could be considered illegal. If, however, a judge had to make his choice from among conflicting opinions because the *halakah* was not yet established, a mistake in law could not be determined for sure. According to the Talmūd a judge has to weigh up conflicting opinions and rule according to the one that was followed in general practice (*mashhūr*). If doing otherwise, this was an error in law; but a *mumḥeh* was free from liability to pay compensation.[41] It is important to note here that a Muslim judge was confronted with the same task since it was also necessary for him to weigh conflicting opinions and to rule

37 Falk 1972: 92.

38 Sanh 5a.

39 Sanh 5a.

40 Sanh 5a, 33a; Mantel 1965: 215–16.

41 Sanh 33a.

according to the one followed in general practice. A Muslim judge, however, was authorized not to follow a *mashhūr* doctrine if he could rely on another doctrine within his own school if it was better suited to a particular case; but he had to provide reasons to divert from the *mashhūr* doctrine.[42]

In **Islamic law** the liability of a judge was not an important issue, perhaps because of procedural reasons. As we have seen the judge was exposed to the witnesses and was called a 'captive of witness' (*asīr al-shāhid*). Liability in factual wrong was, therefore, excluded since it was the responsibility of the party or of the witnesses to testify according to the material truth. Should they abuse their position, it was their liability not that of the proceeding judge. Therefore, the judgment was regarded as valid even when subsequently the truth was revealed and the falsity of the testimony came to light. By contrast, if the judge knowingly and deliberately judged wrongly and acknowledged the 'suppressing' and 'violent' nature (*ẓulm*) of his proceeding he had to compensate the damaged party out of his own property. Moreover, he lost the honesty (*ᶜadāla*) of his office, too. If the mistake was not made intentionally it was the treasury (*bayt al-māl*) or the beneficiary of the judgment who had to compensate the damaged party. In cases of *ḥaqq allāh* it was the treasury that had to bear the burden because the judge acted in the name of the community; therefore the financial responsibility also had to be borne by the community. Otherwise it was the beneficiary of the judgment who had to compensate the damage. The judge, however, was exempt from liability. The liability of the *qāḍīs* was established primarily not for errors in judgments but for squandering and embezzling property in their charge. Since the *qāḍīs* had to arrange for the management and control of the property of orphans and pious foundations, they were financially responsible for any loss in these properties. At the same time there was no effective control mechanism – the only opportunity to discover wrongdoings was the revision of the *qāḍī's* actions by his successor in office, already mentioned. Attempts were made to minimize abuses by establishing ethical requirements and standards for judges. Since the administration of justice served the interests of the entire community (*maṣlaḥa ᶜāmma*) it was thought that the judges' responsibility had to be limited, too.[43] Therefore, only the most outrageous cases came to light, as proven by the following case: an orphaned child turned to the court complaining against his guardian but the judge did not care. When the boy expressed his disillusionment in a satirical poem the judge condemned him to imprisonment. Only when the background of the poem was revealed was the judge suspended.[44]

42 Rosen 1989: 47.

43 Rebstock 1999: 22–34.

44 Schneider 1995: 163.

Chapter 5
The Judge and Jurisprudence

This chapter will discuss the complex relationship of judges vis-à-vis jurisprudence. In doing so it will examine the judges' legal training and qualifications and their role in shaping jurisprudence in their respective societies. Such a comparison will shed light on the judges' 'sociology of knowledge'.

The Judge and Legal Scholars

Islamic Law

As already seen, Islamic law looked on judges as masters of procedure who could manage and conduct lawsuits professionally. It is important to note, however, that the conduct of procedures requires a firm technical knowledge in law but not necessarily a theoretical and well-established knowledge of jurisprudence. Therefore, to outline the distinction between legal knowledge and mastery in jurisprudence is in order.

In Islamic law the judge is not identical to the legal scholar, but is rather an official in the service of the community. To put it differently, one can be a judge without being a legal scholar at the same time, while one can be a legal scholar without ever being appointed to a court. The borderline between the two spheres was not at all impermeable because there were famous legal scholars who served as judges in a certain phase of their life. On the other hand, judges could also meet the qualifications expected of legal scholars and enter the noble circle of scholars.

In Islamic law the legal scholar per se is called *mujtahid*, that is, a person entitled to practice *ijtihād*. Since *ijtihād* is the most difficult mental activity, with its own strict methods in Islamic law, only a minority of legal professionals could participate in *ijtihād*. Consequently the term *mujtahid* indicates a legal scholar of outstanding abilities and knowledge whose social prestige was very high.

Ijtihād cannot be translated or explained as the interpretation of an existing legal norm, for it is rather the study of the sources of law by approaching them through considerations of language, textual context, history and the aim of Islamic law in general. In other words, *interpretatio* as understood in Islamic legal tradition differs fundamentally from the interpretative tradition of other legal cultures. In contrast with a civil law legal scholar who interprets an already existing norm to arrive at its meaning, a Muslim legal scholar is very rarely in such a comfortable position. What he is expected to do is to formulate a legal opinion on the basis of the sources of Islamic law. The rules of Islamic law were not revealed by

God to Muslims in a complete, developed and finished form; therefore, *sharīʿa* rules (*aḥkām sharīʿa*) contain only a fragment of legal norms. This is because – according to Muslim theology – God does not expect humans to adjust to a system of norms received in completion in a servile manner, but rather they are required to participate in the process of 'discovering' these norms. Obviously, God's will and the divine rules cannot be identified by the human mind with full certainty; therefore the outcome of such an intellectual activity could lead only to probability but never to certainty (except in *ijmāʿ*, when the consensus guarantees the certainty of the norm). In short, interpretation in a Muslim context is not the interpretation of existing legal norms but the interpretation of the sources to identify a legal rule. This complex process of deriving law from the sources is called *ijtihād.*

It is important to note that no legal scholar has legislative authority since, according to Islamic legal understanding, God is the sole Lawmaker. Therefore, it is not the legal scholar who makes the law – he only recognizes it in the revealed texts (*naṣṣ*). Divine law exists independently of the knowledge and work of the legal scholar because it was already determined by God. The legal scholar only recognizes the rule in the sacred texts when he is able to identify it in the revealed sources. Thus the legal norm is the product of the legal scholar's intellectual activities in so far as he succeeded in discovering it in the sources where it was hidden. In this sense Schacht was right when he called Islamic law 'jurist's law':[1] it was truly the most outstanding legal scholars who had all theological, methodological and legal competencies to undertake such a difficult task.

Law thus defined, however, was not sure in the sense that it was not possible to know whether the recognized rule was truly identical with divine law or not. Hence the norm thus produced did not belong to the category of *ʿilm* (sure knowledge), but to *ẓann* (opinion). As a consequence *ẓann* doctrines could never rise to the rank of sure knowledge. This was, however, not a hindrance to formulating and implementing legal rules because according to legal theory *ʿilm* was only necessary in the fundamental truths (such as the existence of God, the Prophet's mission); but concerning other issues God was satisfied with as much as man was capable of achieving. If man is unable to explore divine law entirely, it is sufficient to rely on his own wise decision. Therefore a well-considered opinion is also compulsory in issues of law.[2]

Scholarly requirements for *mujtahid*s were primarily of a theoretical nature, while legal practice had a subordinate role. There were some differences in detail among some medieval Muslim authors (Ḥusayn al-Baṣrī, al-Shīrāzī, al-Ghazālī) concerning the qualifications of the *mujtahid*s but by and large the qualifications can be regarded as generally accepted.[3] A legal scholar was not required to be skilled in the field of theology but he had to know the postulates of theology. He

1 Schacht 1964: 209.

2 Weiss 1978: 199–205.

3 The requirements specified by the various medieval authors are discussed in Hallaq 1984: 5–7.

had to know all the legally relevant verses of the Qur'ān, the normative *ḥadīth* and the methods of *ḥadīth* criticism in order to identify the authenticity of traditions. He had to be familiar with all methods of legal interpretation, primarily with the theory of abrogation; methods to distinguish between general and specific rules; and the rules of rational argumentation. A profound knowledge of the Arabic language was rather important, together with skills in lexicography and grammar, so that he could identify the contents of the text precisely. Although it was not a precondition to know Arabic as a linguist would, a legal scholar had to be able to identify differences of dialect and minor differences recognizable in the use of words which could be of decisive significance. Further, he had to know rules defined by consensus so that he should not take a stand in issues that had been closed with certainty previously. In addition to professional qualifications it was taken for granted that he had to be a Muslim and had to be trustworthy (ᶜādl), although a trained scholar with professional qualifications could exercise *ijtihād* without being trustworthy.[4]

Lacking any formal institution in Sunnī Islam, there was no authority that could recognize or name someone a *mujtahid.* The method way of acknowledgement was the licence to teach (*ijāzat al-tadrīs*), issued by a professor, which authorized a legal scholar to teach law. But by far such a licence did not make anyone a *mujtahid.* The acknowledgement of a legal scholar as *mujtahid* depended on both subjective and objective factors. A subjective factor was the self-assessment of a person who presented himself as *mujtahid.* Obviously, if an uneducated person projected himself as *mujtahid* he would become an object of ridicule, thus social control as an objective factor set limits to the rise of self-appointed geniuses. Such a person could easily be defeated in a dispute with legal scholars (*al-jadal al-fiqhī*), which would ruin his social standing. In addition to legal disputes public opinion also played a controlling role, since a *mujtahid* had to establish some kind of social esteem for himself – otherwise people would not turn to him with their questions, a neglect reflecting low esteem. It was not necessary, however, for the *mujtahid* to have disciples who would continue his teaching for generations. Had this been a requirement there would be only four *mujtahids* in the history of Islamic law, the founders of the four schools. There had been innumerable outstanding legal scholars, particularly at the time of the formative and classical period, whose quality as *mujtahid* was never challenged by anyone – yet no school of theirs survived in the long run. The inclusion of this requirement would result in the title of *mujtahid* having to be allocated to these scholars posthumously.[5]

If someone was accepted as *mujtahid, ijtihād* was not only his right but also his obligation. *Ijtihād* was an obligation for the entire Muslim community (*farḍ kifāya*) which was fulfilled by the *mujtahids*. As the representatives of the Muslim community in an effort to identify legal rules no *mujtahid* had the right to retire from *ijtihād* or to accept the view of another legal scholar without proper investigation.

4 Weiss 1992: 688; Hallaq 1997: 118.

5 Weiss 1992: 689–90; Hallaq 1997: 94.

By contrast, a *mujtahid* had to study the sources and formulate his own legal opinion, which would or would not be identical to those of his colleagues. Should they have the same opinion such a consensus would guarantee a firm knowledge of the otherwise probable opinions of individual scholars. Lacking any consensus, the different legal opinions of scholars were considered as valid; meanwhile nobody could ascertain which (if any) of the doctrines was in accordance with divine law. Therefore, the opinion of the majority of legal scholars was wrong in a sense that was not in conformity with divine rules; but it was impossible to ascertain which opinions those were. Consequently, it was not the legal content of an opinion that guaranteed its validity but the methods applied by the scholar who worded it. If an opinion was formulated according to the established methods of legal exegesis, it was considered a sound legal opinion. Legal disputes were important, therefore, because they were forums that controlled the scholars' way of interpretation and argumentation.[6]

Due to the very high standards of qualifications required of a *mujtahid*, there was a radical decrease in the number of *mujtahid*s from the beginning of the third (ninth) century on. To avoid further loss of *mujtahid*s, requirements were reformulated and at the same time a hierarchy within *mujtahid*s was defined, but it led to some confusion because new terms introduced were not established with clarity. Thus the epithet *muṭlaq* was used for an ideal, absolute *mujtahid* meeting all the requirements. The *mujtahid muṭlaq*, however, meant something different for al-Ghazālī and something else again for Ibn Taymiyya. The former understood it as a *mujtahid* capable of interpreting every field of law but working within the framework of his school, whereas in the interpretation of the latter *mujtahid muṭlaq*s were the founders of the four legal schools.[7]

Another accepted category was the *mujtahid fī'l-madhhab*, which meant a legal scholar working within the framework of his own school. It is hardly accidental that this category appeared only later because in this period it was impossible to formulate a doctrine fundamentally differing from the teachings of the established schools which would make sense to the title of an independent (*muṭlaq*) *mujtahid*. In other words, from that period on even the most eminent legal scholar could rise only to the rank of *mujtahid fī'l-madhhab* and could not found an independent school of his own. In addition to distinctions based on general qualifications a distinction by the various fields of law also emerged. As only few could meet the requirement of being a *mujtahid* in every field of law it was made possible for legal scholars to be *mujtahid* only in a particular field of law but not in others. Thus, if someone was an expert in the law of inheritance he could be *mujtahid* in this field but not in others. This authorization with limited competency was called *tajzi'at al-ijtihād*. Though there were several opponents to the acknowledgement of such competency legal scholars defended it, saying that even the Prophet's

6 For the discussion of this topic by al-Āmidī see Weiss 1992: 695–705.

7 Hallaq 1984: 25.

Companions expressed their views only in certain cases and abstained from it deliberately in others.[8]

A *mujtahid* is not to be confused with a *muftī*, although there is a close interrelationship between the two. A *muftī* is a legal scholar who provides legal advice upon the request of laypeople and judges. This process of giving advice was called *futya* – the result of which was the legal scholar's *responsum*, the *fatwā* – and the legal scholar was the *muftī*.[9] As a legal opinion could be expressed by a *mujtahid* it is small wonder that the *muftī* also had to be a *mujtahid*; in other words he had to meet the requirements set for a *mujtahid*. Up to the thirteenth century this was the dominant view; afterwards, however, qualifications set for *muftī*s started to decline.[10]

In addition to the intellectual qualifications expected of a *muftī* the *adab al-muftī* literature (a literary genre explaining the requirements set for *muftī*s) established moral and physical qualities for a *muftī*. Besides the obvious preconditions (adult, Muslim) the requirements of virtuosity, solid ability of judgment, reliability and honest behaviour are underlined. The *adab al-muftī* literature stresses the importance of physical appearance, proper garments and calm behaviour. A *muftī* was not to take up a position in an issue if his physical conditions did not enable him to make a calm assessment – for instance, if he was hungry or angry. His appearance and behaviour became particularly important in public hearings (*majlis*). As the *muftī* was considered an outstanding intellectual and moral leader of Muslim society, a man of loose morals (*fāsiq*) could not be a *muftī* even if his erudition would enable him to act as such. It is worth noting that the doors were wide open for anyone to become a *muftī* because this job could be claimed for slaves, women, and the deaf and mute – people otherwise excluded from the office of judge.[11]

The difference between a *mujtahid* and a *muftī* is to be discerned in their social functions. A *mujtahid* was engaged in *ijtihād* and interpreted the revealed texts in order to identify some doctrines of Islamic law in the framework of a scholarly activity, whereas a *muftī* answered questions put to him by commoners and judges. In doing so he relied on already identified rules of law; in other words, he utilized his knowledge in *fiqh*. Obviously, a person could be a *mujtahid* and a *muftī* at the same time as the greatest *muftī*s were also *mujtahid*s. These legal scholars were engaged in *ijtihād* as *mujtahid*s and gave legal advice as *muftī*s. Both the *mujtahid*s and the *muftī*s were private individuals who accomplished their tasks independently of any state or ecclesiastic authority. They were proud of their independence and stressed its importance. According to their ethos only an independent scholar was able to perform the difficult task of *ijtihād* and legal advice, otherwise political, economic or any other social interest might influence

8 Hallaq 1996: 35-38; Hallaq 1997: 119.

9 Masud–Messick–Powers 1996: 6.

10 Weiss 1992: 718; see also Hallaq 1996: 38-43.

11 Masud–Messick–Powers 1996: 18–20.

the outcome of their study. The independence of the legal scholars (at least, in theory) is in contrast to the office of the judge, who was considered an official of the state losing his intellectual freedom. Therefore, prominent legal scholars refused any office and secured their livelihood with honourable civic occupation. Some of them, like Abū Ḥanīfa, were merchants. Later on, when legal education become more formalized, they also had various jobs in teaching, which resulted in financial dependence on the *waqf* maintaining the colleges (for more on this subject see the next chapter).

Obviously, the demand for absolute independence was rather an ideal but not reality. Legal scholars, no matter how much they wanted to, could not keep away from the influence of politics – whether as supporters of the Caliphs and rulers or as their opponents. Yet the ideal was clear: to attain the greatest possible independence to guarantee that a legal scholar may dedicate his entire life to the study of law. Therefore, aversion from the judge's office became a *topos* of the works of legal theory which was stressed with the help of various anecdotes, too. These stories are about legal scholars who were unwilling to accept the judge's office and were exposed therefore to physical atrocities. This was the fate, among others, of Ibn Farūk, a scholar from Qairawān, who was chained on the governor's order and threatened with being thrown from the ceiling of the mosque in order to force him to accept his nomination to the judge's office. Saḥnūn, a far more famous scholar from Qairawān, was not tortured, yet after having been appointed to court he made such a gloomy face that no one dared congratulate him, and going home he told his daughter that 'today your father is slaughtered without a knife'.[12] Al-Shīrāzī, the first professor at the Niẓāmiya Academy, was also kept under house arrest because he refused to accept the judge's office.[13] The legal scholars' aversion is perhaps best illustrated by the following saying: 'When Allāh has no more use for a creature, He casts him into the circle of officials.'[14]

But politics was only one reason why to neglect the office of the *qāḍī*; the other was fear of committing mistakes and their consequences. This responsibility was not understood as a liability toward the parties and the authorities (which was narrowed down in practice) but as a responsibility toward God. As Kushānī put it, those scholars who refused the office of the *qāḍī* did so 'in dread of the wrath in the world to come, because their deed would anger Allāh',[15] a way of reasoning being in complete harmony with the understanding of Jewish legal scholars.

Now one must place the judges in this cobweb of intellectual environment in order to understand their relationship to jurisprudence and legal scholars. Al-Māwardī in his al-Aḥkām al-Sulṭāniyya w'al-Wilāyāt al-Dīniyya dedicated a separate chapter to the issue of the administration of justice. In this he enumerated seven preconditions for the judge's office:

12 The anecdotes are presented in Coulson 1964: 123–6 and also Coulson 1956: 219.

13 Makdisi 1981: 200.

14 The saying is quoted in Coulson 1956: 212.

15 Quoted in Coulson 1956: 220.

1. adult male
2. sound mind
3. free personal status
4. Islam
5. justice and integrity
6. a proper functioning of the organs
7. knowledge of the sources and rules of law.

As far as the first precondition is concerned only al-Ṭabarī challenged it: according to him women could take up that office in the same right as men. Free personal status was important to exclude slaves from the office of judge because they were exposed to their masters' will and, therefore, it was impossible for them to pronounce an independent judgment. Al-Māwardī stresses that otherwise personal status was no obstacle to studying law and freedom was no precondition to issuing legal opinion. The sixth precondition was disputed since Mālik considered the appointment of a blind man to the office of judge as valid, but majority opinion rejected this. According to al-Māwardī the knowledge of legal sources included familiarity with the rules of the Qur'ān, abrogation, general and specific rules and grammar, whereas familiarity with the prophetic tradition required knowledge of *ḥadīth* literature and methods of *ḥadīth* criticism. In addition to these a judge should know the rules of consensus and analogy, too. This broad scale of requirements actually does not differ from the qualifications expected of a *mujtahid* and al-Māwardī particularly stressed that if a judge was not sufficiently qualified to formulate his autonomous opinion he was also unsuited to passing judgments and, therefore, a decision made by such a judge was null and void.[16]

Al-Jaṣṣāṣ had similar opinion a century earlier. According to him a judge had to be able to identify rules on the basis of the sources with the help of his mastery in jurisprudence. Should he have difficulties he had to ask for advice from a *mujtahid* with proper scholarly training. Al-Shāfiʿī also stressed the importance of legal advice and highlighted that judges should continually consult a *mujtahid-muftī*.[17] Simnānī, a legal scholar living in the eleventh century and acting as head of the secret service of Niẓām al-Mulk, demanded that judges be familiar with both *uṣūl al-fiqh* and *furūʿ al-fiqh*.[18] Ibn Rushd shared his grandfather's view, who demanded the judge have the qualifications for *ijtihād*.[19]

Bearing in mind this intellectual context it is small wonder that the ability of independent reasoning was emphasized by al-Māwardī. In his view a judge's own *ijtihād* was more important than the doctrine of the school he belonged to. According to his own words when a Shāfiʿīte judge concluded contrary to the doctrine of his own school but agreed with the view of Abū Ḥanīfa he had to

16 al-Māwardī: 85.
17 Hallaq 2001a: 77.
18 Schneider 1990: 157; 231.
19 Ibn Rushd 1996: 553.

follow the latter because preference should be given to his own understanding, and imitation (*taqlīd*) was expressly prohibited.[20] According to a then minority view a judge was not entitled to deviate from the teachings of his school but had to follow them. Although al-Māwardī refused this, nevertheless the new approach became predominant during the subsequent centuries, as demonstrated by W. B. Hallaq. Ibn Abī al-Dam already informs us that since there were no longer any *mujtahid*s the qualifications set for *mujtahid*s could not be expected of the judges either. In the fourteenth century a judge had to be a *muqallid*, passing judgments following the doctrines of his school, and that too by considering the *mashhūr* opinion – that is, the most acknowledged and applied legal doctrine.[21]

In the Islamic West this process took place somewhat earlier since it was already acknowledged at the turn of the eleventh and twelfth centuries in Andalusia that a *muqallid* could function as judge but was not empowered to contradict the teachings of his school.[22] Should he wish to do so he could pronounce a judgment in a particular case following another but not *mashhūr* doctrine of his school; but that, too, on the advice of a *muftī* called upon before passing the judgment. The judge's dependence on the *muftī* is indicated by the fact that *muftī*s became permanent figures in court rooms in order to ensure the smooth running of continuous advising towards the end of the classical period. The al-Fatāwā al-Hindiyya recalls the view of some jurists who went so far as to state that the judgment of an ignorant and foolish judge was valid if it rested on the *fatwā* of a *muftī*.[23]

Legal advice for judges was not an invention of the later centuries since numerous scholars of the formative and classical period mentioned it. Al-Shāfiʿī emphasized its importance just as much as his disciple Muzanī did. Al-Māwardī traced advising back as far as the Prophetic times, referring to the Prophet's practice of asking for advice from the people of Medina. Next, following his practice, Abū Bakr and ʿUmar also asked for the opinion of the Prophet's Companions in legal matters. According to al-Māwardī the judge could ask for a legal opinion from any *muftī*, irrespective of whether or not they belonged to the same *madhhab* as he did. In cases difficult to decide he was not only entitled to acquire several opinions but he was also advised to do so and to make his decision after having considered them. In selecting from among the legal opinions presented to him a judge should make his choice along scholarly considerations – but social status, rank and other non-legal elements had to be disregarded since women and slaves could also be masters of law.[24]

The practice of appointing advisors (*mushāwarūn*s) alongside the court became widespread in the Mālikite school, particularly in Hispania and in the Maghreb.

20 al-Māwardī: 86.
21 Hallaq 2001a: 80–84.
22 Serrano 2000: 229–30.
23 Hallaq 2001a: 172–3; 191.
24 Schneider 1990: 95–107.

The advisors constituted a separate body (*shūra*) whose members were appointed by the ruler, usually upon the advice of the judge. The *mushāwarūn*s received a monthly salary from the public treasury. The number of advisors was fixed and a new member could be admitted to the body if an existing member died. Those who were not members of the *shūra* usually gave legal opinion to private individuals and to merchants (*ahl al-sūq*). Advice was given in writing following the request of the judge in which he presented all facts that had been proven and also attached the documents that had been produced. The *muftī*s studied the case and made their proposal about the judgment. When legal opinions differed the judge was free to make his choice from among them. The *mushāwarūn*s did not participate in the procedure personally because they were not present during the proceedings. There was no particular demand for it either, since the conduct of the procedure was the job of the judge even if the advisors happened to be present. Their relief from personal attendance enabled them to be members of several *shūra*s, even in remote cities, at the same time.[25] The proceeding judge could not only ask for the opinion of the *muftī*s appointed to his court but could turn to others as well. It is known that a judge of Marrakesh asked for the opinion of Ibn Rushd, the famous scholar of Cordova. The judges consulted more legal experts, particularly before deciding on capital punishment, in order to avoid hasty judgments.[26]

Now it is clear from what has been said so far that there is an obvious difference between the judge and the *muftī*. In addition to the already mentioned differences in qualifications the *muftī* did not deal with proving facts, but took them for granted; on the other hand, it was the task of the judge to clarify the factual situation and to consider evidence. Moreover, the judge's judgment was always particular and pertained only to a certain case, whereas the *fatwā* was general in a sense that it could be applied also in similar cases. Perhaps the most important difference was that the *muftī*'s opinion was not compulsory – it contained only his interpretation of law, whereas the judgment was legally binding for the parties. When the judgment rested on a *fatwā* it would be compulsory for the parties –not as a *fatwā* but as a judgment of the court.[27] It is, however, important to emphasize that there was no rigid borderline between the two functions because a judge was not excluded from studying jurisprudence if he could meet the qualifications established for a legal scholar. Should he meet all requirements he could participate in the scholarly discourse, not as a judge ex officio but as a legal scholar.

As seen above, a judge adjusted himself to the activities of the *muftī*, relied on his advice and had a subordinate intellectual role compared to the *muftī*. On the

25 Masud–Messick–Powers 1996: 10–11; Müller 1999: 151–4.

26 In one of the disputed cases the question was whether capital punishment could be meted out for a slave who despised the Torāh and thus the Islam indirectly. In another case what caused difficulty was whether a new convert to Islam could be executed for apostasy because he kept objects in his home which were suited for celebrating Mass. The cases are presented in Powers 1993: 94–5.

27 Masud–Messick–Powers 1996: 18–19; Weiss 1978: 205.

other hand it is important to note that the judge also limited the *muftī*'s freedom. In theory, a legal scholar could modify or withdraw his formal legal opinion provided he found new textual proof which encouraged him to do so. By contrast, if one of his legal opinions provided the basis for a judgment he could no longer modify or withdraw it: legal advice given to a judge could not be subsequently modified, even if later the scholar would have developed an entirely different position, because a judgment thus produced is irrevocable.[28]

The reason for this seems obvious: to achieve a certain level of legal security. It is in the interest of society in general and the parties in particular that a legal dispute be settled with certainty; otherwise the entire legal world would be ruined. By guaranteeing the legal scholar could change his mind the freedom of jurisprudence was secured; meanwhile the finality of a judgment provided legal security for society and operability for the legal system. With this clever solution both legal scholars and judges could find their proper place in the Islamic legal system, working together and not against each other.

Now it is clear that profound changes are necessary in the Western interpretation of the office of the *qāḍī*, surrounded by a kind of romantic overtone and sense of cultural superiority. The *qāḍī* is an emblematic figure of Islamic law whom many see as an official sitting under a palm tree, deciding irrationally and subjectively, acting with discretional competency and making decisions just as he pleases. This was the opinion of Justice Frankfurter, among others, a famous United States judge who expounded this view in the *Terminiello v. Chicago* case.[29] A member of the British appellate court, Lord Justice Goddard, expressed a similar view.[30]

These views are not isolated but ultimately go back to Max Weber. We can summarize his views on *qāḍī* jurisdiction as follows:

1. It was an administration of justice by an official exposed to the ruler who could freely interfere into the procedure any time.
2. The judge decided through his own will and discretion both in procedural and substantive questions.
3. People should feel honoured that a judge dealt with their case at all.[31]

Coulson agreed with Weber in respect of political influence coming from the ruler and his high-ranking officials. According to Coulson political influence was possible because the judiciary was not independent but subordinate to the government. Judges appointed by the Caliph were unable to pronounce and

28 Weiss 1978: 204–5.
29 Ziadeh 1990: 80.
30 Rosen 1989: 58.
31 Weber 1972: 486; Weber 1978: 844–5.

implement decisions against members of the political elite.[32] Bryan S. Turner also agreed with some of Weber's claims, although with qualifications.[33]

It was Joseph Schacht who first challenged such simplified views and refuted some of Weber's claims.[34] During the past two decades scepticism has increased due to the works of David Powers, Lawrence Rosen, Farhat Ziadeh and Irene Schneider. The anthropologist Rosen dedicated years to field work in Morocco and modified the Weberian theses based on his own observations; but Rosen's results reflect the present conditions and not those of the classical period.[35] By contrast, the works of Farhat Ziadeh and Irene Schneider pertain to the classical period, and their conclusions drawn from the study of legal sources do not differ from the experiences of the present observer – although we must bear in mind that works on *adab* literature may pertain rather to the ideal and not to the real situation.[36] Studying late medieval Moroccan legal practice based on the *fatwā* collection of al-Wansharīsī, David Powers reached a similar conclusion.[37]

It is clear now that some of Weber's theses should be qualified. Weber was right in saying that the judges were not independent of political influence. The opinion of contemporaries did not greatly differ from this; one should only recall the legal scholars' aversion to entering into the service of political authority as judges and the numerous cases in which judges were dismissed by political considerations upon the will of the ruler.[38] But this was the ruler's only chance to interfere in the business of the judiciary since personal interference in a particular process was unthinkable.

By contrast, Weber's claim concerning discretionary judgments with little or no reliance on jurisprudence should be challenged. As seen above, a judgment was (or at least should have been) based on jurisprudence which was guaranteed either by the judge himself (provided he met the required qualifications) or by legal scholars appointed alongside him as advisors. At the same time the judge guaranteed impartiality and the 'due process of law', the importance of which was emphasized time and again in the *adab al-qāḍī* literature. Therefore, Weber was not right in saying that Kadijustiz 'erstrebt "materiale" Gerechtigkeit, nicht formale Regelung eines Interessenkampfes … und entzieht sich daher in ihren Chancen der Berechenbarkeit'.[39] By contrast, as we have seen, litigation was very

32 Coulson 1964: 121–2.

33 Turner 1974: 107–21.

34 Schacht 1934: 224.

35 Rosen 1989: 58ff.

36 Ziadeh 1990: 80-81; Schneider 1990: 248–52; 1993: 155–8.

37 Powers 1994: 366.

38 For more on this issue see the section about judges and politics in Chapter 6.

39 Weber 1972: 477 – 'aiming at "material" justice rather than at a formal regulation of conflicting interests. It arrives at decisions in accord with consideration of equity even in those cases concerning real property which belong to its jurisdiction. Such considerations are all the more likely where the law is uncodified. Predictability of decisions of kadi justice is thus at a minimum.' Weber 1978: 823.

formal and it was the *qāḍī's* responsibility to implement formal rules of procedure; however it was not his responsibility to establish the material truth, being exposed to the testimony of the parties and witnesses.

What may have misled Weber concerning the incalculableness of a judgment is legal pluralism, unknown to European legal practice. It is true that the same case could lead to different legal solutions and judgments, depending on both subjective and objective factors. To recall only the most important among them:

- It was decisive to the outcome to which legal school the judge and the parties were affiliated.
- It was of importance, too, how an advising *muftī* responded to the queries of the judge and, if more *muftīs* were involved, which opinion the judge followed.
- It was important whether the judge was only a *muqallid* or was qualified enough to engage in *ijtihād.*
- If the judge was a *muqallid*, he was authorized to base his judgment on the generally accepted view of his school (*mashhūr*) or to follow a minority opinion if it was better suited to arrive at a just judgment.

Therefore, there were a lot of choices to be made, the outcome of which was influenced by the judge's personal qualifications, both professional and moral. All these could produce a misleading picture of chaos and arbitrary judgments. But reality was different. Since the boundaries of the legal schools became settled during the centuries there was unlikely to be a Mālikite judge in ᶜIrāq or a Ḥanafite one in Andalusia. Moreover, since the judge had to follow the *mashhūr* opinion of his school – which could be neglected in favour of another, lesser known opinion only exceptionally – the outcome of the procedure was not as unpredictable as it seemed to Weber. In addition, selecting from among a variety of legal doctrines required a profound knowledge of legal literature and jurisprudence; otherwise a judge was unable to find the proper doctrine should he be dissatisfied with the *mashhūr* opinion. Such a selection was, therefore, an intellectual activity and not an arbitrary decision as Weber wanted us to believe – although, obviously, it was not free of some subjective considerations. Moreover, *qāḍīs* had to deal with the cases brought to their tribunals and to judge the cases as soon as possible. The situation is, therefore, just the opposite as Weber understood it and was not 'eine weitgehend freie Gnade, ein Privileg im Einzelfall'.[40]

Weber's Kadijustiz fits more appropriately to the *maẓālim* courts, the members of which were nominated and dismissed by the ruler's own discretion; which was not bound to follow the strict procedural laws of the *sharīᶜa*; and where judgments were not based on the legal advice of *sharīᶜa* experts. Already Schacht has pointed out that features attributed by Weber to the *qāḍī* court fit more appropriately the

40 Weber 1972: 486 – 'grant of legal remedies … as a free gift of grace or a privilege to be accorded from case to case'. Weber 1978: 845.

'weltliche Rechtssprechung der politischen Gewalten',[41] although his wording is not clear enough. But it stands to reason to think, as Irene Schneider does, that his wording refers to the *maẓālim* courts.[42] Therefore, if there is any merit in upholding this Weberian term it should be reformulated as *maẓālim* justice; but *mōbed* justice is another possible candidate since the Sasanian legal machinery was more patrimonial than that of the Caliphate.

Jewish Law

There is no such fragmentation among legal professionals in Jewish law as in Islamic law because Rabbis incorporated the functions of judges, *muftī*s and *mujtahid*s in one person.

In the Second Temple period the relationship between the courts and legal scholars was complicated because there was no homogenous Jewish jurisprudence, different religious groups having their own understanding of law. Competition between the Sadducees and the Pharisees in jurisprudence made it impossible for judges to develop a neutral position because both the Sadducees and Pharisees were present in the *Sanhedrīn*. In other words, judges embodied the differences between these groups. Consequently, a Sadducee judge would naturally support the legal interpretation of the Sadducees and attack the position of the Pharisees, whereas a Pharisee judge would act to the contrary. Therefore the outcome of cases depended on the composition of the court, which determined whether the majority would follow the interpretation of the Sadducees or that of the Pharisees. This is why competition for membership in the *Sanhedrīn* was so important for both the Sadducees and the Pharisees. Concerning local courts this fragmentation was of little or no importance.

The destruction of the Second Temple fundamentally changed this situation as it resulted in the monopoly of the Pharisee legal interpretation in the rabbinic courts. Consequently, the previous legal pluralism was limited to differences inside the rabbinic movement. Regardless of their internal fragmentation, the fact that judges came from the intellectual elite of rabbinism determined the relationship between jurisprudence and legal practice. The Rabbi acting as a judge did not depend on the advice of legal scholars since he was a legal scholar *per definitionem*. It is important to note that it was not the judge who met all the required qualifications established for a legal scholar, but rather it was the Rabbi (that is, a legal scholar) who acted also as a judge – which is a tiny but essential difference.

Now it is clear that Rabbis had different attitudes toward the office of the judge from that of their Muslim colleagues. There is no such aversion, resistance and disdain as observed among Muslim legal scholars. Not that Jewish scholars were enthusiastic about it; by contrast, they considered the judicial function an earthy undertaking taking time and energy away from their more important task

---

41 Schacht 1934: 224.

42 Schneider 1993: 156.

and mission, the study of the Torāh. Since this world was considered a place of decayed morals, where the pious suffer, to engage in the business of this world was no attractive alternative.[43] In addition, Rabbis were afraid of the responsibility of a judge. This responsibility was not of a material nature since Rabbis absolved themselves from financial responsibility for erroneous judgments. Responsibility was exclusively moral in nature, and they were afraid of its consequences. This idea is expressed in a saying attributed to Rava', according to which he wishes to leave the law court as free of guilt as he had arrived there.[44] Despite these essential reservations magistracy was not refused but attempts were made to satisfy its requirements.

At this point the question emerges why the Rabbis did not protest against being appointed to a court and accepted the nomination in the end. As seen previously, Muslim scholars' aversion was fuelled by political considerations – being afraid to lose their independence once entering the service of the state. By contrast, when rabbinic thinking emerged as the leading interpretation of law there was no longer any Jewish state and, therefore, no legal scholar was forced to represent the interests of any state. Moreover, since both the Romans and the Parthians (and later their successors, the Sasanians) guaranteed limited religious and legal autonomy for Jews, by taking official responsibility on themselves they participated in managing the autonomy they gained from their masters. In so doing they joined the respective leaders of the Jewish community, the *nāśī* in Palestine and the *rēsh galūta'* in Babylonia. Although the relationship between the scholars and the *nāśī*/*rēsh galūta'* was at times problematic – burdened with internal struggles for power – at the same time to cooperate with them was something different from entering into the service of the Caliph.

Another problematic issue was the casual interference of the non-Jewish state in the daily legal practice of the Jews. For example, Iranian Jews had no power to execute capital punishment and the Persian government controlled it very strictly. If someone died during the execution of corporal punishment (flogging) the case was immediately investigated by Iranian officials. Therefore, the *rēsh galūta'* did not follow rabbinic legal interpretation in this respect and ordered blinding instead of capital punishment, which was not in accordance with 'academic' jurisprudence – but he could hardly disregard political reality.[45]

Since both the *rēsh galūta'* and the Rabbis represented Jewish autonomy their cooperation was essential for the Babylonian community. Historically, however, the initial cooperation between the *rēsh galūta'* and the Rabbis (Shamū'el) was increasingly replaced by rivalry and hostility. The *rēsh galūta'* even jailed Rav, one of the most famous legal scholars of his age, because he did not implement the law as it was demanded by the *rēsh galūta'*. Thus in the third century the *rēsh galūta'* was unambiguously the leader of the Babylonian Jewry. The relationship with the

43 Neusner 1969: 310.
44 Neusner 1969: 132.
45 Neusner 1969: 186–8.

rēsh galūta' divided the Rabbis: there were some who accepted his leading role and took up his service, whereas others did not. Rabbis in the service of the *rēsh galūta'* wore a distinguishing badge on their clothing in order to show their status symbolically. The 'judges of the *rēsh galūta'*' had great influence both in religious and legal issues. The resistance of the Rabbis of the Academies did not mean any serious problem for the *rēsh galūta'* until he could realize his will through loyal Rabbis and the armed forces obedient to him (which included even Goth mercenaries). The Academies, however, demanded ever greater independence for themselves, hence their relationship with the *rēsh galūta'* became pitched around the issue of who was entitled to appoint the leader of the Academy. During the third century the heads of the majority of the Academies were appointed by the *rēsh galūta'* but the Academies protested against such a practice. The permanent dispute around the issue ultimately led to an ever greater autonomy achieved by the Academies but their status varied according to space, time and school. For instance, the Academy of Nahardea was under the influence of the *rēsh galūta'* in the third century, whereas the Academy of Pumbedita enjoyed relative independence and remained the centre of resistance against the *rēsh galūta'* in the next century. The *rēsh galūta'* and his opponent Rabbis came to terms only in the fifth century, when the persecutions under Yazdagerd II and Pērōz were hitting both sides.[46]

In short, contrary to their Muslim colleagues, some of the Rabbis did not consider being in the service of the *rēsh galūta'* shameful because of political considerations but because of an internal struggle between them and the *rēsh galūta'*. Since both the *rēsh galūta'* and the Rabbis wanted to be the leaders of the Babylonian Jewry, the emergence of the conflict was perhaps inevitable. The *rēsh galūta'* tried to win over some of the Rabbis partly by appointing them into his own court and partly by vindicating the right to appoint the heads of the Academies for himself. It is not to say, however, that Jewish scholars were not divided on the issue of relationships with political authority, too. Though according to their world view being in the service of the political authority meant giving up the legal scholar's intellectual and existential independence, such persons can be found in as good numbers among the Rabbis as among the *mujtahid*s. It is important to note, however, that swapping sides in itself did not result in losing social and scholarly prestige. This aspect was primarily present in Jewish law: recall the life of Shamū'el, the outstanding third-century legal scholar who not only cooperated with the *rēsh galūta'* but also kept up a friendly relationship with the Persian king. And though his behaviour and compromises (such as his principle *dīna demalkūta dīna*) were criticized by many, no one ever doubted his scholarship and eminence in jurisprudence. By contrast, Muslim legal scholars entering state service as officials were condemned by their colleagues because they were turning their back on their common scholarly ethos and giving up intellectual freedom.

In struggling to ensure their independence, Rabbis were more fortunate then their Muslim colleagues because Jewish Academies were at the same time law

46 Neusner 1968: 87–94; Neusner 1969: 73, 77, 116–23; Neusner 1970: 59–60.

courts, too. Here a Rabbi could preserve his independence while remaining in touch with both legal practice and jurisprudence. This is an important aspect which distinguishes Jewish legal culture from its Islamic counterpart, since no *madrasa* was allowed to function as a law court. Therefore, a Muslim legal scholar had nowhere to withdraw to and could refuse the judge's office as the only possible alternative. By contrast, the Academies ensured an institutional background for Jewish Rabbis, where they could remain independent from politics, study law and participate in everyday legal practice.

Another important question is what moved Rabbis to step out of their own academic world and spend their time on unimportant issues of society. Since Babylonian Jews were mainly poor people the majority of cases brought to the law courts were about a few pieces of onion and date-palms.[47] Although these were in fact not matters of major importance, nevertheless they were produced by Jewish community life. Therefore, Rabbis, participating in the daily life of the community, contributed to the survival of the Jewish community either in the Babylonian Diaspora or within the boundaries of the Roman Empire. Moreover, by actively taking part in communal life Rabbis were able to promote their ideal and encourage its realization. Since the relationship between the Rabbis and Jewish society was contradictory and burdened by mutual aversion, social appreciation alone did not prove to be sufficient. The law court was the forum where the Rabbis could assert their influence institutionally. To illustrate: although Rabbis elaborated their ideas about marriage they could not assert them because marriage in Jewish law was a contract of private parties in which the cooperation of the Rabbis was not necessary. By contrast, divorce required the cooperation of the Rabbi as judge who could therefore assert his own views of marriage through judgments. In addition he could also determine this way which marriages were valid and what the legal status of the successors were, issues of importance for a community struggling for survival.[48]

Important as it was to manage everyday legal practice, to study law was the Rabbis' most important duty. In this respect the rabbinic ethos did not differ from that of the Muslim scholars. As seen previously, *mujtahid*s had to make every effort to decipher legal norms contained in some way or other in the *naṣṣ* texts. Jewish legal scholars had a similar task since Biblical law, too, contained only part of the necessary norms. It was, therefore, the task of the Jewish legal scholars to establish the *halakah* with the help of well-defined legal methods and continuous scholarly dispute. Independently of its practical consequences the study of the Torāh became a value in itself in Talmudic times.[49]

Things did not change in the post-Talmudic period. The study of law remained the most important field of knowledge, while disciplines such as theology, philosophy and logic were absent from the syllabus. Legal scholars considered

47 Neusner 1970: 134.

48 Neusner 1969: 195–205.

49 Kramer 1990: 159–69.

academic jurisprudence more important than legal practice, even though they were engaged in it. A Mesopotamian judge was not proud of being capable of performing his complex task but because people came to his town from as far away as Europe to study the Talmūd with him.[50]

It is clear now that Rabbis also exercised '*ijtihād*' and defended their position in scholarly disputes as their Muslim counterparts did. Both systems considered discussion more important than its outcome. Suffice it to recall that in Jewish law it was regarded as an intellectual value to argue against the accepted *halakah* (not to act and pass judgment against it, because it was prohibited) for the sake of intellectual pleasure and for proving one's mastery in argumentation; moreover, it was even permitted to argue against a biblical rule.[51] Here an additional structural similarity could be observed between the two legal cultures. As differences and disputes nurtured the development of the *ikhtilāf* literature in Islamic law – that is, a legal literature whose only objective was to put into writing the differences between legal schools, their reasons and argumentation – so the situation was no different in Jewish law either, for the Talmūd is an encyclopaedic summary of different views and scholarly disputes which obtained its final form as the outcome of the work of several generations. Similarly to the *ikhtilāf* literature the Talmūd is not interested in the outcome of the debate but in the way of discussion and argumentation. The primacy of discussion in the Talmūd makes it a kind of '*ikhtilāf* literature'. The primary significance of the dispute is ensured by the idea that truth cannot be unambiguously identified; therefore the various positions are actually the different aspects of truth.[52] A Muslim scholar could not put it better either since, as seen previously, scholarly opinions were considered only as of probable knowledge and, therefore, no doctrine was superior to the other.

But legal pluralism has its limits in both legal cultures. One such limit was postulates of theology in the respective legal systems. Although these postulates were defined by theologians, not lawyers, at the same time they were such basic tenets that everybody accepted them. For example, no Jewish Rabbi could argue that the Second Temple was destroyed because the Jewry did not accept Jesus because such an argument would have placed him outside the Jewry.[53] Another limitation of legal pluralism was what Muslim legal scholars called consensus. Such consensus emerged when all *mujtahid*s arrived at the same legal solution in their individual research where imitation of one another's opinion (*taqlīd*) was forbidden. Lacking, however, any institutional framework it was not easy to determine whether such a consensus in fact emerged, which made al-Rāzī argue that it was impossible to know that all the *mujtahid*s came to the same conclusion in the huge territory inhabited by the Muslim population and, therefore, consensus

50 Goitein 1988: 416–19.

51 Kramer 1990: 142–3.

52 On the intellectual history of the Talmūd see Kramer 1990; Lightstone 1993; Halivni 1986: 35–49.

53 Kramer 1990: 126.

was of no importance to him.[54] But al-Rāzī's view is a minority understanding and the majority of the *mujtahid*s accepted it, with some variance in their reasoning to support its authoritativeness.[55]

By contrast, Jewish law developed a far more effective and institutionalized solution for closing down the disputes and fixing the *halakah*. The decision of the majority was the tool by which continuous debate could be terminated. When *halakah* was thus established, nobody was allowed to base a judgment on his now minority doctrine and interpretation. Anyone disregarding the majority decision qualified as a 'rebellious elder', which had serious consequences. Worth noting here is the case of R. 'Elīᶜezer Ben Hyrcanus, who did not follow the majority in a dispute evolving around an issue of ritual purity but insisted on his own position. When the *halakah* was established with the help of majority vote scholars called upon R. 'Elīᶜezer, the otherwise highly respected Shammaite legal scholar, to adapt to the majority opinion in the future. As R. 'Elīᶜezer rejected this he was excommunicated and everything he declared pure was burned in fire. R. 'Elīᶜezer's destiny was not changed, although the Heavenly Voice (*Bat Qol*) declared that the *halakah* was in harmony with R. 'Elīᶜezer's teaching and not with the rule accepted by the majority.[56]

This limitation of legal pluralism was effective only in legal practice, not in jurisprudence. That is, a judge could pronounce a judgment only on a rule of the *halakah* established by majority vote, but it was no obstacle to continue a scholarly dispute about it. This explains why, after the *halakah* was fixed, contrary views were also taught and dealt with. As the majority of the rules of the *halakah* were established according to Hillelite teaching the Shammaite doctrines opposed to it lost their practical significance, but since they could also contain the truth to study them was in order.[57] Since to study and teach law was the most important duty of the Rabbis, replacing Temple sacrifice, they started to believe that their work and ethos were of such importance that God and the angels in Heaven also studied the Torāh.[58] Bearing all this in mind it is clear now that jurisprudence meant something other than a solid knowledge of law and legal argumentation. Thus whenever a Rabbi sat in a court room he carried there all the postulates, values and disputes he had come across during his scholarly activity. In this respect a Rabbi as a judge could transform rabbinic ethos and scholarly learning into legal practice in his own right, whereas a Muslim judge could do the same only indirectly, through his advisors.

The judge's qualification was approached from a moral side, too. Causes for exclusion are identical to those applied to witnesses, and the texts (Mishnah, Tōsefta') discuss both categories under the same subtitle. To avoid conflicts of

---

54 Hallaq 1986: 455.

55 On the authoritativeness of Sunni consensus see Hourani 1964 and Hallaq 1986.

56 Gilat 1968: 483–5.

57 Kramer 1990: 139–44.

58 Neusner 1970: 147.

interest, persons interested in the outcome of a case – and close relatives such as father, brother, paternal and maternal uncles, brother-in-law, father-in-law and the husband of the wife's sister – were excluded from judging the case. According to the Tōsefta' eunuchs and those who had no children could judge only in property issues, not in criminal cases; according to R. Yūdah those whose nature was said to be too harsh or forgiving were also excluded.[59]

The tradition of lay adjudication continued in this period, too, but every community had a professional appointed judge, called a *dayyān*. Judges were appointed for a very long period of time, sometimes even for life, but their numbers were rather low because usually one settlement had only one *dayyān* – with the exception of the major commercial centres such as Alexandria and Cairo. It was the privilege of the *dayyān* to interpret legal texts and to pronounce judgments based on his interpretation. A judgment made this way was obligatory for the parties. Ensuring the right of legal interpretation for the judge meant at the same time that his mastery in jurisprudence was also acknowledged. Therefore such *dayyān*s were regarded as outstanding members of the Jewish scholarly elite who functioned like earlier judges of the Babylonian Academies. Their scholarly respect is shown by the fact that the judges were appointed originally by the *ga'ōn* (the head of the *yeshībah*) as judges acting in his name or in the name of his own court, this being a delegation of power. According to Goitein this concept of the delegation of power can be attributed to the influence of the Islamic intellectual environment (as judicial authority was delegated by the Caliph to the judges; see al-Māwardī's theory). In addition to the *dayyān*s, *shōfēṭ*s were also nominated, who were no masters of jurisprudence yet their knowledge in law guaranteed sufficient ground to be judges for smaller, dispersed communities (like in the Yemen); but from the twelfth century onwards references to *shōfēṭ*s disappeared.[60]

The moral responsibility which burdened the judges continued in medieval times. Since according to Jewish moral and legal thinking anyone who made a wrong decision concerning the rules of the Torāh would offend God, judges did not dare pronounce judgments in order to avert this tremendous responsibility (recall the saying of Rava'). This dilemma was bridged by the practice whereby judges did not formally pass judgments but decisions were projected as an agreement of the parties or as a declaration of one of the parties made before the court. While such statements were prepared by the judge, he was nevertheless relieved of his moral responsibility because he did not pass judgment. A text is known from among documents of the Cairo *Genizah* in which a judge accepted his appointment only on condition that he would never have to make a formal judgment.[61]

Finally, to mention responses (responsa) in brief is in order. The term is a loan word from Latin meaning a legal scholar's answers given to a question put to him and furnished with legal reasons and arguments. In its function it

59 Tos Sanh 7:5.

60 Goitein 1999: 312–17.

61 Goitein 1999: 334–5.

corresponds to the *fatwā* issued by a *muftī*. Responsa literature grew to huge dimensions in this period: 460 such writings are known from Maimonides alone and the number of surviving responses is about 300,000. The practice of asking questions to clarify details of law was already in use during Talmudic times. Since these questions were products of everyday legal practice they reflect far more the legal concerns of contemporary society than any other theoretical problems dealt with in academic jurisprudence. Until the Babylonian Academies maintained their scholarly hegemony the questions were addressed to the legal scholars there. Written questions were carried by merchants from distant regions, together with the financial support donated by the senders for the maintenance of the Academies. The Academies' answers were sent back to the sender by the same route. By the end of the ga'ōnic (geonic) period, however, the privileged position of the Babylonian Academies came to an end, which had consequences for the responsa literature. As a result, the earlier tutoring, superior tone was replaced by a more modest form, underlining an advisory nature. Moreover, while in the ga'ōnic period the answers were formulated in the name of the Academy because every member participated in their composition, later the answers were regarded as the opinion of the legal scholar who answered the questions and no longer the interpretation of the Academy (just as the *fatwā* was the individual opinion of the *muftī*). Parallel to this the answers became longer, more detailed and supplied with argumentation.[62]

After the emergence of local scholarly centres legal scholars residing there could also answer these questions, which resulted in an ever growing number of responses. As a consequence of this development we can observe differences between the Muslim West and Muslim East. In the West (that is, west of Egypt) the function of the judges and legal scholars became separated: that is, a legal scholar was not necessarily a judge any longer. It was Goitein who called attention to this important change, demonstrating that while outstanding legal scholars of the West leaving behind a huge number of responses were no judges (such as Maimonides), no such duality could be observed among their colleagues living in Egypt.[63]

Zoroastrian Law

As seen above, efforts were made both in Jewish and Islamic legal systems to preserve the independence of jurisprudence. Muslim legal scholars achieved this aim by rejecting any magistracy and studying law as private individuals, whereas Jewish scholars accomplished it through the *yeshībah*, as the court of an independent academic institution. A judge transformed the principles, postulates and methods of jurisprudence into legal practice either personally (Jewish model) or through experts delegated to the courts (Islamic model).

Such aims were neither established nor achieved in Zoroastrian law during the Sasanian period because Zoroastrian law was administered by the Zoroastrian

62 For more on this issue see Elon 1994, vol. III: 1454–528.

63 Goitein 1999: 326.

Church, which was, in turn, deeply involved in contemporary politics. Since the majority of the judges were priests at the same time, jurisprudence, legal practice, religious and political considerations were not separated, either personally or institutionally. This interdependence is best shown by the fact that it was the high priest, the *mōbedān mōbed*, who was the supreme legal advisor to the monarch. Before making a decision in judicial matters the king was usually advised by the *mōbedān mōbed*, whom he overruled only rarely – usually when personally involved. This is justified by literary (Kār-Nāmag) and historic (al-Ṭabarī) sources and by works of 'political theory' (al-Jaḥīẓ), too. The authority of the high priest in judicial matters was expressed by a symbolic gesture, according to which the ruler knelt down in front of the high priest and swore to accept his ruling no matter how he decided about cases during the hearings of *Nawrūz* and *Mihragān*.[64] But this is only priestly propaganda, not practice. By contrast, as the Kār-Nāmag, shows when a king insisted on his own decision no high priest was able to persuade him to change his mind and return to legality.[65]

Not only judicial practice but also jurisprudence – that is, interpreting legal and sacred texts – was in the hands of the Zoroastrian priesthood. And there was in fact great need for interpretative jurisprudence first of all because the Awesta – being formally the first among the legal sources – could not be applied in this period without constant reinterpretations since its language, social and economic background were extremely different from the social conditions of the Sasanian period. Here, too, Zoroastrian law differs from its Islamic and Jewish counterpart because one cannot see such a robust intellectual effort to tie legal rules to the sacred book, an important aim of both Jewish and Muslim legal scholars. It is worth noting that only two cases are known, out of hundreds, in which direct reference was made to the Awesta (MHD 14. 17–15. 1; 48. 14–16.). By contrast, Zoroastrian jurisprudence rather preferred customs and the legal scholars' teaching (čāshtag) as sources of law and made little effort to ensure their connection to the sacred text.[66]

Persian scholars formulated various doctrines in questions of minor importance, while basic principles and institutions of law seem to be unchallenged and subject to no debate. Resulting from their scholarly debates legal schools emerged, the number of which cannot be determined for certain. Shāyast-nē-shāyast, a scholarly work dating from the end of the Sasanian period dealing with details of ritual purity, is the only source concerning legal schools, but it contains contradictory claims. While paragraph 1.3 mentions three schools, the next paragraph (1.4)

64 See note 79 and related text.

65 This was the situation, for instance, when– according to the Kār-Nāmag – king Ardakhshēr ordered the immediate execution of his pregnant wife for attempted murder even though according to the high priest's warning it was against the law since no pregnant woman could be executed until delivery.

66 Concerning Zoroastrian legal sources and their comparison with Islamic legal theory see Jany 2005.

lists four schools: Ādurohrmazd-Nēwgushnasp, Ādurfarrobay Narseh-Sōshāns, Nēwgushnasp-Mēdōmāh and Sōshāns-Abarag. The author of the Shāyast-nē-shāyast has nothing more to say about the legal schools except these names. But this genealogy of the schools contains identical names at more than one point. If we assume that the same names pertain to the same persons then there were only two schools: the school of Ādurohrmazd-Nēvgushnasp-Mēdōmāh and the school of Ādurfarrobay Narseh-Sōshāns-Abarag.[67] Unfortunately almost nothing is known about these scholars, but Abarag, Mēdōmāh and Sōshāns were known as commentators on the Awesta. As commentators of the Wīdēwdād, Ērbedestān and the Nērangestān[68] they studied the texts of the Awesta and obviously this is what made them known also as legal commentators. It is interesting to note that the MHD+A refers predominantly to Abarag and Mēdōmāh – that is, the representatives of the last generation (the contemporaries of the compiler?) – while previous members of the schools are practically missing from it.

From the rather terse hints found in the Shāyast-nē-shāyast it is impossible, too, to determine the point of birth and history of the legal schools. But a judgment at the beginning of the MHD+A (MHD 1. 2–4) may be helpful because it is the only one that contains both the name of a legal scholar (Sōshāns) and a Sasanian king named Wahrām. Unfortunately there were six kings named Wahrām on the Sasanian throne – Wahrām I (274–76), Wahrām II (293), Wahrām III (293–302), Wahrām IV (388–99), Wahrām V (421–39), Wahrām VI (590) – and in theory any of these rulers could be intended.

Maria Macuch dates Sōshāns to the third century,[69] while Anahit Perikhanian places Sōshāns in the fifth century by thinking that it was Wahrām V who was referred to.[70] In both scholars' interpretation Sōshāns was an early legal scholar who is thus separated from the time of the compilation of the MHD+A by four or two centuries respectively, as that work was completed in all probability during the reign of Khusraw II (591–628).[71] Since we know that Sōshāns represented the second generation of his school, the life of the founding master, Ādurfarrobay Narseh, should be put even earlier. Based on this inference, Ādurfarrobay Narseh should be dated to the beginning of Sasanian history, being a contemporary of Tansar and Kardēr – the two prominent founders of the Zoroastrian Church – or to the beginning of the fifth century.

Accepting these interpretations would mean that the legal schools were established in the third century and that after three generations (about a century) they came to an end. In this case we face questions of why the schools collapsed

67 Tavadia interpreted this also as two schools; see Tavadia 1930: 28–9. See also Kreyenbroek 1994: 10. This section is based on an article about Sasanian legal schools; see Jany 2006.

68 Macuch 1993: 13.

69 Macuch 1993: 29.

70 Perikhanian–Garsoian 1997: 418.

71 Macuch 1993: 9.

suddenly and why was it practically important for a seventh-century lawyer to quote in his compilation a scholar living in the third century, given the enormous social and economic changes that occurred during these centuries. If we place Sōshāns in the fifth century we still have to face these questions, though the time gap would be reduced to two centuries.

By contrast, if we assume that it was Wahrām VI who was referred to, we can answer these questions easily. Following this hypothesis the legal schools need not be dated to the early Sasanian period, but to the last century of its history. Moreover, in this case there was no break in the 'living tradition' of the schools because the representatives of the third generation were contemporaries of the compilers of both the Shāyast-nē-shāyast and the MHD+A (first part of the seventh century). If we count down three generations from this date we arrive at the reign of King Khusraw I (531–79) as the starting point of Zoroastrian jurisprudence. Since it is known that during these decades considerable administrative, social and economic changes took place (following the Mazdakite uprising and the reforms of Khusraw) the emergence of legal schools fits logically into this framework of reforms because old rules had to be adjusted to the changing social reality, which obviously produced different interpretations of legal norms.[72]

Since only the names of legal scholars and some of their legal opinions concerning some questions of problems of minor importance are known, it is impossible to determine the schools' doctrines and on what points they differed from each other. It is also not easy to answer the question of what role the legal schools played in late Sasanian society. A statistical approach offers the following results: in the MHD+A Mēdōmāh's school is mentioned only three times (MHD 17. 14, 50. 15, 51. 15) and Abarag's school only on a single occasion (MHD 50. 13). Mēdōmāh's name occurs five times (MHD 5. 13, 22. 5, 50. 15, 51. 9, 52. 3–9); and Abarag's even less frequently (MHD 5. 14, 22. 5, 52. 3; MHD+A 30. 3). This total of 13 references to the two schools seems rather modest if we recall that the number of references to various scholars is 180 in the MHD+A. Thus, the overwhelming majority of references go to scholars outside the framework of the schools (Pusānweh, Wahrām, Siyāwakhsh, Mardag). By contrast, in the Shāyast-nē-shāyast – a work dealing with ritual law – references to scholars of the schools dominate, while legal scholars dominant in the MHD+A are practically missing. We can infer, therefore, that the schools were active in issues of ritual law whereas in matters other than ritual law the eminence of legal scholars who did not belong to either of the schools could be observed.

The focus on ritual law comes as no surprise because (1) jurisprudence was in the hands of the priesthood practising ritual; and (2) Sasanian Zoroastrianism was ritual centred, where orthopraxis was more important than orthodoxy. These basic institutional features of religion determined the focus of contemporary jurisprudence. Consequently, jurisprudence locked itself into its own academic world, into its ivory tower where the lights of reality rarely penetrated. To prove

72 For more on this subject see Jany 2006: 295–307.

this claim it is perhaps sufficient to refer to the scholarly dispute ongoing on pages of the Shāyast-nē-shāyast in which legal scholars discuss whether or not one should pull out a corpse floating in the water (for water is a sacred element which cannot be polluted with things impure, such as a corpse), and what would be a person's liability for doing nothing in this respect. This example is only an illustration; there are numerous hypothetical cases for academic discussions in this work. To study the hair-splitting disputes of academic learning of law and rite may, perhaps, be interesting to those few modern scholars who are interested in this field, but as the law courts had primarily to decide on mundane issues the results of jurisprudence dealing with ritual law could hardly be of any assistance.

The academic nature of jurisprudence was characteristic not only of Zoroastrian but of Jewish law, too. The Mishnah, the Tōsefta' and the Talmūd also deal with issues which were irrelevant to contemporary social realities. As temple sacrifice was already impossible in this period, dealing with its details reflects only academic interest – yet Jewish legal scholars spent a great deal of their time and energy on studying such questions. Despite this, Jewish jurisprudence was not as inward looking as its Zoroastrian counterpart, possibly because: (1) legal scholars were also judges, hence they had to deal with cases produced in social reality; and (2) they had to answer questions (responsa) put to them by common people and merchants, who were also not interested in problems of academic jurisprudence.

Since there was no literary genre similar to the responsa/*fatwā* literature, Zoroastrian legal scholars were prevented from dealing with questions of everyday legal practice in the Sasanian period. After the fall of the Sasanians, however – when old glory, riches and political authority vanished – church hierarchy (and arrogance) was also transformed and modified. The person heading the community was now called the *hudēnān pēshōbāy* ('leader of those of good religion'), or *dastūr*, who had to give advice also on matters of daily life otherwise he would not have been able to ensure that his surviving community could continue to live according to Zoroastrian ethics and law. Now the *dastūr* was responsible for organizing his community to ensure that individual and community rites were performed properly and social interactions were in accordance with Zoroastrian law. Ecclesiastic hierarchy as experienced during the Sasanian period vanished and there was no essential element in the *dastūr*'s social role which would make him different from a Jewish Rabbi (except in being a priest). This correspondence manifested itself in legal practice, too. Responses called *riwāyat* – a term of Arabic in origin, similar in outlook and function to the responsa/*fatwā* literature – emerged in the post-Sasanian Zoroastrian literature. There are numerous collections of *riwāyat*s because the practice of writing such works continued as late as the seventeenth century. Among these the Riwāyat-i Ēmēd-i Ashawahishtān[73] and the *riwāyat* accompanying the Dādestān ī Dēnīg should be mentioned as particularly important.[74]

73 Safa–Isfehani 1980.

74 Williams 1990.

One can observe considerable changes in discussing the material in these works. It is not the positive law which underwent gradual transformations but the way legal problems were presented and solved. There is no reference to legal schools and scholars any longer in these works. The academic way of legal thinking disappeared together with the hair-splitting argumentations about hypothetical questions. What remained are practical questions produced in everyday life put by the members of the Zoroastrian community to its leader. Answers are as simple as the questions were: the *dastūr* simply outlines the basic norms of Zoroastrian law, mainly in the field of private law – particularly marriage and the law of inheritance. All these are done in a simplistic language understandable to all, free from any sophisticated argumentations. Therefore, these argumentations (if given at all) are not addressed to another legal scholar to prove one's interpretation and familiarity with jurisprudence, as in the case of the Muslim legal scholar's *fatwā*, but to the person putting the question so that he may better understand the answer. In brief: scholarly disputes were replaced by the practice of simple legal advising, the reason for which was the religious and moral imperative to keep the community intact at all cost.[75]

The Judge and Legal Education

Jewish Law

Legal education in Jewish law has a long history, though very little is known about it in the biblical period. The schools hallmarked with the name of Hillel and Shamm'ay were not educational institutions but rather circles of disciples gathered around a master. A more institutional form of legal education was the Academy operating next to the *nāśī* because it was in direct contact with the court. In Palestine *bēt ha-midrāsh* and *bēt talmūd* were terms to indicate institutions usually translated as Academies, the now current *yeshībah* being a latecomer. (*Yeshībah* also means law court and, as seen in Chapter 1, the Academies were related to the courts.) These Academies were open to boys over 13 who were willing to learn more about Jewish tradition and law. Yabneh and Usha – and later on Caesarea, Sepphoris and Tiberias – were centres of Academies, of which the *bēt ha-midrāsh* of Tiberias functioned longest, up to the Islamic period. The first Babylonian Academies are said to have been established in the third century: the Academy of Sura was founded by Rab, a younger contemporary of Rabbi Yūdah, while that of Nahardea was established by Mār Shamū'el. After its destruction the Academy of Nahardea was replaced by the Academy of Pumbedita in the mid-third century. Initially the Babylonian Academies were hardly more than networks

75 This tendency could be observed in modern times in Islamic law, too, since there are *muftīs* who give legal advice in radio and TV broadcasts to persons seemingly unversed in Islamic law; see Messick 1996: 319-20.

of some eminent masters and the disciples gathered around them; therefore they did not essentially differ from the practice of earlier centuries.[76] Ga'ōnic sources indicate that these early Academies were well-established institutions with refined structures and regulations, claims long accepted by modern scholarship. It was Goodblatt who convincingly showed that this view is a historic anachronism and that ga'ōnic sources project conditions and terms of their own back into earlier centuries.[77]

In the Talmudic period and the following centuries these Academies evolved into more complex structures. As the Rabbis working in the Academies were active as legal scholars, teachers and judges this question may deserve particularly attention. The arrangement of the students in the Academies followed the pattern of the court room: here, too, students sat in rows representing their eminence and learning.[78]

Legal education was oral and based on emulation. Students had to learn texts by heart, but a mere lexical knowledge was not sufficient because the material learned had to be used creatively, primarily in debates. Debates constituted an important part of school life and the proper culture of debate was taken seriously. According to R. 'Ashē someone who was rigid and unbending in dispute, who would repeat stubbornly his own truth without being open to his partner's arguments, deserved to be stricken by leprosy.[79]

Practical advice was also given on how to acquire lexical knowledge, which is useful to all students irrespective of space and time, such as paying attention to the teacher, repeating the material before the beginning of the lessons. Constant and continuous repetition was regarded as the most important method of learning, but the advantages of joint learning and group discussion were also underlined so that the students might contribute to common success by helping each other. It was not regarded as expedient, however, to study in the street or in an impure place, due to practical and religious reasons (similar advice was given to Muslim students, too). The *tanna* or repetitor came to the aid of students: he repeatedly recited the text known by him excellently so that the students could hear it several times and learn it. The *tanna*'s knowledge, however, did not go beyond simple knowledge of the texts; he was not considered a legal scholar and merely played the role of a book in this oral culture (precisely as was done by the *muʿīd* in Islamic law). The knowledge of the *tanna*s was not appreciated because they did not participate in legal debates. As a contemporary saying put it: 'the tanna repeats and does not know what he is saying'.[80]

76 Stemberger 1996: 9–12. The term for school was not *yeshībah* but *bēt rab* – that is, the master's house, referring to the very house of the master where education took place; see also Goodblatt 1975: 267–72.

77 Goodblatt 1975: 267ff.

78 M Sanh 4:3–4:4.

79 Sanh 110a.

80 Neusner 1968: 136; Stemberger 1996: 12.

Another important characteristic of education was the principle that the Rabbi's person incorporated the Torāh; he was considered the 'living Torāh': that is, every saying, act and behaviour of the Rabbi expressed the contents and essence of the Torāh. The concept of the Rabbi as the living Torāh ensured high social rank for Rabbis in the eyes of society in general and students in particular. One can observe a variety of social consequences of this attitude. One of them was the enormous respect that surrounded the Rabbi's person among the students. This compulsory respect placed the Rabbi in the parent's, and particularly the father's, position: while a child had to thank his father for his physical existence, he owed his mental development and maturity to the Rabbi, and it was the latter who was regarded as more important. This respect was not only addressed to the Rabbi himself but also to the learning he dealt with. A saying from Amoraic times explicitly expresses this idea: 'The study of the Torāh transcends honouring father and mother.'[81] All this, however, did not mean that students had to give up their personality, and neither was it compulsory to dumb down their critical sense, otherwise legal debates could not have taken place. Compulsory respect therefore did not eliminate the critical attitude, only gave form to it.[82] Another important element of respect toward the Rabbi was that his disciple, no matter how old and professionally advanced a scholar, was advised not to judge a case while his master was still alive.[83]

Another important consequence was the importance of emulation, the essence of which was that whatever the Rabbi did should be learned and emulated, for Rabbis did not act accidentally but due to their knowledge of the Torāh. Every element of their behaviour – their gestures, their use of words and the way they dressed – was an object of observance and imitation. This attitude sometimes resulted in exaggeration, such as in the case of a student of Rav, who hid under his master's bed to observe the sexual life of his master and his wife. When the student was caught and profoundly scolded by his master the disciple answered that it was also Torāh and he needed to learn.[84]

The high social esteem of the masters resulted in the observance of a rigid, obligatory etiquette. For instance, no one was allowed to walk on the Rabbi's

81 Urbach 1975: 612. Now it is worth noting in a short reference that a similar idea developed in India, too. Here the guru, the teacher, enjoys great social respect. This parallel is not only interesting because of the form of respect but also because of its explanation: according to the Indian idea the child owes only his physical existence to his father, but his intellectual awakening and birth are the guru's merit. This is why Hindus are called 'twice born' (*dvija*), since symbolically they are born twice: at first physically and intellectually for the second time. The Indian view, however, mostly eliminated the critical attitude and the master exercised almost total authority over his disciple. Being his spiritual leader, a guru could order everything for his pupil's spiritual development (fasting, several months of meditation in isolation etc.), which was alien to Jewish understanding; see The Laws of Manu II: 194–218.

82 Neusner 1970: 162, 167.

83 Neusner 1968: 146.

84 The case is quoted in Neusner 1970: 166.

right; students could not address the master by name; at the same time the master had to be constantly accompanied on his way, this being one of the students' most important duties. This ritualistic and extremely rigid form of education was taken very seriously; challenging the respect of the master was regarded as a sin. Offending the master could have rather serious consequences because an insulted master could even excommunicate his disciple, which did not only mean that he was divested of participation in education but its social consequences were also damaging. If such a harsh sanction was not necessary, a disrespectful student could be flogged. Small wonder, therefore, that news circulated about merciless and arrogant behaviour of Rabbis which made their disciples' lives miserable. The merciless attitude of R. Sheshet and Rav Yūdah towards their students was well known among their contemporaries. R. Yōsē left his master because he saw how mercilessly he treated even his own children. Rav's opinion that the student had to think about his master bitterly reveals a great deal about the internal relations of master and disciple. Pride, arrogance and self-confidence were personal qualities one often finds when rabbinic behaviour is criticized, whereas their ethos taught modesty and mercifulness. R. 'Ashē taught that arrogance was shameful and the lot of an excessively proud man would ultimately be humiliation.[85]

Students were required to dedicate their entire time and physical and mental energy to the study of the Torāh, which could not be disturbed by any other occupation. During the months dedicated to learning full concentration was required, which created a kind of monastic community among the students. Consequently time spent on learning demanded an ascetic way of life, and celibacy – otherwise alien to Jewish thinking – from the students. In such a community there was no place for women, therefore even married students were required to observe temporary celibacy. It is no surprise, therefore, that women are not to be found among the students, as the study of the Torāh was the privilege of men. Solidarity was expected of the students in this community, even though competition and dispute were accepted and were even basic requirements: friendly behaviour towards beginners was just as much an ethical principle as helping one another by studying in groups. Sudden anger, aggressiveness and humiliation of their fellows in front of others were condemned.[86] Solidarity among students, however, should not be interpreted as equality because the relative order among the students was known to them and was to be respected, which was ultimately expressed symbolically by the seating order of the students.

The schools, and particularly their teachers, competed for talented students. School affiliation was flexible in earlier times since it was common practice to study under several masters and even under representatives of different schools (for instance in the schools of Hillel and Shamm'ay). Apparently the students studied under several masters even in later ages, but attempts were made to restrict this custom, suggesting that while logic and debating skills could be learned from

85 Neusner 1968: 147; Neusner 1969: 297ff; Neusner 1970: 158–9, 170.

86 Neusner 1969: 301–2; Neusner 1970: 162.

several masters it was better to learn oral tradition from one teacher.[87] The same tendency can be observed in Islamic law, where the original freedom to learn from several masters and schools was restricted later.

Learning was a costly affair, primarily because students had to give up working during study times, but enthusiastic persons succeeded. There is a story about a person desirous of learning in the age of Hillel who went up to Jerusalem, withstanding starvation and thirst, just to listen to the master. Perhaps richer students could help their poorer fellows but in the majority of cases the students themselves had to arrange for their livelihood. Therefore they participated in education only during certain periods of the year; the rest of their time was spent at work, primarily in agriculture, and less frequently in commercial activities, which resulted in the seasonality of education.[88] Here, too, the parallel with Islamic legal education is striking: at harvesting time the students went to work in the fields, sometimes with their own master (e.g. Saḥnūn).

Students completing their studies could rise to the rank of legal scholar provided they were given the required ordination (*semikah*). This rite, which consisted of placing one's hand on another person, was the symbolic expression of passing on authority. Moses also passed his leadership to Joshua this way. Through *semikah* the master passed his authority to his student, acknowledging his scholarship. In the third century, when the authority of the *nāśī* and the *rēsh galūta'* grew, the right of *semikah* was exercised by these leaders instead.[89] At the same time ordination by political leaders led to disputes over competency because it had to be decided whether or not an ordination by the *nāśī* was valid in Babylonia. According to the Talmūd, the Palestinian ordination was not valid in Babylonia without being validated by the *rēsh galūta'*, although the *rēsh galūta'* was not entitled to grant *semikah*, only *reshuta*, since there was no *semikah* in Babylonia.[90] Such authorization was important since a judge passing an erroneous judgment was relieved of financial responsibility, as seen earlier. With this, however, the ordination of a former student as a legal scholar and appointment to the court became interlinked. As a result, those who for any reasons did not accept judicial office were not ordained. Therefore, from this time on there could be scholars whose knowledge and reputation were significant yet they were not ordained. Consequently, *semikah* was rather becoming a judicial appointment which relieved the person of financial responsibility and lost its original function. But the Academies insisted on their right to ordain their students, which was an academic acknowledgement and not an official appointment to the court. When the office of the *nāśī* was abolished, the Palestinian Academies continued to exercise the right of *semikah*, which disappeared in this form in the twelfth century but survived among European Jews as an academic acknowledgement and entitlement to decide

87 Urbach 1975: 624.
88 Neusner 1968: 217.
89 Daube: 2000: 599–605.
90 Sanh 5a; Neusner 1965: 109; Mantel: 1965: 215–16; Goodblatt 1975: 168.

on ritual and property issues. The *semikah* consisted of calling the person by his name and granting permission to use the honourable title of Rabbi.[91]

As the chronicle of Natan ha-Bablī and Rav Sherira Ga'ōn's letter prove, the heyday of the *yeshībah*s was unbroken and their internal structure was further refined in the ga'ōnic period, although the fall of the Sasanians and the consequent Muslim conquest produced some chaos in ᶜIrāq. The title *ga'ōn* (head of the Academy) emerged in this period, together with the *dayyāna de-bābā'* (judge of the gate, chairman of the academic court) and the *rabbanan de-metibta'* (Rabbi of the Academies). Rivalry among the Academies for scholarly and legal influence continued and competition for financial support broadened since people asking for responses also subsidized the Academies.[92]

The ancient term *Sanhedrīn* was still used to name the Palestinian Academy, although it had its sessions in Tiberias, not Jerusalem, and moved to the latter venue only later. Because of the Seljūqs' attack in the eleventh century it shifted to Tyre, the richest port of that period (where it was followed by the Shāfiᶜīte school) and then transferred its headquarters to Damascus. Later it is found in Cairo where, after a short time, it was replaced by the school evolving around Maimonides. The Palestinian Academy was also headed by the *ga'ōn*, whose authority was confirmed by the Muslim authorities. The *ga'ōn* appointed local judges and other officials acting in non-legal matters, while the *ab bēt dīn* ('father of the court') came to his assistance in the management of the Academies as its deputy head.[93]

Since Academies in ᶜIrāq still insisted on calling themselves *Sanhedrīn*, a *yeshībah* could only have 70 members, while at the same time the number of scholars linked to the *yeshībah* was higher. The *yeshībah* was headed by the *ga'ōn*, while his work was assisted by the chairman of the court who, in the majority of cases, took over as head of the Academy after the death of the *ga'ōn*. The *rōsh ha-sēder* (head of the rows) designated scholars heading the rows since each row had its own leader. The repetitors' place and function remained intact and became more important as the Talmūd acquired a central role in jurisprudence. Although they were regarded only as men whose knowledge was 'limited' to a huge quantity of texts, their assistance was occasionally helpful even to scholars. The majority of repetitors were poor, blind children blessed with good memories who were trained specifically for this task. The employment of repetitors clearly shows that memorization continued to be an essential element of learning because no intellectual activity could be started without getting over this stage.[94]

In this period the structure of the curriculum underwent some changes. In addition to the Talmūd the works of the outstanding scholars of the period (such as Sa'adya Ga'ōn) were also included for study. At the same time, subjects which

91 Mantel 1965: 206–220.
92 Lightstone 1993: 174ff.
93 Lightstone 1993: 174; Libson 1996: 201–3; Goitein 1999: 201.
94 Goitein 1999: 196-9.

constituted an integral part of the curriculum of Muslim *madrasa*s (such as logics, theology and philosophy) did not figure among the subjects taught.[95]

Contrary to Muslim educational practice no compulsory material was dictated to the students during the course of teaching, but lectures were held from which the students took notes to their liking. A very profound scholarship – that is, professional legal knowledge as a subject on its own – was a prerequisite to obtain a nomination to the judge's office. This consisted not only of the knowledge of positive law which one could learn from various 'manuals', but also knowledge of the sources of law, the Talmūd and the various methods of interpretation. As this was the highest level of scholarship only legal scholars could meet it. On the other hand, since legal scholars were appointed as judges it also corresponded to the scholarly level demanded of judges.[96] To use an Islamic legal term, Jewish judges were continuously expected to be *mujtahid*s at times when the qualifications expected of their Muslim counterparts were limited. It is also true, however, that while Jewish communities were in no need of a large number of judges and could, therefore, insist on their excellent scholarship, the management of the Islamic judiciary demanded more judges – which resulted, quite obviously, in the restriction of their scholarly qualification.

The importance and methods of traditional legal learning were highlighted by Maimonides. According to him the study of the Torāh was compulsory and only women, children and slaves were relieved of it. It was the duty of the head of the family to ensure education, either by personal teaching or by employing a tutor for payment – but this only as an *ultima ratio* because in theory no payment could be expected for teaching law, the reason being that Moses became acquainted with God's revelation free of charge and passed it on (this approach is identical to that of the Muslim scholars). Time dedicated to teaching had to be split into three parts: one part was to be spent on written law; the second one on the study of oral law; and the third one on drawing conclusions and acquiring skills in the methods of legal interpretation. Compulsory respect for the master remained unchanged during the centuries:

- No one could give legal opinion in a given case in the presence of his master.
- A disciple could not address his master by name.
- He had to bow to the master by way of greeting.
- A disciple could not stand next to his master
- When walking he had to follow him at a respectable distance, and could not sit down in his master's presence until permission was given to him.
- When leaving a place he could not turn his back on his master but had to leave the room while facing him.
- He could not go to the same bath as his master.

95 Goitein 1988: 419.

96 Goitein 1999: 196–210.

- At the same time the master also had to be friendly with his disciple.[97]

Finally, to say some words about two peculiar forms of legal education is in order. One of them was called *pirqa*, which was a public presentation held at the synagogue of the Academy on *Shabbāt* or on other festive occasions. These were lectures for a broader audience, whose content did not offer anything new to the students of the Academy. Consequently, debate was prohibited on these occasions but the presence of the scholars was required. Being present at the *pirqa* was therefore not motivated by interest or involvement in learning but by respect for the lecturing scholar. It was considered bad manners and an offence against the lecturer to leave the *pirqa* before it came to an end. The students and scholars for whom the *pirqa* offered nothing new were seated at the back of the room, showing that they did not need the information imparted on the occasion. There is also an example of a scholar dozing off during an overlong lecture. The right to hold *pirqa* belonged to the *nāśī* and the *rēsh galūta'* who, however, delegated this task to members of the Academies. Scholars who held *pirqa* lectures were called *rēshey pirqey* (heads of the *pirqa*s).[98]

The other peculiar form of lecture was called *kalla*, the origin of which goes back to the Yabneh period. Here and at the 'Academy' of Tiberias legal rules were discussed and ultimately established by majority vote, which constituted the basis for the Mishnah in the next century. The Babylonian Academies, however, worked differently and developed a peculiar form of scholarly session called *kalla*. The Babylonian *kalla* was a scholarly conference of learning aimed at the discussion of a particular tractate of the Mishnah. In order to ensure that the participants prepared for the discussion in advance it was made public which tractate of the Mishnah would be the subject of debate before the *kalla* started. Therefore *kalla*s were held at particular times of the year, adjusted to weather conditions and agricultural specifics of Babylon. As cereals were sown twice a year (early spring and early autumn) and rice was regarded as a summer crop, the time of the *kalla* was set for a date when agricultural work allowed for staying away from the land, for the months of 'Elul (August–September) and 'Adar (February–March). This way education was split into two 'semesters' and the last month of each semester was the time for the *kalla*. During the *kalla* not only current members of the Academies gathered but also former students and legal scholars coming from more distant places. As a result, the *kalla* was a scholarly occasion for the Academy, when it could present its full intellectual power and refinement. The scholars were seated in rows during the discussion, as were the students. The president of the Academy chaired the session of the *kalla*. The *pirqa* held on Saturdays was not eliminated even at the time of the *kalla* and these occasions rather gained special significance compared to lectures held on other Saturdays. These sessions attracted crowds but it was Jacob Neusner who pointed out that since the time of the *kalla* corresponded

97 Maimonides 1981a: 57a–62b.

98 For more on *pirqa* see Mirsky 1959: 376–87.

to the time of the collection of the head-tax, some people attending the *kalla* – and thus away from home – were presumably motivated by reasons other than jurisprudence.[99]

The institution of the *kalla* survived for a long time with little modification. Scholars gathering for the spring *kalla* discussed questions sent to the Academy and after the discussion they answered them in writing. Its significance was that right after Easter the missionaries could immediately set out with the answers. All this cannot be observed in Palestine, for there it was the annual pilgrimage to Jerusalem which ensured that Academy members living far away (in Egypt or Syria) could meet.[100]

Islamic Law

Initially legal education was free of formalized structures and was imparted in the mosque from the first century on. Here various circles (*ḥalqa*) evolved, the members of which dedicated their attention to different Islamic disciplines. Larger mosques affiliated several *ḥalqa*s by thematic classification, thus separate *ḥalqas* came into being for the study of grammar, *ḥadīth* and *fiqh*. The number of members of these circles depended on the size of the settlement and of the mosque, on the popularity of the teacher and on the subject taught. Obviously, *ḥalqas* of the greatest mosques were frequented more than the mosques of smaller towns. Teachers were paid by the Caliph. Students could freely participate in the study of the various circles, being subject only to the master's permission. Teaching was supported by a library – designated by various names – which also served as the venue for social and scholarly meetings.[101] Ḥalqas were informal entities:

- Admission was only due to the professor's permission and there seems to have been no restriction on the size of the *ḥalqas*.
- *Ḥalqas* were open to anybody interested in the subject – no social, economic or ethnic background played a role in admission.
- No official curriculum existed; professors could select from the texts which one they wanted to teach and comment on, the latter being the essence of their teaching activity.
- An intimate relationship (*ṣuḥba*) emerged between professors and students or between scholars of equal standing.

The *madrasa*, the most characteristic educational institution of Islam, emerged from this rudimentary structure. With the coming of the *madrasa* the organizational structure was modified while the subjects and methods of education remained

99 Mirsky 1959: 395–401; Neusner 1969: 384–5; Goodblatt 1975: 155–96.

100 Goitein 1999: 198–201.

101 Triton 1957: 30-32; Makdisi 1981: 9–27.

practically unchanged, since *ḥalqa*s continued to be the forum of education – *madrasa*s providing only an external legal framework for operation.[102]

The network of *madrasa*s extending over the entire empire was organized by Niẓām al-Mulk, the vizier of the Seljūqs of Iranian descent. The Madrasa Niẓāmiyya founded by him in Baghdad was for long a reputed centre of Islamic scholarship, where it was an honour to have a teacher's job. However, the initial aversion against the new *madrasa* structure is indicated by the fact that after the opening of the Niẓāmiyya in Baghdad, al-Shīrāzī – one of the most respected Shāfiᶜīte scholars of his age – at first rejected an invitation to teach law there and accepted the job only upon the persuasion of his students. Scholars of Transoxania also rejected this innovation. The Shāfiᶜīte Madrasa Niẓāmiyya's opponent was the Ḥanafite *madrasa* founded in the same year (1067), which evolved around the shrine of Abū Ḥanīfa.[103] Despite this initial aversion to *madrasa*s soon they were founded all over the Muslim world: by the end of the twelfth century there were more than 30 *madrasa*s in Baghdad alone; Cairo had 32 in the thirteenth century; 25 *madrasa*s were in operation in fourteenth-century Bursa; while the number of *madrasa*s in sixteenth-century Istanbul was 142. In the following centuries the number of *madrasa*s shows a more rapid growth, their number being counted in thousands.[104]

Teachers enjoyed high social esteem and were regarded – in line with Jewish tradition – as superior to fathers.[105] Teachers of law were called *mudarris*, while teachers of other disciplines were not. A person taking up this job was recommended by the former *mudarris* from among his most eminent students. But recommendation alone was insufficient: the agreement of the local scholars was also necessary, which could be obtained by proving one's professional qualification, mostly in debates. A newly appointed *mudarris* gave an inaugural lecture in which he demonstrated his professional qualities, knowledge and ability in discussion. This inaugural speech was one of the most important means and occasions for gaining broad acknowledgement for a well-prepared *mudarris*, while it was torture and humiliation for a less talented one. The inaugural speech was an outstanding social event, attracting legal scholars, prominent officials and the local nobility. Appearance at the inaugural speech itself was a sign of acknowledgement and honour; this is why biographies of legal scholars favoured recording the fact that a huge audience was present on the occasion. By contrast, if this information was missing from the biography of a scholar or it was underlined that only few people were present it could be a sign of professional, political or some other resentment. The inaugural speech took place amidst festive externalities as it was accompanied by a reception and the handing over of a robe of honour.[106]

---

102 Hallaq 2009: 135–41.

103 Makdisi 1981: 27–34; Triton 1957: 102.

104 Hallaq 2009: 141–2.

105 Triton 1957: 48.

106 Makdisi 1981: 153–9.

In the formative period the income of the *mudarris* was secured by the students' payments. Later on, he received his salary primarily from the *madrasa* and the *waqf* (pious foundation) maintaining the school, though the students' contributions were not entirely wound up. *Mudarris*es were not among the rich, their salary being usually half of what a physician received. Therefore they had several jobs simultaneously, a practice criticized by many because they employed deputies while they were absent. A deputy's education (*nā'ib al-mudarris*) was no lower than the legal scholar's in whose name he was teaching. As usually there was only one *mudarris* in each *madrasa* (in bigger *madrasa*s there was a separate post for every legal school) deputies were often forced to be satisfied with this lower status and the related lower income. As this subsidiary and exceptional institution became increasingly widespread voices of criticism became louder, seeing in it the evasion of the system and a practice of abusing the *nā'ib*s which greatly contributed to the rapid decline of the level of education.[107] There are reports of a scholar who was a professor in Damascus and Jerusalem simultaneously; another scholar was professor in six different colleges in Damascus. Professors were sometimes judges at the same time.[108]

Since Islamic legal education, too, was primarily oral, repetitors called *muᶜīds* were among professionals who came to the assistance of students. A *muᶜīd's* task was identical to that of the *tanna* in Jewish legal education. *Muᶜīds* repeated the texts and explained the passages more difficult to understand in the lecture of the *mudarris*. A *muᶜīd* was usually a graduate lawyer from among the most eminent students of the *mudarris* or a student who had already advanced in his studies. To appoint a talented student to the office of a *muᶜ*īd was at the same time a means in the hand of the *mudarris* to eliminate competition in the future, since very talented students could challenge their position. Several legal scholars started their professional career as *muᶜīds*; one among them was al-Shīrāzī, who was a *muᶜīd* in the school of al-Ṭabarī.[109]

Social and scholarly prestige was linked to the knowledge of texts: persons learning such extensive quantities of texts and capable of reproducing them at any time were called 'oceans' (*baḥr*) of learning, while those who depended on the help of books were not appreciated. It is small wonder, therefore, that students were supplied with various useful pieces of advice on how to learn. Accordingly, one was to study at dawn rather than at night, possibly on an empty stomach and not after a good fill, but serious fasting was also to be avoided because it diverted one's attention. A similarly diverting effect was due to a physical environment of constant motion and of vegetation, therefore one could learn best in an empty room and not on a river bank, in a forest, at the wayside or in a similar place. The greatest help to memorizing, however, was constant repetition. One had to repeat a text at least 50 times so that the material learned might sink deeply into one's mind.

107 Makdisi 1981: 159–65, 188–90.

108 Triton 1957: 118.

109 Makdisi 1981: 193–5.

Constant practice, recalling and the mutual assistance of students by reciting the text aloud, and putting questions in relation to the material (*mudhakara*) were also indispensable. Discussing the material learned was also regarded as an important aid if it was not victory over fellow students but mutual help which was the aim of the discussion. Written notes were taken but they served only as tools for the not always perfect memory, since written materials had by far less repute than texts learned by heart.[110]

As a result of an interpersonal way of education a close interpersonal relationship between a master and his disciples developed which substituted for a sophisticated institutional structure during the formative period. People interested in the teachings of Islam in general and law in particular spent years with famous teachers, and they did not only listen to the masters but also came into close personal contact with them. ᶜAmr ibn Dīnār, a legal scholar of Mecca and a transmitter of *ḥadīth*, had himself carried by his students into the city; at the same time he prohibited them from putting down in writing anything from his lectures.[111] Saḥnūn, a well-known legal scholar of the Mālikite school, is another example: this broad-shouldered, long-haired scholar tilled his land with his own hands even when he was a successful scholar in Qairowān. During almost half a century of his teaching career he gave lectures in front of the entrance of his house, but the seasonality of agriculture strongly influenced teaching, and when there was work out in the fields teaching stopped and sometimes he was assisted in the fields by his students.[112]

Education was a rather costly affair because students had to cover the costs of living and accommodation, and occasionally they also had to pay tuition fees, though this was subject to debate. According to the ethos of Muslim scholars religious science should not be taught for a fee and, therefore, some were reluctant to accept it. Ibn al-Naqur, for example, was unable to secure a living for his family because he refused to be paid for teaching but due to his teaching activities was unable to make a living from other sources. Therefore al-Shīrāzī issued a *fatwā* on his behalf in which he declared it lawful to accept a fee for teaching. Al-Ghazālī, by contrast, considered it prohibited by law because religious teachers had to follow the example of the Prophet and teach religion for free.[113] The reference that teachers took no payment for teaching in general or for teaching the Qur'ān in particular is a frequent one in biographical works, although sometimes it looks like a literary topos, not social practice. On the other hand, however, sources show a judge who refused to accept the witness testimony of a teacher because he took fees for teaching the Qur'ān.[114] It should be noted here, however, that al-Ghazālī's

110 Triton 1957: 47; Makdisi 1981: 99–105.

111 Motzki 2002: 264.

112 Talbi 1996: 843.

113 Makdisi 1981: 161.

114 Triton 1957: 9–10.

line of argument resembles that of the Jewish scholars who argued the same way, reflecting Moses.

Despite these controversies payments had to be made and these burdens could only be afforded by better-off parents or by those students who inherited considerable wealth. Often the poor but talented students were looked after by their own teachers: Abū Ḥanīfa supported Abū Yūsuf with money; al-Juwaynī devoted his own inheritance to supporting his students and sometimes supplemented it with part of his teacher's salary. Occasionally rich patrons came to the aid of students and trusted the *mudarris* with the distribution of their subsidies. Caliph Hārūn al-Rashīd provided a large sum at the disposal of al-Shaybānī so that he could support his talented disciples. It may not have been an easy task at times because the number of students could be as high as 20 in the bigger *madrasa*s but by and large student members depended on economic conditions: in a year when yields were poor or insufficient the number of students also dropped drastically.[115]

Teaching continued on each day of the week with the exception of Fridays; a longer break was possible only at Ramaḍān. Legal scholars adjusted the Friday break for scholarly discussions and for issuing *fatwā*s. The duration of teaching was not specified and varied by teacher, with the exception of the four-year basic studies compulsory for all. Ranking of the students was symbolically expressed by the seating order: the closer one sat next to the teacher the greater appreciation he enjoyed. The seating order reflected time spent at studies as well, for those studying for a longer time obviously qualified as more advanced in learning. As anecdotes show, it also happened that some outstanding students were selected by the teacher himself and seated next to him during the lectures. Such a public transfer in the seating arrangement was regarded a great honour, as the case of al-Mutawallī, a prominent student of al-Sarakhsī, shows. After he excelled himself in debates his master ordered him closer, finding himself quite near to his teacher at the end. It was such a great honour that, according to his own words, such a privilege happened to him only once more during his entire life, when he was appointed to head the Niẓāmiyya Academy.[116] In the Middle Ages law students organized themselves and, as a result, a new post called *nā'ib al-fuqahā'* came into being who was an agent on behalf of his fellow students. This post was not universally recognized throughout the whole Islamic word but could be proven in the law colleges of Damascus.[117]

Besides learning huge amount of texts by heart, scholarly discussions played a prominent role, too, in legal education. As there was no time left for thinking, for selecting the proper arguments and their textual verification, one had to refute the claims of his partner immediately and persuade him that his views were wrong, thus winning him over to the other position. As in many cases, these disputes were held in public; those not skilled in discussions could be forced to give up their

115 Makdisi 1981: 180–87.
116 Makdisi 1981: 92–105.
117 Stewart 2008: 203–5.

position and thus lost their social appreciation. Regular discussions were usually held on Fridays, but scholarly debates were also organized on public holidays or on occasions dedicated to the memory of a famous master. Legal scholars frequently welcomed their partners for discussion in their own house and continued their discourse under private conditions sometimes even for decades. Important discussions lasted for a long time, sometimes from dawn to dusk. There were permanent partners for discussions, but the appearance of new scholars obviously made debates far more interesting. This happened when a scholar passed through a region or city and matched himself against the local representatives of learning. The disputes were regarded as verbal combat, therefore the similarity between discussions and bravery in the battlefield was expressed by metaphors. This is why Ibn Surayj was given the name 'grey falcon' (*al-bāz al-ashhab*) and al-Shīrāzī won the title 'the knight of dispute' (*al-fāris al-munāẓara*). Competition sometimes did not stop at the verbal level: when the participants could not control their emotions the discussion turned into a quarrel. Passions let loose caused some problems, therefore Caliphs sometimes prohibited public debates and the sale of books on dialectics.[118]

In the classical period, when education became more institutionalized, the licence to teach (*ijāzat al-tadrīs)* was introduced. After this time a *mudarris* could be appointed only when he was granted such a licence. *Ijāzat al-tadrīs* was issued by a master who was convinced of the suitability of the candidate. Such a licence could be obtained not only for teaching but also for issuing *fatwā*s or for both. Suitability had to be proven by writing a work on jurisprudence and in scholarly debates. The licence was not issued immediately on the termination of studies but after a longer period of time, after the candidate had obtained some legal practice and life experience, usually in his thirties or forties. Though there were some legal scholars authorized to teach law and issue *fatwā*s very early (al-Awzaᶜī was 13 and al-Subkī was 18), this was exceptional by all means. As issuing the licence also contained subjective elements the way was open for abuses: candidates could attempt to obtain a licence with some form of corruption while on the other hand licence-givers could abuse their authority. Since former students with *ijāzat al-tadrīs* immediately became competitors of their masters they were not willing to invest their younger colleagues with such a licence. Several anecdotes have it that scholars did not issue licences but rather deterred the candidates by telling them that they had not acquired the necessary qualifications because they had performed inadequately in the final exam. Since, however, every master could issue a licence and not only the students' professor candidates could ask for a licence from any recognized scholar. One could do so even if already possessing an *ijāzat al-tadrīs* issued by another master.[119] It should be emphasized, however, that this licence pertained primarily to teaching and to participation in legal disputes and was not an appointment to a judicial position, which was the right of the Caliph regardless of the *ijāzat al-tadrīs*.

118 Makdisi 1981: 130–37.

119 Makdisi 1981: 147–52; 170–71.

Politics was also involved in legal education. As seen above, Jewish leaders made efforts to control legal training and jurisprudence with the help of ordination, by nomination of the heads of the Academies and by employing loyal legal scholars in various administrative offices. No Caliph was able to follow this pattern of influence since there was no ordination in Islam. Therefore, political authorities chose another method of *indirect* influence: control through financial channels. It was the very novelty of *madrasa*s that authorities made legal education dependent on the financial aid they offered them. Scholars of Transoxania were clearly aware of this and lamented that from then on people would teach for money and not for its own sake, which would result in the degradation of learning.[120]

In sum, Islamic legal education shows a variety of similarities with Jewish legal education both in its underlying principles and structure. The oral nature of both legal cultures ensured an eminent place for memorizing, for the precise learning and recitation of huge quantities of texts. To this end similar good advice was given to students on how to learn and, what is more, an official repetitor (*tanna*, *muʿīd*) came to their assistance who was not regarded a legal scholar. In addition to memorizing important significance was attributed to legal disputes, as discussion among students and with their master was an integral part of education. These discussions determined the ranking of students, which was expressed by the seating order in both cultures. The various schools were originally no more than a personal relation between masters and disciples in both cultures which developed into a more institutionalized structure only at a later phase of their development. In the formative period students could learn from several masters belonging to various schools, a right which was restricted only later, when both Islamic and Jewish schools became more formalized entities. Teaching was marked by seasonality, primarily determined by the rhythm of agriculture in which students and sometimes even their teachers participated in order to ensure their livelihood. Scholarly acknowledgement and granting licences to graduate students were the right of the scholarly community. The *ijāzat al-tadrīs* authorized a person to teach law, to issue *fatwā*s and to participate in scholarly discourse. *Semikah* had similar functions in Jewish law, entitling the person to use the title of Rabbi and to enjoy the scholarly and social privileges pertaining to it. Perhaps the only important difference is that while Jewish legal students could enter the court in exceptional circumstances no Muslim law student was authorized to do so.

Both Jewish and Muslim authorities wanted to control legal education to some extent, therefore institutions of learning lost their former independence witnessed earlier. But political influence was *indirect*, through the channel of nomination and financial aid, while authorities did not want to interfere in the daily business of the Academies and *madrasa*s directly. The curriculum, for example, remained unchanged for centuries since it was the business of the schools and no authority saw it as suitable to influence or regulate the matter. When, however, in recent

---

120 Triton 1957: 102. For more on politics and legal education see Hallaq 2009: 126–58.

times state authorities interfered more directly in the inner life of the *madrasas* (e.g. the nationalization of al-Azhar in 1961), *madrasas* became more and more involved in politics from Egypt to Pakistan.[121]

Zoroastrian Law

Legal education in Zoroastrian law differed from the Jewish and Islamic models, although one may find some similarities. One of the most important differences between the Jewish-Islamic and Zoroastrian model is that in Zoroastrianism legal education was not independent of other training but was part of priestly education. It is small wonder if we recall that jurisprudence and the administration of law was the terrain of the Zoroastrian priesthood and new generations of priests had to be taught about different topics such as ritual, theology and law. It was the ērbed (teacher) whose task was to educate young priests. This explains why ērbedestān meant a place where training was imparted and at the same time denotes also a text about education and other, loosely related topics.

The relationship between a teacher and his student (*hāwisht*) was determined by unconditional respect for the teacher and subordination to him. It might be no coincidence that the text uses the word *tarsagāh* to define this relationship, which is a derivative of the verb 'to fear'.[122] Subordination of the students is reflected also in corporal punishment meted out to students for sinful neglect of duties or for the disregard of rules of proper behaviour (such as chatting while eating). In such cases sanctions established for petty crimes (e.g. *ardush*) had to be implemented.[123] Since scholars were at the same time religious superiors (*rad, dastwar*) and spiritual leaders,[124] this personal authority made the Zoroastrian system similar to the Indian model but distinguished it markedly from the Jewish and Islamic systems where legal scholars were not spiritual leaders.

The work entitled Panč hēm ī asrōnān (The five virtues of the priests) explains qualifications expected of priests. These are:

1. incorruptibility
2. goodness in thoughts, words and deeds (a reference to the basic principles of Zoroastrian ethics expected of every believer)
3. to have a spiritual leader as a wise guide
4. to worship according to ritual
5. to contend with opponents.

121 Hefner 2007: 32. On problems of modern *madrasas* see Zaman 2002: 60–86 and the numerous scholarly articles about *madrasas* in various Muslim countries in Hefner–Zaman 2007; see also Fair 2008.

122 Ērbedestān 0.3.

123 Ērbedestān 16.12; 17.1. On the classification of crimes see Jany 2007: 362–73.

124 Kreyenbroek 1994: 7–15.

To this end priests had to know the sacred texts by heart: that is, the Awesta and its commentary, the Zand, which together comprise an enormous quantity of texts. It is the *dastwar* who knows by heart this corpus of texts most profoundly and without any written aid. Therefore, the most important task was to memorize the texts, an attitude proven by both fourth-century Greek sources and tenth-century Arabic reports. As this remained a basic requirement educated priests still know these texts by heart in the twentieth century. Thus it is not surprising that besides heresy, laziness and forgetfulness are sins that could be committed by priests.[125] It is also true, however, that modern priests who still know the texts by heart sometimes do not understand a word of them because they are composed in a dead language out of use for a millennium or more. The rather deficient level of knowledge of modern-age priesthood is proven by both the observations of nineteenth- and twentieth-century travellers and recent surveys of scholars.[126]

Due to the oral nature of the (legal) culture the deaf and dumb were disqualified,[127] and absence from learning was permitted only in the case of *force majeure* (starvation, thirst, drought, cold).[128] Memorization was realized by the joint recital of the texts by teacher and students, but the repetitor known from the Islamic and Jewish legal education was missing. After the teacher and the students repeated the text thrice and the student was able to repeat it a fourth time on his own the text was considered as learned.[129]

Such a close relationship between master and his disciples guaranteed the proper transfer of the oral tradition while at the same time prevented unauthorized persons learning the Zoroastrian tradition. Non-Zoroastrians and foreigners could not be taught; only some part of the tradition could be revealed to them – and that, too, only when the teacher was on the brink of death by starvation and could secure his livelihood only by the 'tuition fee' paid to him. The extent of the material taught, however, could not be more than what was necessary for the teacher's survival.[130]

By contrast, women could participate in education – which may come as a surprise in a patriarchal society as the Persian no doubt was in the Sasanian period. Yet the Ērbedestān is clear about this issue and claims that either husband or wife can participate in education. But one of the spouses had to stay at home, namely whoever was better suited for the management and increase of family wealth. If this person was the head of the family then his wife could go to study, and vice versa.[131] Perhaps this rule is related to the principle that the 'management' of property was better than pursuing religious studies (*khwāstag sālārīh weh ku*

125 Bailey 1943: 158–65.
126 Stausberg 2004: 103–8.
127 Ērbedestān 16.1–2.
128 Ērbedestān 17.3.
129 Ērbedestān 13.5, 13.15.
130 Ērbedestān 12.38–39, 19.3–9.
131 Ērbedestān 5.1–5.6.

ērbedestān kardan).[132] Management of family wealth was an important issue during studies, therefore the Ērbedestān devotes an entire chapter to discussing this problem from different angles. Accordingly, a student who was absent from family business should return every four months to look after affairs, but if he knew that his wealth was not in good hands he was obliged to break off his studies.[133] To ensure moral standards among students a person who caused damage to anyone's property could not participate in education.[134]

While in Jewish and Islamic culture studying law was regarded as the most eminent activity, its standing was subject to debate among Zoroastrians. According to one view religious studies are as meritorious as ritual. Another opinion has it that religious studies are as beneficial as *khwēdōdāh*, that is, marriage between close relatives, being in high esteem among *mōbed*s; but a third opinion denies it, saying that religious studies are not as important as *khwēdōdāh*.[135] Since it is known that ritual in general and *khwēdōdāh* in particular were regarded as the most meritorious acts, with benefits for the world to come, placing religious studies on an equal footing with them means high esteem for learning. This might be the ideal of priestly authors, while the view that business activity is superior to religious learning, an opinion already quoted, might reflect social reality.

The duty of education rested on close relatives (*nabānazdisht*), who made themselves responsible and committed sin if they did not comply with a student's request for education. Their responsibility was in accordance with their level of relationship to the would-be student.[136] The explanation of this peculiar ruling may perhaps be that the priestly class was an elite group with caste-like features. To refuse to educate a young family member could be interpreted as abandoning family ties and social cohesion within the family and the priestly class, an act contrary to the interests of the priestly class which could not be tolerated.

Education did not last for long; it took only a year.[137] This, however, may only pertain to elementary studies because it is impossible to learn the entire tradition within such a short time. Further studies were continued with the help of a prominent master, who was a teacher and a spiritual leader at the same time. Students gathered around such scholars and after completing their studies carried on the master's teaching. The (legal) schools of Abarag, Sōshāns and Mēdōmāh can be understood in this context. These Zoroastrian legal schools were not institutions with refined structures but could rather be regarded as a close relationship between masters and their disciples, similar to early Jewish and Islamic legal schools.

Students could learn from several masters (similar to the original concepts of Jewish and Islamic legal training); moreover, it was an expressly recommended

132 Ērbedestān 3.2.
133 Ērbedestān 4.2–4.3.
134 Ērbedestān 2.29.
135 Ērbedestān 2.25–7.
136 Ērbedestān 15.6.
137 Ērbedestān 12.1.

form of learning. Students who had already learned everything from their teacher could continue their studies with another scholar in order to learn more: they could go to two or even three teachers for this purpose.[138] It was the teacher's duty to teach his students but he had to render only assistance that was necessary to complete the studies and was not obliged to do more. At the same time, similar to the Jewish attitude, it was regarded the teacher's fault if students did not progress properly in their studies.[139]

Disputes, so important in both Jewish and Islamic legal education, were missing from Zoroastrian legal education. Obviously, legal problems were debated among legal scholars belonging to different schools but there is no reference to discussions between masters and their disciples: the disciples' task was to follow the master's guidance, to memorize texts and to accept him as intellectual and spiritual leader. It was, therefore, not eminence in disputes on which the ranking of the students rested, if there was any formal ranking at all. There is no mention in the sources of seating the students in rows either, thus matters concerning the daily routine of Zoroastrian legal education remain in the dark.

Sources also reveal nothing about political influence on legal education. Perhaps the silence of the sources indicates that there was no attempt by the king to do so. It is likely because legal education was in the main the business of the Zoroastrian Church, the inner life of which was not the terrain of the ruler but that of the *mōbedān mōbed*. Interfering in the affairs of the Church could be more harmful than beneficial for the monarch. If there was anything a ruler wanted to achieve in the Church he could arrange it through the chief *mōbed* without personal involvement. As due to its political, social and ideological prestige the Zoroastrian Church was a more or less autonomous body, it stands to reason to think that Zoroastrian legal education was free from direct political influence – this, however, at the cost of a hierarchical organization and a strong doctrinal adherence required from all the participants. No Persian king was interested in manipulating legal education through financial aid or ordination since it was not his business to educate young priests but that of the Zoroastrian Church, which accomplished this task due to its own interests.

Until now this study has looked at three models of education: the Jewish-Islamic and the Zoroastrian. For the sake of comparison, however, some words about contemporary Christian education are in order. Christian Academies were found close to the Western border of the Sasanian Empire, in the cities of Edessa and Nisibis run mostly by Persian Christian intellectuals. These Christian Academies were not established for legal education but for teaching biblical exegesis, liturgy, grammar, music and medicine, the latter being considered a somewhat secondary discipline. The school of Nisibis had a well-organized structure: it was headed by the *mepashqānā*, elected from among the teachers, whose work was assisted by the *rabbaitā*, an executive officer managing daily affairs. The head of the school

138 Ērbedestān 13.1–2, 14.2.

139 Ērbedestān 14.5, 15.1–2.

decided on the most important issues with the agreement of a 'board' as a kind of an advisory body, consisting of the most prominent teachers. Several statutes of the school have been handed down, enabling us to learn about the administrative structure of the school, the way of education and the life and duties of the students. Accordingly, this school constituted a temporary monastic community where celibacy was the rule. Teachers and students lived in cells large enough for several people. Full hermitage was, however, not allowed: learning and meals were regarded as community events. Commercial activity, including usurious loans, was forbidden for the participants, who had to live primarily through manual labour. Here, too, education was seasonal, adjusted to the rhythm of agriculture (the school was closed between August and October, which more or less corresponded to the Jewish custom). Offences against school statutes were punished by corporal punishment. A characteristic punishment, however, was exclusion and exile from the school and the city. Laziness was harshly punished here too, just as in the Zoroastrian system. Members of the school were almost hermetically isolated from the city: they were not allowed to reside in Nisibis, could not beg in the city and could not visit inns and public parks. If they happened to wander into a public place they had to be recognizable immediately by their garments and haircut: they could not let their hair grow; they were not allowed to shave their head clean either, but had to have tonsure and wear modest clothing (not specified in detail). Women were excluded from the community; no social interaction with them was allowed, including meeting and talking to them in the street.[140]

Thus, concerning underlying principles the Jewish model of education seems to be very close to its Christian counterpart. The monastic community, part-time celibacy, the panic caused by women, exclusion for the sake of learning and a constant struggle to maintain independence against authorities (*rēsh galūta*, bishop) are features shared by both Jewish and Christian models which are somewhat alien to the Zoroastrians and Muslims. Islamic education seems to share institutional similarities with the Jewish educational system, while the Zoroastrian model shares only a few similarities with these systems. It is remarkable since it was Zoroastrian converts, Iranian in origin, who played the leading role in shaping contemporary Christian education.

140 See the canons of Narsai and Henānā in Vööbus 1962: 73–102. For the history of the school of Nisibis see Vööbus 1965.

Chapter 6
The Judge and Society

Judges and Social Customs

To arrive at a proper judgment theoretical postulations of jurisprudence are insufficient, therefore a judge has to pay attention also to everyday legal practice of his society. Judges were aware of this and tried their best not to alienate the judiciary from contemporary social practice. In doing this, however, they were faced with postulations of legal theories which regarded social customs in legal life differently.

In **Islamic law**, when after al-Shāfiᶜī's work the four sources of law were established with the exclusion of social customs, some attempts were made to encapsulate social practice into the circle of legal sources formally, too, but in vain. Though formally not accepted, they were nevertheless regarded as legal sources materially, a situation which had to be taken into consideration by both legal theory and legal practice.

Social custom (*ᶜāda*, *ᶜurf*) was therefore no source of Islamic law, though it could find its way into positive rules through the accepted legal sources. Several methods were known to achieve this: the content of a custom was either introduced in the form of a prophetic *sunna* or could be made accepted by *ijmāᶜ*. A third technique to introduce customs was asserted in contractual law, according to which customs were interpreted as legal background to the contracts signed by the parties. In other words, if there was no condition or rule specified in a contract differing from local practice it was assumed that the rules of local customs were parts of the contract; otherwise the parties would have made differing stipulations. As the parties did not do this the rules of the customs were regarded as contractual conditions. This solution was primarily applied in legal disputes between merchants. The fourth technique to implement local customs was achieved by *istiḥsān*, an established method of legal reasoning, according to which in doubtful cases a solution more advantageous to people should be favoured. The more advantageous solution for people was understood as rules being in harmony with local practice. Thus the acknowledgement of custom as a substantial source meant the *de facto* acknowledgement of custom while evading all problems of legal theory to accept it as a *formal* source of law. These methods were primarily favoured by members of the Ḥanafite school; other schools devoted less attention to customs.[1]

It is small wonder, therefore, that it was Abū Yūsuf, one of the most prominent members of the Ḥanafite school, who made some attempt to acknowledge custom

1 Libson 1996: 131–42; Libson 2003: 68–72, 76–8.

also as a formal source of law. Abū Yūsuf went as far as considering customs having priority over the *naṣṣ* texts in case of collision. Abū Yūsuf's position was not only rejected by the majority of legal scholars but also by members of his own school. According to al-Marghīnānī the relationship between these two sources is different because *naṣṣ* texts are established legal sources and cannot be disregarded in favour of customs, which are not. Another prominent representative of the Ḥanafite school, al-Sarakhsī, held a similar view. At the same time no one saw any obstacle to applying customs when they did not contradict the textual sources.[2] This led to al-Sarakhsī's broadly acknowledged thesis, according to which 'what is known through custom is equivalent to that which is stipulated by the clear texts of revelation'.[3] The popularity of this thesis is demonstrated by the fact that the Ottoman 'civil code' (Majallat al-aḥkām al-ᶜadliyya), enacted during the Tanẓimāt reforms of imperial Turkey, repeated it almost word for word and recognized it also as a formal source for Turkey but, obviously, not for Islamic law in general.[4] It is important to note that the influence of local legal customs remained in effect in some parts of the Islamic world until modern times. This is the situation in, among others, Nigeria, Java, Tunisia,[5] the Berber-speaking regions[6] and Yemen, where people settle their conflicts with the help of elected tribal courts and not in courts implementing Islamic law.[7]

Social custom is not to be confused with legal custom of the courts referred to as *ᶜamal* (act). Reference to *ᶜamal* can be observed primarily in the Mālikite school. In Andalusia references are made to the customs of certain cities (such as Cordoba), whereas in Morocco the implementation of *ᶜamal* has been far more widespread since the fifteenth century. It was impossible to make *ᶜamal* a source of law because decisions had to be made on established legal sources and not on how judges proceeded earlier. Yet, in Morocco the rulings of earlier judges could be considered when a new decision was being made. Reference, however, was not made to a precedent, because it is alien to Islamic law, but rather to legal opinions known as 'favoured' (*rajīḥ*) or 'isolated' (*shaḍḍ*) views. As seen earlier, legal pluralism was tolerated not only between schools but also within schools. As a result, several legal doctrines emerged, one of which was called *mashhūr* (lit. famous) – that is, a doctrine followed and preferred by and large by the members of the school. At the same time other doctrines contradicting the *mashhūr* view were not considered null and void; they were merely referred to less frequently. A judge was required to base his judgment on a *mashhūr* doctrine in the majority of cases but had the right to refer to *rajīḥ* or *shaḍḍ* views if they better suited customs, the public good or the interests of the parties. A judge had to reason why

2 Libson 1996: 145–7; Libson 2003: 73–5.

3 Quoted in Hallaq 2001a: 222.

4 Mejelle, Preface, Part II, 45; Hakim 1993: 147; Libson 2003: 78–9.

5 Coulson 1959: 19.

6 Bousquet 1986: 170–71.

7 Serjeant 1995: 46–8.

he did not follow the *mashhūr* opinion and favoured a lesser known legal view of his school instead when resolving a particular dispute. In such reasoning judges referred to the practice of earlier judges who ruled the same way as they did in such cases. Legal customs of the courts were, therefore, taken into consideration in everyday legal practice though never accepted as a formal source of law. As the product of the local practice of the courts, *ᶜamal* is an expressly pragmatic law, being sometimes closer to the daily life of Moroccan society than the occasionally less practical rules of Islamic law.[8] It is no wonder, therefore, that a particular literature of *ᶜamal* emerged in Morocco. These works contain brief descriptions of problematic cases and the related opinion of lawyers, thus supplying judges with practical information and guidance. Worth mentioning among these works are Lāmiyya, a manual of procedure by ᶜAlī al-Zaqqāq (fifteenth to sixteenth centuries) and the work of al-Fāsī (seventeenth century) entitled Al-ᶜamal al-fāsī, containing several hundred rules set in verse for the sake of easier memorization.[9]

What is common in *ᶜada* and *ᶜamal* is that they both reflect the interest of a community, whether a local community (town, area) or a community of a particular profession (merchants). Muslim lawyers, however, also developed legal techniques to realize the interest of private individuals through lawful means. These were called *ḥiyal*, a plural of *ḥīla* meaning strategy, a device to achieve a particular aim. In legal literature *ḥiyal* means lawful legal techniques by which extra-legal ends could be achieved. It was the merchants driven by business considerations who wished to apply these techniques for the first time, and some jurists were ready to give them a helping hand. To give an example: it is well known that Qur'ānic rule prohibits interest, a norm resting on revelation no one risked to disregard. At the same time business activities were burdened by this rule. Therefore the needs of commerce were satisfied by a simple technique of *ḥiyal* known as double (or dual) sale. Accordingly, the debtor sells something to the creditor for an agreed price and then buys it back for a higher sum. Thus the interest of both parties could be satisfied simultaneously: the debtor obtained the required loan; the difference figuring in the price embodied the interest; and the object of the contract functioned as security to the demand. Here are two lawful contracts (purchase), the legality of each being beyond question, while the whole legal construction was aimed at overcoming a Qur'ānic rule. The letter of the law was respected while its ideal content was evaded.

The technique of dual sale and purchase was already known in Medina at the time of Mālik in the eighth century. The vast majority of legal techniques, which number several hundred, were not such simple transactions, but consisted of a complex system of transactions following each other in a definitive order established by the parties and their legal advisors. These transactions and contracts were lawful in themselves, but taken as a whole resulted in an entirely different final outcome. In order to follow the process properly documents were produced

8 Berque 1986: 427–8; Rosen 1989: 47; Serrano 1996: 188.

9 Berque 1986: 428; Rosen 2000: 25–6.

in each phase of the transaction and deposited in the hands of a trustworthy person who had to guarantee that the final aim of the entire process should be realized. In order to safeguard the parties against each other the 'trustee' handed over to the parties only those documents which were indispensable to the realization of the next phase in this complex system of transactions. The techniques of *ḥiyal* belonged primarily to the arsenal of the Ḥanafites, who did not moralize about them because they were convinced of their legality. It is the reason why members of the Ḥanafite school were masters of *ḥiyal*, and are among the authors of *ḥiyal* literature. Already the disciples of Abū Ḥanīfa, Abū Yūsuf and al-Shaybānī are among the authors of *ḥiyal* literature, and al-Sarakhsī, too, figures among the commentators on *ḥiyal* literature. Al-Khaṣṣāf, the legal advisor to Caliph al-Muhtadī, belongs to the most influential authors of *ḥiyal* literature. The success of the Ḥanafites in this subject forced the other schools to change their position, despite the fact that al-Shāfiʿī expressly disregarded *ḥiyal* and Mālik spoke in an ambivalent manner about it (for instance he prohibited the above-mentioned dual purchase and sale). The traditionalists, however, insisted on the spirit of Islamic law and took up a position expressly against *ḥiyal*; they prohibited it as a means, insisting only on the letter of law but not on its content and morality.[10]

Since custom (*minhāg*) was acknowledged as a legal source in **Jewish law** there emerged no theoretical problems similar to Islamic law. Customs played a significant role already in the Second Temple period, proven by a saying attributed to Hillel: 'Leave it to Israel: if they are not prophets, they are the descendants of prophets.'[11] Customs had a triple function in Jewish law:

1. Customs supplemented existing law when there was no rule of *halakah* pertaining to a particular case.
2. If there were concurrent legal doctrines the relevant view was chosen from among the different views on the basis of customs (similar to *istiḥsān* known from Islamic law).
3. They defined rules being formally *contra legem* in nature but to be followed in particular circumstances (this was rejected in the end in Islamic law but can be observed in Zoroastrian law; see below).

In addition to this the principle was established that custom overrode the law (*minhāg mebattēl halakah*), but only in secular legal matters (*mamōna'*), meaning that one could neglect biblical rules on the basis of the freedom of contract as they were only *ius dispositivum*. As far as *issura'* (ritual issues) was concerned, biblical rules remained *ius cogens*, never to be overruled by custom.[12]

Jewish courts did their best to conform to contemporary social reality and customs and not to implement rigid rules of academic jurisprudence. To understand

10 Schacht 1986: 510–12.

11 Quoted in Elon 1994: 882.

12 Elon 1994: 880–907.

this attitude recall the fact that Jews were living in the Diaspora for many centuries and it was in their interest to embrace the opportunity of legal autonomy granted to them. Since it was open to Jews to turn to non-Jewish courts, if Jewish legal scholars wanted to dissuade their fellows from doing so, they had to run a flexible judiciary which did not neglect social customs. For example, pilgrimage was encouraged by declaring the road from Babylon to Palestine as pure. To understand the significance of this we should remember that according to law a way going through lands inhabited by non-Jews was impure. Since the maintenance of this rule would have meant placing crowds on pilgrimage to Palestine in a difficult situation, the road used by pilgrims was declared pure.[13] Other attempts were also made to make Jewish courts attractive: the Jewish courts were, contrary to Muslim courts, free of charge; and as they consisted at least of three members they offered a greater chance of objectivity.[14]

In the *ga'ōnic* period several forms of customs were distinguished, including the customs of the Academies; the customs of ancestors, scholars and localities; and those of professionals (such as merchants). As Jewish merchants concluded accords with Muslim merchants, too, Islamic courts extended their legal authority over these transactions. Therefore Jewish merchants became acquainted with the rules of Islamic law, some of which were more advantageous to them than the Jewish norms. Consequently Jewish merchants were inclined to turn to Muslim judges to settle their disputes. To thwart this, Jewish courts were ready to recognize Muslim legal customs, first of all in the law of commerce, but resisted any foreign influence in family law. With the slow decline of the Babylonian Academies and the emergence of local centres in North Africa, Hispania and Europe local customs evolved here and were considered in judgments. Consequently, one can no longer speak about uniform Jewish customs, but only about their local variants – about which responses and *takkanah*s offer valuable information.[15]

In **Zoroastrian law** nothing is known about theoretical reflections on customs as a legal source, either because there was no attempt to clarify this issue or because texts about such questions of legal theory were lost. By studying the MHD+A, however, it becomes clear that customs did in fact modify the law and its implementation. Customs of the courts were designated with the term *kardag* (from the verb 'to do') and the compiler deliberately distinguished it from other sources of law. When presenting a case the compiler of the MHD+A presented first the leading legal doctrine about the issue, if there were such a doctrine, followed by competing views when several legal doctrines were formulated. Only at the end of the presentation of the case did he refer to *kardag* and how the case was to be decided according to it. Since this order is almost uniform in the whole compilation (*kardag* being referred to at first when legal doctrines were missing), it

13 Urbach 1975: 582.

14 Goitein 1999: 311–12.

15 See Libson 2003: 92–112, where the author illustrates the incorporation of Muslim legal customs into Jewish legal life with examples.

is reasonable to think that it refers to a hierarchy of legal sources – although no such term can be found in Zoroastrian legal literature. When no doctrine is mentioned and *kardag* rules immediately follow the presentation of facts of a particular case, the custom of the courts obviously filled the gap of law in order to decide on cases for which otherwise there was no rule. What is more, however, *kardag* rules were sometimes at variance with traditional legal doctrines and succeeded in modifying them. To refer only to one example: according to *kardag* a letter of divorce (*hisht-nāmag*) was regarded valid even when the husband declaring divorce did not name in the document the person who would exercise guardianship over his wife after divorce. According to the traditional doctrines such a letter of divorce was invalid. By contrast, *kardag* regarded such a document as a valid bill of divorce.[16] By granting legal effect to such documents *kardag* implicitly established the right of women to be independent persons in no need of any guardian, although it is not known whether or not this was the deliberate aim of the courts. It was the law of inheritance (*stūrship*, čagar – marriage) which was modified by *kardag* also in important points, while other branches of law – such as the law of procedure, rules concerning petty crimes etc. – belong to the less important alterations. Taken as a whole, the effect of these legal changes was that during the next centuries *kardag* rules became dominant while the old doctrines were abolished in daily practice. Curious as it is, later on *kardag* norms were taught as if they were legal doctrines. In sum, *kardag* norms became an autonomous corpus of law in the last century of the Sasanian Empire, representing a more flexible attitude than legal doctrines of academic jurisprudence. Therefore, Persian judges contributed by their legal customs to social changes in contemporary society and promoted further legal changes whose effects could be observed even in the subsequent centuries.[17]

To say some words about corruption in a chapter about the relationship between the courts and society is in order. Unfortunately, but understandably, legal works dealing mostly with legal theory and problems of positive law hardly allow any insight into this important issue. Nevertheless, the corruptibility of Persian courts was already mentioned in Antiquity. There is a reference to the corruptibility of Persian courts in the Babylonian Talmūd in a dialogue between two Jewish legal scholars. It reveals that Persian courts were in fact corruptible, at least until the *pursishn-nāmag* was sealed.[18] The fact that the situation was known to Jewish scholars in such technical detail does not only show that Jewish legal scholars knew the daily routine of Persian legal administration but also that the corruptibility of Persian courts was broadly known in Mesopotamia. Other officials of legal administration could be bribed also. As seen earlier, in al-Ṭabarī's chronicle Kawād was freed from prison by bribing his warder and the Syrian Acts of Martyrs also refer frequently to bribing warders.[19]

16 MHD 4.9–10; Macuch 1993: 82.

17 For more examples of *kardag*'s effect on Zoroastrian law see Jany 2005: 310–13.

18 Gittin 28b.

19 Braun 1915: 81, 125, 177.

By contrast, reference to the corruptibility of Jewish courts comes up rarely in the sources, either because they kept quiet about it or because corruption was in fact the exception, as is assumed by Neusner[20] and Goitein.[21] To understand this we should bear in mind that Jewish courts did everything to prevent the parties turning to non-Jewish courts, but this effort could be undermined heavily by corrupt judges. As Jewish courts were no supervisors of wealthy foundations, they were not tempted to misuse their rights to their own benefit either. Consequently no abuses of this nature are heard about. Moreover, Jewish *dayyān*s owed their authority to their learning and not to nomination by a ruler and were in no positions of power, contrary to Persian and Muslim judges. Therefore, they were not tempted to misuse their power.[22]

Traces of corruption are rare also in the *ga'ōnic* period. The case of a judge who accepted money (from both parties) provoked great consternation, particularly because he also stole books and carpets. Such cases, however, were rather rare: as pointed out by Goitein, the fact that there are hardly any hints of complaint among the Cairo Genizah documents shows that corruption was in fact not characteristic in the law courts. By contrast, the overwhelming majority of complaints against judges were formulated because people thought that judges considered their office too seriously. Overly severe judgments; rigid, literal implementation of law; disregard for the parties' will and for changing circumstances were the major complaints against judges, who, in many cases, were so unable to find harmony with their own community that they rather left it, together with their judicial function.[23]

Corruption in Muslim courts was more widespread. Bilāl, a descendant of an early ᶜIrāqī governor, was the first documented corrupt judge in the history of Islamic law. In my opinion the reasons for corruption are numerous. For one thing, Muslims had to turn to an Islamic court; therefore, there were no constraints on corruption building up in the system as in Jewish law (see above). Moreover, only a small number of Jewish judges were nominated to communities living in the Diaspora who could be selected from among the learned and the most honest, while Muslim judges were far greater in number who could not be selected with such safety as their Jewish colleagues. To this should be added that Muslim judges had to supervise the wealth of orphans and *waqfs*, a task that opened the way to abuse and corruption on a larger scale. In fact, numerous cases were revealed which prove that judges sometimes abused their authority. Anyone protesting against such corrupt practices was punished by the same judge, who therefore abused his judicial authority even more. In this respect the already mentioned case of an orphan boy making fun of a corrupt judge in a poem should be recalled: he

20 Neusner 1970: 269.
21 Goitein 1999: 318–19.
22 Goitein 1999: 319.
23 Goitein 1999: 318.

was released from jail only after the background to his poem was revealed and the judge condemning him was suspended from office.[24]

Besides supervising pious foundations, lawsuits also offered sufficient opportunities for corruption. Judges, however, usually did not commit their abuses alone but in collaboration with others. It was primarily the official witnesses (*ʿudūl*) who could be considered as partners since it was their task to authenticate the documents of private parties as witnesses and to justify them in the lawsuit. With the passage of time it became a highly lucrative job and people involved were ready to pay big sums to acquire the position of official witness. As professional witnesses had to work with the judge they had to 'agree' with him first and foremost. Sources show a judge who dismissed his professional witnesses, only to reemploy them the next day in exchange for a greater sum of money.[25] Often judges and professional witnesses acted in concert to misuse their power and to profit from their public offices.[26] There was little chance of legal remedy in such cases: only a new judge could revise the decisions of his predecessor in office but this happened rather infrequently (see Chapter 3 about legal remedy).

Besides political influence corruption was the reason why legal scholars usually rejected appointments, at least according to their somewhat idealized biographies. Although *adab al-qāḍī* literature did its best to promote proper and modest behaviour for judges it was not sufficient to stop abuses. It happened not by chance that al-Ghazālī turned his back on public life for this reason and chose the life of a Sufi for ten years.

Judges as Public Authorities

In both Jewish and Zoroastrian legal systems judges were also public authorities, but this common feature can be traced back to different reasons: Jewish legal scholars were public authorities because there was no Jewish state, while Persian legal scholars were public authorities because there was a Persian state.

Since there was no **Jewish** state, public authority meant that Jewish legal scholars participated in managing legal autonomy granted for the Jewry not only through courts but through other offices, too. These were outside the judiciary but legal knowledge was a precondition to fulfil the task properly.

As seen previously, Jews had their political leaders (*nāśī*, *resh galūta'*) who represented the community and organized the observance of all duties the Jews owed to their changing but militarily always superior masters (Romans, Parthians, Byzantines, Persians and Muslims). These political leaders relied on the cooperation of the legal scholars both as advisors and officials. Although the

24 Schneider 1990: 120–21; Schneider 1995: 163; see also Chapter 4, note 44 and related text.

25 Makdisi 1981: 202

26 Ziadeh 1990: 84.

relationship between them was not always free from internal struggle, the leading role of the legal scholars was never challenged by anyone. The only niggling question was whether the jurists could claim their position in their own right or through the delegation of the political leader's authority. There is no uniform answer to this question because it varied by space and time: when the political leader was strong enough legal scholars played a rather subordinate role; recall the third century when prominent authorities such as Shamū'el and Rav were the representatives of the *rēsh galūta'* and had the duty to implement the leader's decision. In subsequent centuries the political leader's influence declined (in Palestine the office of the *nāśī* was even abolished), hence leadership increasingly shifted to the hands of the Academies, the heads of which became prominent authorities in the early Islamic period (*ga'ōn*). In this respect the legal scholars' function as market inspectors is worth mentioning: they supervised merchants and artisans to respect basic ritual rules, controlled prices in the market and organized the supply of basic foodstuffs in order to avoid famines (for instance Shamū'el, as *agoranomos*, supplied the city of Nahardea with food at times of famine). Control of weights and measures was also part of market inspection, the reason being to limit competition and protect local merchants and craftsmen. The Rabbis could issue decrees regulating the order of the market and merchants were obliged to obey them.[27]

In **Zoroastrian law** judges were no public authorities: *mōbed*s did not take upon themselves administrative tasks because they were judges but because they were at the same time priests, legal scholars and advisors to the king. Their activity was not motivated by the need to maintain legal autonomy but rather to secure their enormous influence and contribute to the proper governance of the Sasanian kingdom. In other words, Jewish legal scholars took administrative functions upon themselves because they participated in upholding the autonomy granted for the Jews, while *mōbed*s did the same because there was a Persian state which relied on their contribution as reliable public authorities and ideologues.

As a result, *mōbed*s were appointed at times to rather important jobs in public administration: there were *mōbed*s who were leaders of a city and there was a *mōbed* who governed the important western province of Adiabene. The monarch expected the *mōbed*s to accompany him on his military actions. This task, however, seems to be a distinction and a duty of religious leaders in general: sources show that Mani accompanied his patron Shābuhr on several of his campaigns, and the *Catholicos* was also expected to do so during the Byzantine campaign of Khusraw II.[28] In the trials against Iranian Christians *mōbed*s were not only judges, but also investigators, attorneys and prosecutors who supervised the executions (see Chapter 3 on criminal procedure).

Islamic law differs from the Jewish-Zoroastrian model because a *sharī'a* court was bound to enforce Islamic law and not the policy of any state which had its own

27 Neusner 1969: 141–3; Neusner 1966: 113; Neusner 1968: 300.

28 Shaked 1990: 268–71.

organs to implement its rulings. Taken as a whole, Islamic law was an autonomous and independent body of law with its own domain (ritual, private law) which enabled the Caliph to issue edicts (*qānūn*) on a broad range of problems of public administration (finance, tax, governance, crimes etc). By contrast, Zoroastrian law was more intertwined with the Persian monarchy, which resulted logically in a more active role of *mōbed*s in public administration. As a consequence of the separation of Islamic law from *qānūn* both bodies of law were administered by their own officials. Therefore, *qāḍīs*, being the specialists and trustees of Islamic law, were not charged with the implementation of state law since the state had its own officials to do so. To clarify this by way of an example: Muslim states recognized the need to control and regulate the affairs of the market place, as the Jewish community did, but reacted differently. As seen earlier, the task of the *agoranomos* was fulfilled by Rabbis, whereas in the Muslim state an independent official called *muḥtasib* was charged with this difficult job instead.

But this is only a tendency, not a rule. Since no separation of powers was established in theory, the judiciary was not separated from public administration either in theory or in practice. Nevertheless, courts were not authorized to fulfil administrative tasks, though some judges were. Ibn Ḥujayra, for example, was a judge, preacher and head treasurer at the same time in Egypt at the end of the seventh century.[29] His accumulation of jobs in various branches of administration was his personal achievement without intertwining the institutions he headed. We know of other judges who also held other jobs simultaneously. There were *qāḍīs* sitting in the *maẓālim* courts, too – particularly in the ᶜAbbāsid period, after the fall of the Barmakids when the power of the Muᶜtazilī *qāḍīs* was at its peak.[30] Consequently, judges were sometimes allowed to have several jobs at the same time in various branches of administration, but it was not the court which had administrative functions. By contrast, institutions of public administration such as the *muḥtasib* and the *maẓālim* court had very wide competencies, including, among others, jurisdiction.

Economic Background of Judges

It was well known among theorists of **Islamic law** that a solid financial background of judges was an important precondition to guarantee the professional quality of jurisdiction and to eliminate corruption as much as possible. It is small wonder, therefore, that authors on legal theory (such as al-Khaṣṣāf) emphasize the importance of the salary given to judges, which had to be financed by the treasury (*bayt al-māl*) because judges were fulfilling a community task.[31] Ibn Abī al-Dam expressed the same view and highlighted also the remuneration of a proper

29 Wadād al-Qāḍī 2009: 22.

30 Nielsen 1991: 933–5.

31 al-Khaṣṣāf 1978: 109.

sum.[32] Al-Māwardī also advocated payment by the treasury: according to him the remuneration of judges was 100 dirhams per month at the time of Caliph ᶜUmar, which was raised to a monthly sum of 500 dirhams during the Caliphate of ᶜAlī.[33] Recent research has shown that the salaries of judges (*rizq*) varied according to place and time. Meanwhile in Egypt and Syria judges were paid in dīnārs, the gold currency; in ᶜIrāq in dirhams, the silver currency (the ratio being approximately 1:12 in the eighth century). One can witness a drastic rise in judges' salaries in Egypt in 150 years between 680 and 830 (from a monthly 16 dīnārs to 168 dīnārs). By contrast, salaries in ᶜIrāq remained relatively stable at around 200 dirhams in the same period.[34] This is, perhaps, due to several economic reasons but further research is needed to clarify the issue.

State remuneration, however, resulted in losing financial independence and made the judges dependent on state authorities, which was among the reasons why legal scholars wishing to preserve their independence rejected appointments. At the same time Muslim theorists thought that a judicial office was incompatible with any active participation in commercial activities, primarily because it significantly damaged the judges' social prestige. Reality, however, was different. Muslim judges did participate in commercial activities, particularly when the state was unable to ensure their salary due to its financial difficulties. This rather unfortunate situation did not escape the attention of legal theorists who were unable to solve the contradiction. Al-Māwardī, wishing rather to prevent losing face than to present a proper solution to the dilemma, suggested that judges should not participate in business life directly and personally but through agents because in this way the judges' person would remain hidden and therefore their prestige would not be damaged.[35]

Prominent legal scholars not appointed to any court guaranteed their livelihood by civic occupations such as agriculture (Saḥnūn), commerce (Abū Ḥanīfa) or entered the service of the Caliph (Abū Yūsuf, al-Khaṣṣāf). More fortunate scholars such as al-Shaybānī, al-Juwaynī and al-Ṭabarī inherited considerable wealth, which guaranteed a solid material background to their scholarly career. By contrast, *mudarris*es participating in institutionalized legal education were usually poor people whose income was ensured by *waqfs* financing the *madrasa*, provided they had sufficient resources. Therefore, the teachers' income was dependent on the wealth and management of the *waqfs* which could not be influenced by them. Some scholars became indebted at the end of their life and were compelled to sell their house in order to ensure their livelihood. A part of their livelihood could be guaranteed by fees paid by students but – as seen previously – this practice was subject to debate. The heart of the matter was an underlying principle according to which (legal) education was not aimed at educating legal professionals for

32 Ibn Abī al-Dam 1987: 57–8.

33 al-Māwardī 1972: 295–6.

34 Wadād al-Qāḍī 2009: 17, 28–9.

35 Schneider 1990: 69–75.

lucrative jobs in the judiciary and public administration but at the acquisition of religious knowledge, which could not be dependent on the financial condition of the students. Unfortunately, not everyone was so honest in the service of the community, which is proven by ironic anecdotes about illegal modes of utilization of *waqf* property. The most frequently applied method of scholars wanting to ensure their livelihood without corruption was the accumulation of jobs in several *madrasas*.[36]

A similar approach could be discerned in **Jewish law**, since according to rabbinic understanding no one could make money out of the study of the Torāh because it was a sacred activity, the aim of which was not to acquire material advantages. As they put it: the Torāh is not 'a spade wherewith to dig'; moreover, those who profit from the words of the Torāh would destroy their own life.[37]

Reality was, however, more complicated. Similarly to Islamic law, financial support received from the political leader divided legal scholars: those entering the service of the *nāśī* and his Academy received their remunerations from him, which clearly resulted in a subordinate position.[38] These Rabbis of the *nāśī*/*rēsh galūta'* came into conflict with members of Academies preserving their independence. Independent Academies worked under more difficult circumstances because Jewish courts were free of charge. In the Islamic period the practice of responses contributed to some material relief because people putting questions also supplied the Academies with money. Towards the end of the Second Temple period one can find some rich people among the legal scholars, particularly among the Sadducees, who represented the wealthy upper class of society. This is why they could afford to be in judicial offices, primarily in the *Sanhedrīn*, without receiving a salary. By contrast, the Pharisees were more modest. These legal scholars provided for their livelihood with civic occupations, usually in commerce, as the example of Shimᶜeōn b. Shetaḥ shows.[39]

Commerce remained a source of living for centuries. In the *tannaic* period scholars participated in an international silk trade reaching from Nisibis to Arabia and India. This trade was facilitated by local synagogues offering accommodation to travelling merchants. The silk trade was further strengthened by commercial bases and a background industry in Syria and Palestine, from where silk could be transported to Rome. Silk trading was sometimes concentrated in the hands of larger families whose members were also members of the *nāśī*'s court. The silk trade of the period contributed to the strengthening of the two centres in Palestine and Babylon and to the improvement of their relationship. Thus the dispersion of Jews over a larger geographic area proved to be favourable commercially for those who were able to take advantage of the new situation, such as R. Yūdah and his

36 Makdisi 1981: 159–70; Triton 1957: 118.

37 Urbach 1975: 609; Neusner 1968: 126. This ethos is referred to also in Maimonides 1981a: 59b: 10.

38 Urbach 1975: 601.

39 Urbach 1975: 568, 572.

family in Palestine. Scholars who did not participate in commercial activities lived on agriculture – such as R. Ḥiya, who owned a large estate in the neighbourhood of Tiberias.[40]

Babylonian legal scholars such as Rav and Shamūʾel also participated in international trade. Rav in his admonitions addressed to his son advised him to focus on commerce instead of agriculture as it was a family tradition. Due to his skills in commerce and good family relations with the *rēsh galūtaʾ* (his daughter married the son of the *rēsh galūtaʾ*) he was appointed as market inspector (*agoranomos*). His opponent, Shamūʾel, was also a wealthy man who took an active part in trade and owned huge estates which he had cultivated by hired labourers and by his own slaves.[41]

Obviously, not everybody came from a rich family: R. Ḥisda started his career as an agricultural labourer; later he became a rich man as a beer brewer. Others rose to the prominent group of the rich by marriage. A few of them, such as R. Naḥman, became famous through their lavish circumstances and way of life.[42] R. Papa enriched himself as a brewer.[43] Ravaʾ, while he characterized himself as a person exclusively dealing with the study of the Torāh, was in fact a wine merchant owning land, slaves and boats and was on good terms with the royal court.[44] Some scholars, however, insisted on guaranteeing their livelihood by agriculture, though it lost its significance in the Babylonian economy. Rav Huna cultivated his land personally; when people went to him for adjudication he would request someone to irrigate his field instead of him[45] (in Islamic law it was Saḥnūn who represented this type of legal scholar).

Commercial privileges established by the Rabbis for themselves promoted their success and enrichment in commerce: scholars could put their goods in the market before other merchants arrived there; they were exempt from taxation, as a result of which they could keep their prices at a lower level than others. Moreover, as market inspectors they could easily assert their privileges. A further opportunity for gaining material benefit was that it was believed to be a pious act to bequeath larger sums of money to Rabbis in testaments, which was in fact done by rich testators.[46]

The system of taxation granted further financial advantages to Rabbis. Religious minorities like the Jews and the Christians had to pay a poll tax (*karga*). Collecting this tax was the task of the head of the community, and the sum was fixed in an accord concluded by the king and the community representative. This tax primarily hit the poor, as taxes usually do. Since the majority of the Babylonian Jews lived

40 Neusner 1965: 88–93.

41 Neusner 1966: 114–15, 135.

42 Neusner 1968: 127.

43 Neusner 1970: 173.

44 Urbach 1975: 613.

45 Urbach 1975: 610.

46 Neusner 1968: 126–30.

on agriculture and were poor this tax led to serious financial difficulties for many. Being unable to pay this tax, many people were forced into debt slavery. The rich who paid the tax for the poor made them work in their fields in exchange. This practice of abusing the situation of the poor was not considered to be a violation of the prohibition of usury because some wealthy Rabbis also took advantage of it. As a result, a particular group consisting of people of half free and half slave status emerged, the legal status of which caused a lot of headache for Jewish legal scholars in respect of wealth, marriage and other important legal considerations. It is no coincidence that the Talmūd contains several cases related to this problem.[47] It is worth mentioning in brief that in Zoroastrian law, too, there were persons being free and enslaved at the same time, who could have such a mixed status in a variety of proportions (e.g. 1/2:1/2; 1/10:9/10 etc.).[48]

Since the tax agreed upon had to be paid to the Persian king in due time (who did not care whether there were some people among the Jews who were exempt by their own laws), the exemption of Rabbis from taxation caused a serious problem for the *rēsh galūta'*. As a result, he had to levy the Rabbis' share on the rest of the society who, as shown, could hardly pay even their own share. Rabbis tried to justify their exemption from taxes with references to the Bible. In this respect Rava's opinion is perhaps the most extreme: according to him a rabbinic disciple may tell lies in the interest of tax evasion; moreover, he can even deny being a Jew. It is not known, however, whether Rava's opinion was shared by his colleagues and whether anyone availed himself of this opportunity. Therefore, as pointed out by Neusner, it is highly probable that Rabbis also paid their poll tax and the vehemence of rabbinic sources is only a theoretical protest which was never realized. What complicates matters is that there were Rabbis loyal to the *rēsh galūta'* who did not only pay their taxes but were also appointed as tax collectors by the *rēsh galūta'* (R. Ḥisda, R. Naḥman).[49] In addition to the poll tax other kinds of taxes had also to be paid, such as the bridge tax collected by a tax officer (*bazbāna*). Rabbis were exempted from the payment of this tax, which also gave them significant advantages together with their other privileges. These privileges were supported by the *rēsh galūta'*; otherwise he would have given them a salary for which he would have had to levy further taxes on the population.[50]

Rabbis did not have only poor people to work for them; they had also slaves. Therefore slavery was not condemned and Rabbis did nothing to improve the miserable situation of slaves. Some Rabbis did not even regard their slaves as humans: R. Ḥisda gave them to Arabs for sexual services; and according to R. Naḥman slaves were not even worth the bread they consumed. Rav Yūdah went as far as to declare that the liberation of a slave was a violation of a biblical rule

47 Neusner 1968: 25–7.

48 For more on this issue see Jany 2009.

49 Neusner 1969: 86–91.

50 Neusner 1969: 314–15.

(Lev. 25.46).[51] Other legal scholars joined this view, although argued differently: according to them refraining from the liberation of slaves was equal to observance of the *Shabbāt*; or, as Rabbah put it, their liberation was equivalent to the violation of the *Shabbāt*. There were, however, opinions running against this view: Abaye rather interpreted the texts in the interest of slaves, while according to Rava' a slave once liberated cannot again be forced into slavery by the creditor of his former master.[52]

Donations by the rich contributed to the income of the Rabbis, who tried to promote this practice by all means. According to R. 'Elīᶜezer, for instance, a person never giving any gift to scholars will never see a sign of blessing; moreover, ordinary people (*ᶜam hā-'āreṣ*) can only ensure resurrection for themselves this way.[53] In this regard Rabbis seem to follow the path of the Zoroastrian priesthood, who also claimed that donations given to them were pious acts (*ahlawdād*) helping the donator in the world to come.

Regarding finances, no basic change can be observed in the Islamic period. For instance, a noted legal scholar of the Academy, Nahray b. Nissim, was a merchant and a banker, just as the judge Hananel b. Shamū'el was. Maimonides, who made his living as a physician,[54] highlighted the importance of privileges granted to scholars.[55]

As far as **Zoroastrian** law is concerned, there is no information whatsoever so every important question remains in the dark. Although the Zoroastrian Church in general and some Fire-temples in particular were very rich due to donations given to them by the king and rich donors, the economic conditions of judges and priests working in remote parts of the land are unknown.

Judges and Politics

Politics was an important issue among **Jewish legal** scholars. Towards the end of the Second Temple period politics was among the factors which divided the Sadducees and Pharisees: the former favoured a pro-Rome policy and cooperation while the latter were famous for their anti-Roman attitude, ending sometimes in bloodbaths.

The policy toward Rome and Roman occupation continued to be a reason for division among legal scholars when Phariseeism became dominant. The followers of Hillel are said to have preferred a more peaceful policy based on compromise, while the followers of Shamm'ay advocated a policy of resistance instead. This may be an oversimplification and generalization. We know that legal scholars

51 Neusner 1968: 27–8.

52 Neusner 1969: 247.

53 Urbach 1975: 628.

54 Goitein: 1998: 419.

55 Maimonides 1981a: 63b: 10.

were divided about the revolt at the end of the Second Temple period: Rabban Simeon b. Gamalī'el supported it but R. Yōḥanān ben Zakk'ay did not. The latter came into contact with Vespasian and, after having been convinced that Jerusalem and the Temple were not to be saved, he left the city and received permission to settle in Yabneh, at the seat of the *bēt dīn*.[56] The uprising led by Bar Kokba' was supported by R. ᶜAqībah, who declared its leader Messiah – but had to pay for this with his life in the end. Other scholars were less enthusiastic and warned him about the consequences of his actions, but in vain. Revolts and battles were nevertheless only exceptions and Rabbis' involvement in politics can be observed in peaceful times, too. Some prominent Babylonian Rabbis had good relations with the Arsacide dynasty, whereas Shamū'el, the representative of the next generation of scholars, was a friend of the Persian King Shābuhr I.

Judges (*dayyān*) had political functions in the Islamic period as well because the judge was the representative of the local community, representing the interests of the Jews to the local authorities and sometimes even to the central government. These negotiations were far more political than legal in nature.[57]

Persian *mōbed*s participated in contemporary politics directly. As supporters of the royal power they ensured legitimacy and an ideology on which Sasanian power rested. In foreign policy they represented the king in diplomatic negotiations and performed important services to the king as emissaries. When war broke out they accompanied the ruler on his armed campaigns. When, however, a Sasanian king changed his policy and made some attempt to restrict their political influence, the leaders of the clergy immediately turned against him. When internal conflicts escalated, leading *mōbed*s did not stick and imprisoned a legitimate ruler or killed him, with which the Persian nobility gave them a helping hand. When only local interests were at play, some local potentates resisted royal authority on a district level. We know that Gufrashnasp, the mōbed of Adiabene, revolted against King Wahrām II and had a stronghold built in the mountains which the royal army was unable to conquer by military means.[58]

In **Islamic law** the political role of the judges was different. Since the *qāḍī* was appointed to implement Islamic law as an independent judge, he had (at least in theory) nothing to do with politics. Moreover, according to their own ethics, judges had to resist any political influence on their activities. Similarly to Jewish and Persian scholars Muslim scholars and judges sometimes represented the ruler in important diplomatic negotiations because they were well versed in debating techniques and were experts on how to argue in order to achieve a particular aim. Therefore, rulers rightly expected to profit from their routine in talks with partners of negotiations. Muslim rulers, however, generally refrained from sending them on negotiations to non-Muslims, which was probably due to the religious nature of the *qāḍī*'s office.[59]

56 Urbach 1975: 595–7.

57 Goitein 1999: 216.

58 Shaked 1990: 265–71.

59 Secall 2000: 250–51.

In crisis situations, when a state collapsed or was near to it, *qāḍīs* filled the power vacuum and took over political authority spontaneously as the only legitimate public authority. This happened in Hispania in the eleventh and twelfth centuries when the area, falling apart into smaller kingdoms, sank into anarchy. The rule of judges in the eleventh–twelfth centuries in the various cities lasted until the political situation was resolved and once again governance was taken over by ruling dynasties.[60]

On the other hand, judges were dependent on political authorities since the source of jurisdiction was the Caliph and not the judge. According to the well-known theory of delegation – elaborated by, among others, al-Māwardī – a judge acts only as a delegate of the authority who has nominated him for office. Therefore, a nomination could be withdrawn at any time and a judge could be deposed by the authority who had nominated him by his own will, this power being subject to no institutional control. In the first century judges were nominated by the governors but the ᶜAbbāsid Caliphs insisted on exercising this right personally, even in periods when their power was in decline.[61] If we add to this that judges were financially dependent on the treasury – receiving their salary from it or, worse, receiving nothing due to the financial situation of the budget – a dependency on the political authorities is clear. To these we can add that a *qāḍī* was dependent on the authorities in implementing his decision, particularly when a party concerned was of high social standing or had political influence. Therefore, although Weber was not right in saying that political authorities could freely interfere in a procedure before a *qāḍī*, he was nevertheless right in claiming that there was a chance for a kind of political manipulation since judges could be dismissed at any time – a right for an authority which could lead to abuses[62] – and was unable to implement his decision against persons of influence.

Social Environment of Judges

Concerning the social background of judges, Islamic and Jewish legal systems share the common feature of social mobility: that is, the office of judge was relatively open to anybody who could meet the required qualifications (disqualified persons were non-believers, women, slaves and the blind), while the Zoroastrian system resembled a caste-like rigidity. In respect of the social role and influence of judges, however, it is Zoroastrian law which is similar to the Jewish legal system while Islamic law is different because Jewish and Persian scholars had a variety of social responsibilities but Muslim judges had none.

---

60 Source material: al-Jokhanī 1914 and Ibn al-Hatīb 1970. See also Fierro 1994: 104–10.

61 Schacht 1991: 1.

62 Schneider 1993: 156.

Regarding the social background of judges, two parallel tendencies in **Jewish law** are noticeable. On the one hand there was openness with the help of which persons not belonging to learned dynasties were also welcomed, mostly from members of the *ᶜam hā-'āreṣ*, because the rabbinic ethos wanted to extend the knowledge of law to the entire society. Following from this attitude everyone was accepted into the circle of scholars who wanted to participate in learning. This openness was characteristic of Phariseeism and rabbinism since representatives of every social class could be found among its members: there were children of priests, rich landowners, merchants, hired labourers and even of proselytes.[63] One of the most famous legal scholars, R. ᶜAqībah, came from among the members of the *ᶜam hā-'āreṣ*; as a *homo novus* he became one of the most faithful representatives of the rabbinic worldview.[64] Shemᶜayah and 'Abṭalīōn, masters of Hillel, were children of converts – as was R. Me'īr, the respected debater.[65]

On the other hand, rabbinic families entertained closed ties. For example, all of the five noted Babylonian legal scholars participating in the court of R. Yūdah belonged to a single family (Ḥiyya, Rav, Rabba, b. Ḥana and the two sons of Ḥiyya) that played an important role not only in shaping jurisprudence but also in international silk trade.[66] The leadership of the Academies was in the hands of only a few families for generations. The continuation of family tradition meant also that a male child learned from his father or from a close male relative if they were noted Rabbis. R. Huna, head of the Sura Academy, himself taught his son, who later became a legal scholar as well as a judge. The sons of R. Naḥman and R. Ḥisda had similar careers. Abaye, the best-known scholar of his day and head of the Pumbedita Academy, also studied in a family circle. Rava', his major intellectual adversary, was the son of a Rabbi and came from a very rich family. At the same time the father of R. Naḥman b. Isaac did not belong to the narrow circle of scholars, though he was linked to them through the maternal line. In brief, despite the fact that Rabbis did not constitute a caste with rigid borders, the building of family networks with close social ties was characteristic of them: the majority of noted legal scholars were relatives or descendants of earlier scholars. Legal scholars knew one another since childhood and often they studied under the same master. Moreover, the children of rabbinic families intermarried, thus strengthening their previous bonds. As a result, a strong sense of belonging emerged.[67]

Family background was only an advantage; but talent, the acquisition of knowledge and proficiency in debates were indispensable. Therefore, a family tie in itself was not sufficient; scholarly and administrative functions could not be inherited easily. Consequently, a person of little talent was not kept up by his background, just as an outstanding scholar was not hindered by his common origin

63 Urbach 1975: 574.

64 Urbach 1975: 631.

65 Maimonides 1981a: 2a.

66 Neusner 1965: 93.

67 Neusner 1969: 286–90.

either. Ultimately competitive spirit was the decisive factor and family background was only of secondary significance. Since they supported the education of poor but talented students, this led to the paradox that while scholars despised and abused members of the ᶜ*am hā-'āreṣ*, a large number of their successors came from the common people who, as *homo novus*, picked up all the attitudes of scholars and shifted to the other side of the barricade. This is how they succeeded in properly providing for fresh blood and how they broke through the barrier stretching between them and society, avoiding their own shrinking into a real caste-like social class.[68]

The emergence of this sense of group identity did not hinder members in taking up positions against each other, for which scholarly debates ensured a proper forum. Since in these debates social prestige was also at stake, scholars attempted to gain the upper hand not only by legal argument but also by offending each other. Despising each other, using defamatory adjectives etc. naturally depended on how heated the debate was and also on the human qualities of the actors; therefore no generalization is in order. Rēsh Laqish, for instance, humiliated Rav by ostentatiously pretending not to know him (Who is this Rav? I do not know him), whereas others designated their adversaries mockingly 'a black pot', 'untrained judges' and 'foolish Babylonians'. Consequently some people were of the view that scholars died early because they constantly offended each other – but clashes stopped at that and no physical force was tolerated. We know only of one case in centuries when in a heated debate the followers of the school of Shamm'ay pulled out their swords and forced the Hillelites to accept their opinion.[69]

Despite this, there were more things linking scholars than separating them. Scholars formed close social groups – with their own style of speech, clothing, ways of walking and common eating habits – because they spent most of their time together at the Academy (for instance no fresh vegetables were to be consumed before the fourth hour, rejecting wine drinking, prohibiting the throwing of food, saying table blessings before eating). The Rabbis' appearance, behaviour, way of speech were regarded as precedents worthy of emulation in rabbinic circles, and particularly among students.[70]

The social role of Rabbis was complex. As far as *religion* is concerned, the sages vindicated prophetic functions for themselves because, according to their understanding, after the destruction of the Temple the prophetic function was performed by the scholars. Therefore, mystic experiences were just as much linked to the scholars as the ability to see into the future or to hear the Heavenly Voice. As a result, they considered themselves to be higher than prophets who were no scholars well versed in law.[71] The religious functions of legal scholars and judges continued

---

68 Neusner 1968: 103.

69 Urbach 1975: 620–24; 595. Rēsh Laqish seems to have been a troublesome fellow: according to a narrative in the Talmūd two legal scholars ascended to an upper chamber and took away the ladder in order to prevent him following them: Sanh 26a.

70 Neusner 1970: 150–57.

71 Urbach 1975: 578–9.

in the Middle Ages, when *dayyān*s were engaged in sermons and public lectures. Though this was not their exclusive competency, according to the documents of the Cairo Genizah this task claimed a considerable part of their time and energy.[72]

In *legal* practice the Rabbis' influence can be described by the following paradox: in areas where their cooperation was not needed they could hardly assert their influence, as they only had the opportunity of making moral appeals, exhortations and threats. Where, however, it was impossible to avoid the court's assistance – such as the declaration of divorce or in legal disputes deriving from contracts – they could influence legal practice enormously.[73] Rabbinic influence was considerable particularly in criminal law through the moderation and humanization of punishments and the introduction of new punishments. For instance, they introduced strangulation because it was a far less spectacular form of execution and as a result it could be hidden from the Roman authorities. Stoning was also reinterpreted and the original form of execution was replaced by pushing the condemned off a cliff. The criminal act called 'stubborn and rebellious son' was constantly reinterpreted. Since the original biblical commandment could not be changed, its preconditions were interpreted so restrictively that it was practically impossible to commit this crime.[74]

In a broader social context Rabbis had a series of social functions: they visited the sick[75] and, though they did not have any particular medical education, they were sometimes engaged in healings. Moreover, Rabbis also functioned as holy men bringing rain. In addition the interpretation of amulets and dreams was also part of the competencies of Rabbis, just as they were familiar with astrology, too.[76]

Thus, the social functions of Rabbis were extremely complex and society solicited their cooperation in a large number of problems. Yet the relationship between Rabbis and society was sometimes clouded, and occasionally mutual hatred and aversion would better qualify their feelings. The Rabbis' economic and tax privileges on the one hand, and their abuse of the poor and of slaves on the other, gave sufficient grounds for aggravating mutual conflicts. Arrogance of Rabbinic circles, which was regarded by many as their most characteristic feature, further enhanced internal tension. According to Liebermann rabbinic literature is a reflection of the ongoing war between Rabbis and the rest of society.[77] Examples of it abound: according to R. Me'īr a person giving his daughter to an *'am hā-'āreṣ* is like his throwing her in front of a lion; according to R. Hiyya a person studying the Torāh in the presence of an *'am hā-'āreṣ* is like a person raping his

72 Goitein 1999: 216.

73 Individual cases are analysed in Neusner 1968: 272–317; 1969: 191–251; 1970: 294–320.

74 M Sanh 8:4. This is why the Tōsefta' says that there has never been and there never will be such a son: Tos Sanh 11:6.

75 Urbach 1975: 607.

76 Neusner 1969: 330–70.

77 Referred to in Neusner 1968: 148.

fiancée. This view is also expressed symbolically in that Rabbis did not show up in the street together with *'am hā-'āreṣ*. A similar aversion of society was present at the same time, as animosity sometimes was greater than aversion felt towards non-Jews. As it was believed by R. 'Elīᶜezer, if the *'am hā-'āreṣ* did not need them for commerce, they would kill them.[78] Yet, as seen above, a high proportion of scholars actually came from among the *'am hā-'āreṣ*, though they rapidly acquired all aspects of the rabbinic way of life. Compulsory respect was attempted to be forced by administrative means: if someone did not show respect he could be excommunicated for 30 days (*nidduy*).[79]

The social standing of **Persian** *mōbed*s was different from that of the Jewish and Muslim legal scholars, first of all because they were priests. Moreover, a Zoroastrian priestly office was inherited in priestly families, which led Zaehner to regard *mōbed*s as a caste based on heritage, the aim of which was to safeguard the national religion.[80] This caste-like feature of the Sasanian period is still true today since priests of the Indian Parsees are members of priestly families who can trace their priestly ancestors back centuries. Therefore, social mobility witnessed among Jewish and Muslim scholars is lacking.

Being priests, *mōbed*s' primarily social functions were linked to various cults and rituals, while legal matters were only of secondary importance. Therefore, it was not a judge or a legal scholar who had various extra-legal social functions but it was a priest who fulfilled legal tasks, too – this being a tiny but important difference. Organized into a hierarchical church organization, Zoroastrian priests in general were not private individuals proud of their intellectual freedom and independence, but subordinate priests subject to control of the chief *mōbed* appointed by the monarch.[81] Moreover, as the Zoroastrian Church was linked to the Sasanian state with a variety of ties, the interest of the state was an additional factor which limited their intellectual independence. And it was in criminal law that the interests of the Persian state could be advocated and defended most successfully. As a result, contrary to the Jewish legal understanding, an opposite tendency could be discerned in criminal law: while Jewish scholars were advocates of the humanization of penalties, Persian *mōbed*s became the spokesmen of unlimited state power in criminal law, ending in torture, dehumanization of penalties and cruel methods of execution. When, however, the Sasanian state vanished and penalties could no longer be implemented, only some rhetoric threats remained which had no effect on post-Sasanian society, as acknowledged by the author of the Riwāyat-i Ēmēd-i Ashawahishtān (REA) himself.[82]

---

78 The various opinions are presented in Urbach 1975: 634–5.

79 Mantel 1965: 225. The neglect of a court decision to pay a debt could also result in excommunication.

80 Zaehner 1965: 164–5.

81 Gnoli 1989: 170.

82 REA 4: 6.

Despite these important differences, the social role of *mōbed*s shows some similarities with that of the Rabbis, particularly as far as their extra-legal functions are concerned. *Mōbed*s, just like Rabbis, were considered wise men by both the king and society at large and, therefore, their wise counsel was appreciated. Both Sasanian and post-Sasanian sources (Kār-Nāmag, al-Ṭabarī) prove that *mōbed*s were astrologers who calculated the king's coronation day, calculated the best time for a decision to be made and deciphered the dreams of the monarch.

In **Islamic** law extra-legal social functions of legal professionals are sporadic. As already seen, judges became professional technicians of Islamic law, masters of procedure – a position which did not enable them to escape the boundaries of their competencies. On the other hand, given the religious significance of Islamic law, *qāḍīs* were involved in the religious life of Muslims, which is why preachers can also be found among them.[83] *Qāḍīs* were also expected to visit the sick and to take part in funerals.[84]

Competencies expected of legal scholars did not go beyond the boundaries of law either because theology, grammar, medicine and other disciplines belonged to the competencies of other scholars. There were polymaths who were well versed in medicine, theology, philosophy and jurisprudence simultaneously (Ibn Sīna, Ibn Rushd), taking part in various activities (such as healing); but they were only exceptions and legal scholars were not expected to do more than they were qualified for. Making rain, interpreting omens and dreams, calculating astrological constellations and similar tasks were anyway contrary to their understanding of Islam, and were rather part of folk Islam they were fighting against.

Concerning their social background, we can find a similar social mobility as witnessed in Jewish law. Contrary to the Zoroastrian model, Muslim legal professionals formed no caste-like grouping. Anyone could become a Muslim legal scholar; it was just a matter of talent and diligence – particularly recalling that in theory a blind man, a slave or a woman could also become a legal scholar (but not a judge). Obviously, this is only theory because the educational system hindered women in acquiring the necessary knowledge. The way, however, was in fact open to slaves: one of the most prominent figures of early Islamic jurisprudence, al-Awzāʿī, is known to have been the descendant of an Indian slave.

Family relations were important among Muslim legal scholars, just as they were among Jewish Rabbis. Examples which prove that family relations were decisive in scholarly careers are numerous. To refer only to some well-known personalities: the Shāfiʿīte al-Juwaynī took over as head of the *madrasa* from his father; the Ḥanafite al-Kāsānī studied under al-Samarqandī, his father-in-law, and became his successor. There were also examples of legal scholars heading *madrasas* handing down their offices to their less talented offspring instead of a learned scholar, but these cases are presented by Muslim sources as cases of

83 Wadād al-Qāḍī 2009: 22.

84 Schneider 1990: 91–2.

abuse and corruption. Family relations were of importance also among judges, as witnessed by the emergence of *qāḍī* dynasties particularly in Andalusia.[85]

Another similarity between Jewish and Muslim legal scholars is that their social prestige rested on their knowledge and not on their priestly office as in Zoroastrianism. As a result, scholarly debates were organized to decide on both professional qualifications and legal questions, while in Zoroastrian law it was the Church which had to solve internal conflicts. Despite skirmishes and fragmentation by political and school affiliations, a sense of group identity and internal group solidarity emerged among Muslim legal professionals. This is illustrated in the unwillingness to revise the judgments of a former judge by his successor in office. As seen previously, chances of subsequent revisions dropped to the minimum and were limited to judgments obviously violating divine law. In sum, Jewish and Islamic law was 'more democratic' as far as access to knowledge and the social background of scholars are concerned, while Zoroastrian *mōbed*s organized themselves into a caste-like grouping forming a church hierarchy closed enough to prevent common people entering.

Finally, we can observe similarities between the Jewish and the Muslim legal scholars' religious understanding, too. Both Jewish and Muslim legal scholars considered themselves the heirs of the Prophet(s), embodying true religious knowledge – an intellectual monopoly they could vindicate for themselves because of the lack of any priesthood. Both Jewish and Muslim legal scholars followed the middle path. The Pharisees and later the Rabbis rejected both the attitude of the Sadducees advocating a literal interpretation of the texts and that of the Qumranians professing strong elitist views. The Pharisees and the Rabbis developed a more flexible interpretation of the Bible in legal matters than the Sadducees. On the other hand, they rejected the isolationist views of the Qumranians and stood for social participation, since their aim was to persuade all Israel about their views. They took effective measures against the Karaite movement emerging in the Middle Ages, too.

Muslim jurists also followed a similar middle-path attitude: they rejected both the theses of the *ahl al-Qur'ān* movement accepting exclusively the Qur'ān (which functionally corresponds to the 'only the Bible matters' attitude of the Sadducees) and those of the extreme traditionalists. Groups rejecting analogy, and hence even the possibility of rational argumentation (such as the Ẓāhirites), found themselves just as much outside orthodoxy as members of the *ahl al-Qur'ān*, or those of the *ahl al-naẓar*, advocating reason exclusively. Thus both the Rabbis and the *mujtahid*s advocated a method of interpretation by which they succeeded in maintaining the rule of the canonized texts, while they were flexible enough to ensure adaptation to the constantly changing conditions.

In Zoroastrianism there was no need for such a balancing because the hierarchical church organization could guarantee orthodoxy and orthopraxy by administrative means.

---

85 Müller 1999: 156–9; see also the chronicle of al-Jokhanī 1914.

Chapter 7
Conclusions: Lessons in Legal Sociology

Despite theological postulations and claims of legal theories Islamic, Jewish and Zoroastrian laws are jurists' law irrespective of the fact that the foundations of these legal systems were laid down in holy books (the Bible, the Qur'ān and the Awesta). *Fiqh* law is a jurists' law established by *mujtahid*s. Post-biblical Jewish law is also jurists' law, blossomed in the intellectual centres of the Palestinian and Babylonian Academies. The situation is similar in Zoroastrian law, with the significant difference that the rules of the Awesta put less emphasis on everyday legal practice than those of the Qur'ān and the Bible.

All three legal systems witnessed a transformation from customary law to 'religious law' by the subsequent theologization of existing norms. This process was linked to one person in Jewish and Islamic law despite the fact that it was a long process stimulated by different social and historical circumstances, while in Zoroastrian law such a person was missing. This conceptualization prevented political authorities from interfering in the realm of the law by lawmaking which was substituted by the law-finding activity of legal scholars. Therefore the efficiency of these legal systems depended on the quality of jurisprudence.

This primacy of jurisprudence cannot be compared to the position of Roman legal scholars whose interpretative activities only supplemented but did not substitute legislation. By contrast, in the legal systems studied here state legislation was absent and new rules were 'discovered' (that is, established) by legal scholars primarily on a case-by-case basis, through solutions of particular 'hard cases' and not as a result of broad-scale legal reforms. Since legal scholars were at the same time active in everyday legal practice as judges and legal consultants, new doctrines defined by them rested on their practice and were supported by scholarly reasoning. Consequently, 'lawmaking' and legal practice were not separate but intertwined, which resulted in a flexible understanding of law. This flexible attitude to law is proven by the fact that various legal doctrines were formulated on social practice, and were sometimes adjusted to the demands of the respective societies.

All this could not have been achieved without great personalities; moreover, the entire system was built on them. This is the reason why such great emphasis was laid on the qualification of legal scholars and judges and on legal education, during which not only already established legal norms but also legal theory, grammar and the techniques of interpretation were studied. Besides learning by heart, scholarly disputes were important during the course of education, aimed at preparing students for constant legal debates inside the courts and among legal scholars. The ultimate end of these debates was to establish legal rules but they rarely resulted in a full agreement. Therefore, majority rule as an auxiliary mechanism was introduced in Jewish law but Islamic law insisted on consensus. By contrast, in Zoroastrian law – where ecclesiastic hierarchy reduced scholarly debates – the autonomy of jurisprudence was narrowed.

The creativity of great personalities, a relatively free finding of law in the texts and the subsequent scholarly debates were the main factors which contributed to legal pluralism present in all three legal cultures. This legal pluralism was manifest both horizontally and vertically: horizontally among the various schools; vertically within the schools among scholars belonging to them. Taken as a whole, Islamic and Jewish legal systems are more pluralistic than Zoroastrian law in two important aspects. First, on the level of legal doctrines: in both Islamic and Jewish legal systems legal schools were developed with their own doctrines and methods, a fragmentation of utmost importance for Islamic law even today. By contrast, there are no such entities in Zoroastrian law – only legal debates on some irrelevant problems of ritual law which remained on an academic level but did not result in *madhhab*-like entities.

Second, if legal pluralism is taken as an opportunity for 'forum-shopping' (a term recently introduced by Ido Shahar),[1] – that is, litigants could choose from among a variety of legal forums where to turn – it is again Islamic and Jewish law which is more pluralistic. In the Islamic context a litigant could turn to the *qāḍī*, the *maẓālim* court, but could also rely on arbitration. In Jewish law, too, there are several forums at the disposal of the litigants: beside the rabbinic court one could turn to arbitrators, lay judges and to the Roman or Muslim courts, depending on historical circumstances. By contrast, in Sasanian Persia the competencies of the courts, *rads* and *mōbeds* were established and a litigant had to turn to these forums but not to others. Only arbitration was a way out for the litigants, but parallel forums were not at their disposal. This is in line with the interest of the Persian state and the Zoroastrian Church, both struggling for centralization, manifested in a hierarchical and less plural structure of the judiciary. If we remember that it is only Sasanian law where the system of appeal could be discerned – at least in a rudimentary form (from the *dādwar i keh* to the *dādwar i meh*, the chief *mōbed* and ultimately to the king) – the theory first formulated by Martin Shapiro seems to be confirmed by this additional argument. According to Shapiro, the judicial hierarchies serve the interest of the central government by reinforcing the ruler's legitimacy and extending his authority to the more remote places of his realm and by guaranteeing control over his officials. Therefore, wherever a central government exists, the emergence of an appellate court is very likely.[2] Sasanian Persia is a very good example to prove this claim. This line of reasoning could be supported from the opposite angle, too: it is Jewish law which has no appellate court, while at the same time there were no Jewish central governments. Islamic law is somewhere in between: although Caliphs wished to establish a central government they failed to do so at the end, notably during the second part of the ᶜAbbāsid period. And it

1 Shahar 2008: 123ff.

2 Referred to in Powers 1992: 315–16.

is exactly Islamic law where we can find a half-hearted solution: though *maẓālim* courts sometimes dealt with appeals they were not organized as courts of appeal.

While legal pluralism was an important element guaranteeing the autonomy of jurisprudence, at the same time it resulted in difficulties in the legal practice of the judiciary. Therefore, contrary to Weber's understanding, judiciaries in these legal systems produced no arbitrary judgments based on the personal will of the judge; but sometimes the problem was that 'too much jurisprudence' was involved: horizontal and vertical legal pluralism, based on long traditions of jurisprudence, offered various legal solutions for an individual case and a judge was sometimes in trouble deciding which to follow. It is, however, not arbitrary judgment but a rational choice from among the legal doctrines.

This is not to say, of course, that there were no abuses motivated by political, religious or personal reasons. They were, however, not system errors but the result of corruption or abuse of power from which Jewish law seems to be the most free. It is because Jewish courts operated in the service of various Jewish communities independently of any state intervention. By contrast, Zoroastrian courts served the interest of the state religion and the Persian monarch, which resulted in a less independent judiciary. *Sharīʿa* courts were somewhere in between, having a semi-autonomous position which was disturbed from time to time by both political reasons and personal corruption.

The flexible understanding of law was promoted by finely developed techniques of legal interpretation in both Jewish and Islamic legal cultures, while in Zoroastrian law less emphasis was laid on them. Contextual and grammatical interpretation of canonized texts – supplemented by other interpretative methods such as analogy, a fortiori argumentation and assumptions – ensured the intellectual basis which lent adequate flexibility to argumentation. Argumentation, in its turn, was focused on the result: at first the end result was defined, followed by the selection of the texts which could be interpreted with a variety of techniques by which one could 'reach' the required result. There are innumerable examples to prove this result-centred approach in all three legal systems.

Flexible legal understanding was restricted only by revealed legal norms; but this claim, too, needs some qualification. In the Zoroastrian system the Awesta, containing almost no legal rules, was definitely no obstacle. In Jewish law, it is true, the Bible defines legal rules, but by interpreting them as *ius dispositivum* in secular legal matters there was no hindrance to conclude agreements with rules no longer contradicting them. Established rules of *halakah*, too, were sometimes overruled: the Babylonian Talmūd contains about 30 cases in which judgments were at variance with legal norms.[3] *Contra legem* judicial decisions are also known from Zoroastrian Persian law.[4] Islamic law is perhaps more flexible. According to some Muslim legal scholars a collision between *naṣṣ* texts and the interest of the entire community is an issue worth considering. The basic principle was

3 Jackson 2002: 39.

4 See Chapter 6 about *kardag*.

already laid down by al-Ghazālī (eleventh–twelfth centuries), according to whom a *mujtahid* could disregard a norm of the *naṣṣ* texts provided the judgment was absolutely necessary and definitely followed the interest of the entire community of Muslims (*maṣlaḥa*). Al-Ṭawfī (fourteenth century) argued similarly: according to him the aim of the rules of the legal system was to serve the interest of the Muslim community; therefore, when a collision between a *naṣṣ* text and the interest of the community emerges jurists could consider the latter one. But this only in respect of secular matters because religious norms were only within the competency of God (this argumentation is similar to that of the Jewish legal scholars). Al-Jawziyya, a disciple of Ibn Taymiyya, was of a similar view. It is important to see, however, that with this line of argumentation no *mujtahid* wanted to provide a theory on how to disregard *naṣṣ* norms; they only wanted to show the flexibility of Islamic law.[5]

Politics was an important factor but not in a way Weber wanted us to believe. No Caliph was entitled to interfere in the course of the process in a *sharīʿa* court. Political considerations might enter the judiciary through the nomination and dismissal of the *qāḍīs*, a discretionary power of the Caliph guaranteed to him by the theory of delegation. Politics sometimes hindered the proper operation of the *sharīʿa* courts, which were sometimes weak enough to implement their judgments against persons of higher social standing and political influence, one of the factors which led to the establishment of the *maẓālim* courts. This court, however, does not fit into the *sharīʿa* system and is alien to Islamic legal theories. Therefore, it rather resembles the Persian model of centralization and implementation of state authority, a practice vehemently disputed and refuted by some Muslim legal scholars. By contrast, politics was sometimes an important factor in Sasanian litigation, notably in criminal cases in which Persian kings participated personally following political motivations. In so doing, neither institutional organization nor rules and postulates of jurisprudence could hinder a judgment based on discretion. Therefore, what Weber called Kadijustiz fits rather to the Persian courts of higher instances led by the king and the *mōbedān mōbed*.

The net results of the findings of the present study are summarized in Tables 7.1–7.6.

5 Poya 1998: 236–41.

Table 7.1 Ontology

Islamic law	**Jewish law**	**Zoroastrian law**
Basic principles of the legal system are defined by revelation and a holy book (Qur'ān)	Basic principles of the legal system are defined by revelation and a holy book (Torāh)	*Some* basic principles of the legal system are defined by a holy book (Awesta)
Revelation contains substantial legal norms, too; God as Lawmaker, no legal changes possible in this set of norms	Revelation contains substantial legal norms, too; God as Lawmaker, no legal changes possible in this set of norms	Revelation contains *no* legal norms, only the underlying principles and the notion of cosmic order, called *arta*
Substantial legal norms are rooted mainly in legal practice, the theologization of law being a later development	Substantial legal norms are rooted mainly in legal practice, the theologization of law being a later development	Substantial legal norms are rooted mainly in legal practice, the theologization of law being a later development
Theologization of law was the result of a long process and legal debates; Muslim tradition, however, sees it as the work of a single person (al-Shāfiʿī)	Theologization of law was due to a long process and political changes; Jewish tradition, however, emphasizes the role of one single person (Ezra)	Theologization of law was due to a long process, but Zoroastrian tradition knows no individual playing an extraordinary role in it
The theory of the divine origin of the non-Qur'ānic law: prophetic *sunna*	The theory of the divine origin of the non-biblical law: oral law	There is *no* theory of divine origin of the non-Awestic law
Jurists' law: in the absence of formal lawmaking the elaboration of the substantial part of the legal system was the work of generations of legal scholars; outstanding importance of legal reasoning and flexible interpretation	Jurists' law: the elaboration of the substantial part of the legal system was the work of generations of legal scholars; only limited role of formal lawmaking, outstanding importance of legal reasoning and flexible interpretation	Jurists' law: the elaboration of the substantial part of the legal system was the work of generations of legal scholars; *flexible* interpretation of legal texts having only *secondary importance* in contrast to the conservatism of theological-legal doctrines; only sporadic evidence for formal lawmaking
The culture is based on textual coherence	The culture was based originally on ritual coherence, later changed to textual coherence	The culture is based on *ritual coherence*, textual coherence having only secondary importance
Law defined as a way to God	Law defined as a way to God; the idea of the covenant with God	Law is *not* regarded as the way to God; no proof for the idea of the covenant with God
Law as the most important part of the religion	Law as the most important part of the religion	Not law but ritual is the most important element of the religion
Leading role of non-priestly individuals: legal scholars (*mujtahid*); lack of formal, ecclesiastic institutions	Leading role of non-priestly individuals: legal scholars (Rabbi); lack of formal, ecclesiastic institutions	Leading role of the priesthood; formal ecclesiastic organizations

Table 7.2 Legal procedure

Islamic law	Jewish law	Zoroastrian law
Distinction between private and criminal procedure	Distinction between private and criminal procedure	Distinction between private and criminal procedure
Very formal procedure and procedural law	Very formal procedure and procedural law	Very formal procedure and procedural law
High-ranking elaboration of procedural legal terms	High-ranking elaboration of procedural legal terms	High-ranking elaboration of procedural legal terms
Professional judge	Professional and lay judges, an attempt to disqualify the latter	Professional judge
Only one judge in the court	3, 23, or 71 judges sitting together in the court	No clear rules, sometimes only 1 judge, sometimes more; 3 institutions in the court system (*rad, dādwar, mōbed*)
Legal academy is only the place of study, not of judgment	Legal academy is at the same time a court	Legal academy is only the place of study, not of judgment
No appellate court system; later revision of the judgment only by the next judge in the same position	No appellate court system; later revision possible only by a higher court composed of more outstanding legal scholars	Revision of the judgment by the king or high priest on a non-regulated basis
No laypersons attached to the courts	No laypersons attached to the courts	No laypersons attached to the courts
Legal experts attached to the courts: *shūra*	No legal experts attached to the courts because the judge is a legal scholar at the same time	The high priest as the legal advisor to the king; his ruling is, in theory, binding for the ruler
Apprentices take no part in the procedure	Apprentices could take part in the procedure	Apprentices take no part in the procedure
The trial is considered the duel of the parties; to establish the material truth is not the task of the judge	The trial is considered the duel of the parties; to establish the material truth is not the task of the judge	The trial is considered the duel of the parties, but to establish the material truth is the moral obligation of a judge
The importance of compromise and friendly termination of the procedure	The importance of compromise and friendly termination of the procedure	No proof of preferring compromise
Oral procedure	Oral procedure	Oral procedure
The importance of the oral testimony of the witnesses, written documents playing only secondary role	The importance of the oral testimony of the witnesses, written documents playing only secondary role	The importance of the oral testimony of the witnesses, written documents playing only secondary role

Number of witnesses: 2, 4	At least 2 witnesses	Sometimes the testimony of 1 witness is enough for judgment
Control of the witnesses: both their testimony and personal dignity during and outside the trial	Control of the witnesses: both their testimony and personal dignity during and outside the trial	No information in this regard, but there was no control in politically motivated criminal procedures
Detailed legal norms to disqualify unworthy judges and witnesses	Detailed legal norms to disqualify unworthy judges and witnesses	No information
Professional witnesses	Professional witnesses	No professional witnesses
Oaths playing only auxiliary role	Oaths playing only auxiliary role	Greater emphasis on oaths and ordeals
Assistant personnel attached to the court	Scribes attached to the court	Scribes attached to the court, the official of the oaths (*war sālār*)
Negative attitude towards advocates	Negative attitude towards advocates	Negative attitude towards advocates
No torture in criminal procedures	No torture in criminal procedures	Torture allowed in criminal procedures
In implementing the sentence in a criminal case both the witnesses (stoning) and the injured party (and relatives) take part (retaliation)	In implementing the sentence in a criminal case the witnesses take part (stoning); the role of the injured party (and relatives) is debated	Implementing the sentence in a criminal case is the task of the armed forces (royal guards, soldiers)
The existence of prisons, not for sentences but only for preventive detention	The existence of prisons, not for sentences but only for preventive detention	The existence of prisons, not for sentences but only for preventive detention
No bail	No bail	Bail in criminal procedure
The proper behaviour of the judges regulated in works of a literary genre: the existence of the *adab al-qāḍī* literature	No such a literary genre, but the proper behaviour of a judge set in the legal literature	No such a literary genre; no existing source contains such norms
The emphasis on the judge's neutrality towards the parties	The emphasis on the judge's neutrality towards the parties	Penalties for the party who breaks the rules of proper conduct during the trial
Detailed norms set for judges concerning toilet, behaviour and greeting forms during the trial	Detailed norms set for judges concerning toilet, behaviour and greetings during the trial	No proof of norms for judges concerning toilet, behaviour and greetings during the trial
Negative attitude towards women appearing in court	Negative attitude towards women appearing in court	Negative attitude towards women appearing in court
Days for trials: Monday, Thursday	Days for trials: Monday, Thursday	No proof for preferred days
The parties are seated during the trial	The parties stand; only by permission could take a seat	The parties stand, three steps away from the court

No positive discrimination of a legal scholar when judging his case	An attempt at positive discrimination of a legal scholar in his own case	No information in this regard
Judges are, in theory, responsible for their judgments materially and personally, but in practice removal of a judge rarely happens	Rabbinical judges are materially not liable for their judgments; financial liability of lay judges for wrong judgments	No information in this regard; in modern times, however, revision of the judgment is possible; social boycott of the judge also happens
Great deal of extra-procedural functions: supervision of endowments (*waqf*), marrying widows, management of the wealth of orphans, guardianship of insane persons, supervision of prisons	Limited number of extra-procedural functions: guardianship of the wealth of orphans, widows and insane persons	Great deal of extra-procedural functions: supervision of endowments, marrying widows, guardianship of the wealth of widows and orphans

Table 7.3 Judges and jurisprudence

Islamic law	**Jewish law**	**Zoroastrian law**
The study of law is a value in itself	The study of law is a value in itself	The study of law is not a value in itself
Study as the most valuable activity	Study as the most valuable activity	Ritual is more important than the study of law
The function of a judge and a legal scholar is separated: *qāḍī, mujtahid, muftī*	The function of a judge and a legal scholar is not separated	The function of a judge and a legal scholar is separated
High-level professional qualifications for judges and legal scholars alike; later the level of qualification – most of all for the judges – was lowered	Permanent high-level professional qualification	The professional qualification of a judge and a legal scholar was distinguished
A judge could be a legal scholar, but not ex officio	A judge is a legal scholar at the same time	A judge is not necessarily a legal scholar
The early emergence of the legal schools: originally personal, later doctrinal schools	The development of the legal school is a relatively late phenomenon; personal and doctrinal schools	The development of the legal school is a late phenomenon; personal and not doctrinal schools
Legal scholarship focuses on both ritual and civic aspects of life	Legal scholarship focuses on both ritual and civic aspects of life	Legal scholarship focuses mainly on ritual law
Topics of legal scholarship are problems of everyday legal practice: less academic discipline	Topics of legal scholarship are in part problems out of touch with reality: semi-academic discipline	Majority of the topics of legal scholarship are irrelevant to everyday life: academic discipline

Legal pluralism: all doctrines of the legal schools are operative and have legal effect	Legal pluralism: all doctrines of the legal schools are operative and have legal effect	Legal pluralism: all doctrines of the legal schools are operative and have legal effect
Emergence of a legal genre to compare the various doctrines of the legal schools: *ikhtilāf* literature	No *sui generis* legal genre to compare the doctrines of the schools, but its topics are incorporated into the legal literature: Talmūd	No *sui generis* legal genre to compare the doctrines of the schools, but its topics are incorporated into the legal literature: Shāyast-nē-shāyast
Importance of scholarly debates: the informal assessment of scholarly qualification	Importance of scholarly debates: the informal assessment of scholarly qualification	Scholarly debates are less important
Formal guarantee of qualification: *ijāzat al-tadrīs*	Formal guarantee of qualification: *semikah*, *rēshūta'*	Qualification formally guaranteed by the ecclesiastic hierarchy
Consensus (*ijmāᶜ*) of the scholars is a legal source	A legal norm could be established by majority vote, no need for consensus	Consensus (*hamdādestānīh*) is a source for judgment
Development of legal theory (*uṣūl al-fiqh*) as a discipline	No legal theory as a discipline in itself	No legal theory as a discipline in itself
Jurisprudence's link to society through individual requests for legal solution: *fatwā*	Jurisprudence's link to society through individual requests for legal solution: *responsa*	Jurisprudence's link to society through individual requests for legal solution: *riwāyat*
New legal literature: the *fatwā*-collections	New legal literature: the responsa collections	New legal literature: the *riwāyat*-collections
Legal scholars are private individuals; the neglect of all administrative posts (including the court) because they are perceived as a threat to scholarly independence	Legal scholars are private individuals; an ambivalent attitude toward administrative posts	Legal scholars are members of the clergy
Judgments are not arbitrary, but rest on high-level legal scholarship	Judgements are not arbitrary, but rest on high-level legal scholarship	Politically motivated judgments are sometimes arbitrary (criminal cases), otherwise rest on legal scholarship
Legal scholars afraid to commit wrongly while judging and therefore a tendency not to judge	Legal scholars afraid to commit wrongly while judging and therefore a tendency not to judge	No trace of such an idea

Table 7.4 Legal training

Islamic law	Jewish law	Zoroastrian law
Legal training is independent of other training and discipline	Legal training is independent of other training and discipline	Legal training is part of the education of the priesthood
A separate place and institution for study: mosque, *madrasa*	A separate place and institution for study: *bēt talmūd, bēt midrāsh, yeshībah*	A separate place and institution for study: ērbedestān
Form of education: orality	Form of education: orality	Form of education: orality
Method of education: to learn by heart	Method of education: to learn by heart; the Rabbi as a source of imitation and as the living Torāh	Method of education: to learn by heart
Centrality of legal debates during education	Centrality of legal debates during education	No place for legal debates during education
Repetitors to help students: *muʿīd*	Repetitors to help students: *tanna*	No repetitors, no formal aids to help students memorize the texts
Academic grade of the students established by legal debates in classes	Academic grade of the students established by legal debates in classes	No formal academic grade of the students
Seating in the classroom as the symbol of students' academic grade	Seating in the classroom as the symbol of students' academic grade	The absence of such a symbol
Less ceremonial respect for the professor	Ceremonial respect for the professor	No information in this regard
Ambivalent relationship between professor and student: rivalry and assistance	No friendly relationship between professor and student	The professor's full authority over the student's life: a spiritual master
No corporal punishment of the students	The right to corporal punishment of the students	The right to corporal punishment of the students
The cyclic nature of education depends on the seasonality of agriculture	The cyclic nature of education depends on the seasonality of agriculture: semesters	The cyclic nature of education: 3–4 months
No monastic community during the education	A monastic community evolves during the study time	No information
Study lasts for years	Study lasts for years	Study lasts for years
No women in the classes	No women in the classes	The right of women to study
Scholarly debates, *fatwā* on Fridays	Scholarly debates during the break between two semesters: *kalla* month	No information

No scientific lectures for the general public	Scientific lectures for the general public on holidays: *pirqa*	No scientific lectures for the general public
Studying is a material burden on the student	Studying is a material burden on the student	Studying is a material burden, but business has predominance in education
No tuition fee in theory because religious education is free, referring to the Prophet's teaching activities	No tuition fee in theory because religious education is free, referring to Moses	No such theory
Professors are underpaid legal scholars, sometimes judges, too	Professors are judges at the same time; they make their living not from education	Professors are priests
Indirect political influence by financial aid	Indirect political influence by nominations	Political control and influence through church organization

Table 7.5 Judges and society

Islamic law	**Jewish law**	**Zoroastrian law**
Practice (*ᶜada*) is not a formal source of law, but the courts take it into consideration in judging a case	Practice (*minḥāg*) could be in certain circumstances a source of law; courts take it into consideration during litigation	Practice could be a source of a judgment
Existence of the legal practice of the courts (*ᶜamal*), but no precedent law	No precedent law, but former decisions could affect later judgments	Existence of the legal practice of the courts (*kardag*), but no precedent law; practice could overrule legal doctrine
Lawful means to achieve unlawful gains: widespread use of legal techniques called *ḥiyal* to assist business activity; *ḥiyal* literature as a genre	Lawful means to achieve not strictly lawful gains: flexible interpretation of existing norms	Lawful means to achieve unlawful gains through *kardag*
Judge as public administrator: not ex officio	Some public administrative function of a judge: supervision of the market	Public administrative functions: *mōbed* as the head of a city or province
Monthly salary for a judge from the budget (*rizq*)	No salary from the state	No information
Business activity of the judges: condemned but tolerated because of the insufficiency of their salary	Business activity of judges is accepted as the basis for their livelihood	Business is a despised activity for priests
Judges are not wealthy persons	Some of the Rabbis are wealthy persons: businessmen, landholders, owners of slaves	High priests are wealthy persons

Judges have no business privileges; they are advised not take part in business activities	Business privileges: being exempt from tax, market privileges	No privileges
Judges and legal scholars are sometimes envoys of the ruler; independent political role only during political crisis	Judges and legal scholars are representatives of the community; political negotiations with foreign rulers (the Roman emperor included)	*Mōbeds* as diplomats, political advisors to the king
Social mobility: legal scholarship is open to all	Social mobility: legal scholarship is open to all	*No* social mobility; caste-like nature: priestly dynasties even in modern times
Group identity and professional cohesion which prevents establishing liability for wrong decisions or sentencing corrupt judges	Group identity and professional cohesion which guarantees privileges for the members	Group identity and professional cohesion which guarantees privileges for the members
Awareness of superiority, but no sign of confrontation with society at large	Arrogance, disdain, confrontational attitude towards society	Awareness of superiority; hierarchical relation towards society; in modern times: degradation of priestly office; law-rank social prestige among people
Symbols of group identity: special attire	Symbols of group identity: special attire, behaviour and speaking manner	Symbols of group identity: special attire
Non-priestly person, religious significance is the consequence of social position	Non-priestly person, religious significance is the consequence of social position	Priest
No extra-legal social functions	Variety of extra-legal social functions: physician, holy man	Variety of extra-legal social functions: astrologer, political advisor, interpreter of dreams
Independent in the conduct of a particular case	Independent in the conduct of a particular case	Not independent in the conduct of a particular case: a king could be personally involved
Exposed to outside political influence by the ruler's right to nomination and dismissal	Not exposed to outside political influence	No reliable information
Wide-scale corruption	Almost no hint to corruption	Wide-scale corruption
Possibility for forum-shopping	Possibility for forum-shopping	No possibility for forum-shopping

Table 7.6 Legal sociology

Islamic law	**Jewish law**	**Zoroastrian law**
Jurists' law, no formal lawmaking	Jurists' law, formal lawmaking only exceptionally	Jurists' law, formal lawmaking only exceptionally
Doctrines of jurisprudence is a legal source	Doctrines of jurisprudence is a legal source	Doctrines of jurisprudence is a legal source
Flexible adaptation to social reality	Flexible adaptation to social reality	Flexible adaptation to social reality
Outstanding role of great personalities both in legal practice and legal scholarship	Outstanding role of great personalities both in legal practice and legal scholarship	Outstanding role of great personalities both in legal practice and legal scholarship
Freedom and independence of jurisprudence	Freedom and independence of jurisprudence	Freedom and independence of jurisprudence *restricted* by ecclesiastic hierarchy
Importance of legal training to uphold tradition	Importance of legal training to uphold tradition	Legal training is less important to uphold tradition
Flexible legal system guaranteed by legal pluralism and flexible methods of interpretation	Flexible legal system guaranteed by legal pluralism and flexible methods of interpretation	Legal system is *less* flexible, but capable of renewal; restricted legal pluralism; less flexible methods of interpretation

As it is evident from the above systematic comparisons, Jewish and Islamic legal theory and legal practice share a great many common characteristics, while Zoroastrian law is a somewhat similar but distinct legal culture.

Bibliography

Primary Sources

Ammianus Marcellinus (1940): *Rerum Gestarum Libri XXXI*. Translated by J. C. Rolfe. The Loeb Classical Library. Harvard University Press: Cambridge, MA and London.

Bāqir aṣ-Ṣadr, Muḥammad (2003): *Lessons in Islamic Jurisprudence*. Translated by Roy P. Mottahedeh. Oneworld Publications: Oxford.

Bazak, J.–Passamaneck S. (1978): *Jewish Law and Jewish Life. Selected Rabbinical Responsa*. Union of American Hebrew Congregations: New York.

Boyce, M. (1968): *The Letter of Tansar*. Istituto Italiano per il Medio ed Estremo Oriente: Rome.

Braun, O. (1915): *Ausgewählte Akten Persischer Märtyrer*. Kempten; Munich.

Firdausī (1379): *Sh*āhnāme (ed. Mohl). Tehrān.

Gershevitch, I. (1959): *The Avestan Hymn to Mithra*. Cambridge University Press: Cambridge.

Al-Ghazzālī (1351): *Nasīhat al-mulūk*. Galāl al-Dīn Hemmātī: Tehrān.

Herodotus (1921): *History*. Translated by A. D. Godley. The Loeb Classical Library. Harvard University Press: Cambridge, MA and London.

Hoffmann, G. (1880): *Auszüge aus syrischen Akten Persischer Märtyrer*. Abhandlungen für die Kunde des Morgenlandes, VII Band, No. 3. Leipzig.

Humbach, H.–Elfenbein, J. (1990). Ērbedestān. *An Avesta-Pahlavi Text*. Munich.

Ibn Abī al-Dam (1987): *Kitāb adab al-qāḍī*. Bayrūt: Libnān.

Ibn al-Hatīb (1970): *Kitāb ᶜamāl al-ᶜalām. Islamische Geschichte Spaniens*. Übersetzung *der ᶜamāl al-ᶜalām und ergänzende Texte* von Wilhelm Hoenerbach. Artemis Verlag: Stuttgart and Zürich.

Ibn Isfandiyār (1942): *Tārikh-i Ṭabaristān*. ᶜAbbās Iqbāl: Tehrān.

Ibn Rushd (1994): *Bidāyat al-mujtahid*. The Distinguished Jurist's Primer, vol. I (tr. Nyazee, I.). Center for Muslim Contribution to Civilization. Garnet Publishing Ltd: Reading.

Ibn Rushd (1996): *Bidāyat al-mujtahid*. The Distinguished Jurist's Primer, vol. II (tr. Nyazee, I.). Center for Muslim Contribution to Civilization. Garnet Publishing Ltd: Reading.

al-Jokhanī (1914): *Historia de los jueces de Córdoba*. Texto árabe y traducción española por Julián Ribera. Madrid.

Josephus Flavius (1963): *Jewish Antiquities*. Translated by Ralph Marcus–Allen Wikgren. The Loeb Classical Library. Harvard University Press: Cambridge, MA and London.

Kay Qābūs (1342): *Nasihat-nāme* (Qābūs-nāme). Tehran (ed. Saᶜid Nefisī).

Kent, R. (1953): *Old Persian. Grammar, Lexicon, Texts*. American Oriental Society: New Haven.

al-Khaṣṣāf (1978): *Kitāb adab al-qāḍī*. The American University in Cairo Press.

Khadduri, M (1961): *Al-Shāfiᶜī's Risāla. Treatise on the Foundations of Islamic Jurisprudence*. Translated with an Introduction, Notes, and Appendices. Baltimore.

Kotwal, F. M. (1969): *The Supplementary Texts to the Šāyest-nē-šāyest*. Copenhagen.

Kotwal, F. M.–Kreyenbroek. Ph. (1992): *The Hērbedestān and Nērangestān, vol. I. Hērbedestān*. Studia Iranica, Cahier 10. Paris.

Kotwal, F. M.–Kreyenbroek. Ph. (1995): *The Hērbedestān and Nērangestān, vol. II*. Nērangestan, Fragard 1. Studia Iranica, Cahier 16. Paris.

Kotwal, F. M.–Kreyenbroek, Ph. (2003): *The Hērbedestān and Nērangestān, vol. III*. Nērangestān, Fragard 2. Studia Iranica, Cahier 30. Paris.

Macuch, M. (1981): *Das Sasanidische Rechtsbuch 'Mātakdān I Hazār Dātistān' (Teil II)*. Steiner Verlag: Wiesbaden.

Macuch, M. (1993): *Rechtskasuistik und Gerichtspraxis zu Beginn des siebenten Jahrhunderts in Iran. Die Rechtssamllung des Farrohmard i Wahrāmān*. Harrassowitz: Wiesbaden.

Maimonides, M. (1981): *Pīrūš ha-Mišnayōt li-ha-Rambīm. Maskot Sanhedrin*. Edition: Rosner, F. (1981): *Maimonides' Commentary on the Mishnah. Tractate Sanhedrin*. Sepher-Hermon Press: New York.

Maimonides, M. (1981a): *Mishneh Torah* (*Yad ha-ḥazakah*). Edition: Hyamson, M. (1981): *Mishneh Torah. The Book of Knowledge*. Feldheim Publishers: Jerusalem and Nanuet, NY.

Mālik ibn Anas (1987): *Muwaṭṭa'*. Bayrūt. *Al-Muwaṭṭa of Imam Malik ibn Anas. The First Formulation of Islamic Law*. Translated by A. A. Bewley. Kegan Paul International: London, 1989.

al-Masᶜūdī (1989): *Murūj al-dhahab wa ma'ādin al-jawāhir fī-l tārikh*. Bayrūt: Libnān.

Al-Māwardī (n.d.): *Al-Ahkām al-Sultāniyya w'al-Wilāyāt al-Dīniyya*. Bayrūt: Libnān.

Al-Māwardī (1972): *Adab al-qāḍī*. Maṭbuᶜat al-ᶜānī: Baghdād.

Majallat al-aḥkām al-ᶜadliyya. Translated by Tyser, Demetriades and Effendi. The Other Press: Kuala Lumpur: Malaysia, 2001.

Al-Miṣri (1994): *ᶜUmdat al-Sālik*. Translated by Nuh Ha Mim Keller. Amana Publications: Beltsville, MD.

de Menasce, J. (1973): *Le Troisiéme Livre du Dēnkart*. Klincksieck: Paris.

Neusner, J. (1988): *The Mishnah*. Yale University Press: New Haven and London.

Neusner, J. (2002): *The Tosefta*, vol. I–II. Hendrickson Publishers: Peabody, MA.

Nöldeke, Th. (1879): *Geschichte der Perser und Araber zur Zeit der Sasaniden*. E. J. Brill: Leiden.

Nyberg, H. S. (1964): *A Manual of Pahlavi*. Harrassowitz: Wiesbaden.

PERIKHANIAN, A.–GARSOIAN, N. (1997): *The Book of A Thousand Judgements. A Sasanian Law Book*. Persian Heritage Series, No. 39. Mazda Publishers: Costa Mesa, CA and New York.

SAFA-ISFEHANI, N. (1980): *Rivāyat-i Hēmīt-i Ašawahistān. A Study in Zoroastrian Law*. Harvard Iranian Series, vol. 2. Harvard University Printing Office: Cambridge, MA.

AL-SHĀFIᶜĪ, M. I. (1940): *Risāla*. Cairo.

SHAKED, SH. (1979): *The Wisdom of the Sasanian Sages (Dēnkard VI)*. Persian Heritage Series 34. Westview Press: Boulder, CO.

AL-SHAYBĀNĪ (1975): *Kitāb al-siyar: al-qānūn al-dawlī al-islāmī* (ed. MAJID KHADDURI). Bayrūt: Libnān.

KHADDURI, M (1966): *The Islamic Law of Nations. Shaybānī's Siyar*. The Johns Hopkins Press: Baltimore.

SMITH, B. K.–DONIGER, W. (1992): *The Laws of Manu*. Penguin Books: London.

TALMUD (1987): *Hebrew–English Edition of the Babylonian Talmud. Seder Nezikin, Sanhedrin*. The Soncino Press: London.

TAVADIA, J. 1930. *Šāyast-nē-šāyast. A Pahlavi Text on Religious Customs*. Walter de Gruyter: Hamburg.

VAHMAN, F. (1986): *Ardā Wirāz Nāmag. The 'Iranian Divina Comedia'*. Curzon Press: London.

VÖÖBUS, A. (1962): *The Statutes of the School of Nisibis*. ETSE: Stockholm.

WEST, W. (1885): *Menog i Khrad. The Spirit of Wisdom*. Sacred Books of the East 24, Oxford. (Today West's interpretation is untenable on several points; a new and complete edition of the text has not yet been published.)

WILLIAMS, A. V. (1990): *The Pahlavi Rivāyat Accompanying the Dādestān ī Dēnīg. Part I: Transliteration, Transcription and Glossary. Part II: Translation, Commentary and Pahlavi Text*. The Royal Danish Academy: Copenhagen.

Secondary Literature

ALBERTZ, R. (1997): Die Theologisierung des Rechts im Alten Israel. *Religion und Gesellschaft. Studien zu ihrer Wechselbeziehung in den Kulturen der Antiken Vorderen Orients*, 115–31. Ugarit-Verlag: Münster.

BAILEY, H. W. (1943): *Zoroastrian Problems in Ninth-Century Books*. Ratanbai Katrak Lectures. Oxford University Press: Oxford.

BAKHTIAR, L. (1996): *Encyclopaedia of Islamic Law. A Compendium of the Major Schools*. ABC International Group: Chicago.

BARTHOLOMAE, CHR. (1922): *Zum sasanidischen Recht IV*. Heidelberg.

BERQUE, J. (1986): ᶜAmal. *The Encyclopaedia of Islam*, vol. I, 427–9. E. J. Brill: Leiden.

BLENKINSOPP, J. (2001): Was the Pentateuch the Civic and Religious Constitution of the Jewish Ethnos in the Persian Period? *Persia and Torah. The Theory of*

Imperial Authorization of the Pentateuch (ed. Watts, W.), 41–62. Society of Biblical Literature No. 17. Atlanta.

Bousquet, G. H. (1986): ᶜĀda. *The Encyclopaedia of Islam*, vol. I, 170–73. E. J. Brill: Leiden.

Burton, J. (1990): *The Sources of Islamic Law. Islamic Theories of Abrogation.* Edinburgh University Press: Edinburgh.

Boyce, M. (1975): *A History of Zoroastrianism*, vol. I. E. J. Brill: Leiden.

Calder, N. (1993): *Studies in Early Muslim Jurisprudence.* Clarendon Press: Oxford.

Carlsen, B. H. (1984): The cakar marriage contract and the cakar children's status in Mātiyān I Hazār Dātistān and Rivāyat I Emēt I Ashavahishtān. *Middle Iranian Studies* 16, 103–14. Leuven.

Cohen, A. (1991): *An Introduction to Jewish Law.* Feldheim Publishers: Jerusalem and Nanuet, NY,

Cohn, H. (1974): Bet Din. In: Elon, M. (1974): *The Principles of Jewish Law.* Keter Publishing House: Jerusalem.

Cohn, H. (1974a): Practice and Procedure. In: Elon, M. (1974): *The Principles of Jewish Law.* Keter Publishing House: Jerusalem.

Cohn, H. (1974b): Blood-avenger. In: Elon, M. (1974): *The Principles of Jewish Law.* Keter Publishing House: Jerusalem.

Cohn, H. (1974c): Capital punishment. In: Elon, M. (1974): *The Principles of Jewish Law.* Keter Publishing House: Jerusalem.

Cohn, H. (1974d): Witness. In: Elon, M. (1974): *The Principles of Jewish Law.* Keter Publishing House: Jerusalem.

Cohn, H. (1974e): Perjury. In: Elon, M. (1974): *The Principles of Jewish Law.* Keter Publishing House: Jerusalem.

Cohn, H. (1974f): Oath. In: Elon, M. (1974): *The Principles of Jewish Law.* Keter Publishing House: Jerusalem.

Coulson, N. J. (1956): Doctrine and practice in Islamic law: One aspect of the problem. *Bulletin of the School of Oriental and African Studies (BSOAS)*, 18, 211–26.

Coulson, N. J. (1959): Muslim custom and case-law. *Die Welt des Islams* 6, 13–24.

Coulson, N. J. (1964): *A History of Islamic Law.* Edinburgh University Press: Edinburgh.

Dandamaev, M.–Lukonin, V. (1989): *The Culture and Social Institutions of Ancient Iran.* Cambridge University Press: Cambridge.

Daube, D. (1960): *Texts and Interpretation in Roman and Jewish Law.* A Special London University Lecture (School of Oriental and African Studies, 21 November 1961). Published in: *Collected Works of David Daube*, vol. 1 (ed. Carmichael, C.), 173–204. University of California Press: Berkeley, 1992.

Daube, D. (1960a): Three notes having to do with Johannan ben Zaccai. *Journal of Theological Studies* 11, 53–62. Published in: *Collected Works of David Daube*, vol. 1 (ed. Carmichael, C.), 425–37. University of California Press: Berkeley, 1992.

DAUBE, D. (1971): Dissent in the Bible and Talmud. *California Law Review* 59, 784–94. Reprinted in: *Collected Works of David Daube*, vol. 1 (ed. CARMICHAEL, C.), 425–37. University of California Press: Berkeley, 1992.

DAUBE, D. (1986): Witness in Bible and Talmud. Oxford Centre for Postgraduate Hebrew Studies. Reprinted in: *Collected Works of David Daube*, vol. 1 (ed. CARMICHAEL, C.), 401–24. University of California Press: Berkeley, 1992.

DAUBE, D. (2000): The Laying on of Hands: *Collected Works of David Daube*, vol. 2 (ed. CARMICHAEL, C.), 599–616. University of California Press: Berkeley.

DHALLA, M. N. (1922): *Zoroastrian Civilization*. Oxford University Press: Oxford.

ELMAN, Y. (2003): *Returnable Gifts in Rabbinic and Sasanian Law*. (Presentation at the Irano-Iudaica conference on 16 September 2003, Piliscsaba.)

ELON, M. (1974): *The Principles of Jewish Law*. Keter Publishing House: Jerusalem.

ELON, M. (1974a): Arbitration. In: *The Principles of Jewish Law*. Keter Publishing House: Jerusalem.

ELON, M. (1994): *Jewish Law. History, Sources, Principles*, vols I–IV. The Jewish Publication Society: Jerusalem.

FALK, Z. (1972): *Introduction to Jewish Law of the Second Commonwealth*. E. J. Brill: Leiden:

FAIR, C. CHR. (2008): *The Madrassah Challenge. Militancy and Religious Education in Pakistan*. United States Institute of Peace Press: Washington DC.

FIERRO, M. (1994): The Qāḍī as Ruler. In: *Saber Religioso y Poder Politico en el Islam. Actas del Simposio Internacional* (Granada, 15–18 October 1991), 71–117. Madrid.

FIKENTSCHER, W. (1980): Synapeik und eine synepeische Definition des Rechts. *Entstehung und Wandel Rechtlicher Traditionen* (ed. FIKENTSCHER–FRANKE–KÖHLER), 53–119. Verlag Karl Alber: Freiburg and Munich.

FREEDMAN, D. N. (1990): The Formation of the Canon of the Old Testament: The Selection and Identification of the Torah as the Supreme Authority of the Postexilic Community. *Religion and Law. Biblical-Judaic and Islamic Perspectives* (ed. FIRMAGE–WEISS–WELCH). Eisenbrauns: Winona Lake, IN.

FREI, P. (2001): Persian Imperial Authorization: A Summary. *Persia and Torah. The Theory of Imperial Authorization of the Pentateuch* (ed. WATTS, W.), 5–41. Society of Biblical Literature No. 17. Atlanta.

FRIED, L. (2001): 'You Shall Appoint Judges': Ezra's Mission and the Rescript of Artaxerxes. *Persia and Torah. The Theory of Imperial Authorization of the Pentateuch* (ed. WATTS, W.), 63–89. Society of Biblical Literature No. 17. Atlanta.

FRIED, L. (2004): *The Priest and the Great King. Temple–Palace Relations in the Persian Empire*. Biblical and Judaic Studies, vol. 10. Eisenbrauns: Winona Lake, IN.

FYZEE, A. A. A. (1974): *Outlines of Muhammadan Law*. Oxford University Press: Oxford.

GILAT, D. (1968): *R. Eliezer Ben Hyrcanus. A Scholar Outcast*. Bar Ilan University Press: Ramat-Gan, Israel.

GLENN, P. (2000): *Legal Traditions of the World. Sustainable Diversity in Law*. Oxford University Press: Oxford.

GNOLI, G. (1989): *The Idea of Iran. An Essay on its Origin*. Istituto Italiano Per Il Medio Ed Estremo Oriente: Rome.

GOITEIN, S. D. (1955): *Jews and Arabs. Their Contacts through the Ages*. Schocken Books Inc.: New York.

GOITEIN, S. D. (1988): *A Mediterranean Society*, vol. II. University of California Press: Berkeley, Los Angeles, London.

GOITEIN, S. D. (1999): *A Mediterranean Society*, vol. V. University of California Press: Berkeley, Los Angeles, London.

GOLDZIHER, I. (1890): A hadísz kialakulása. *Az iszlám kultúrája* I. Budapest, 1981, 192–490.

GOODBLATT, D. (1975): *Rabbinic Instructions in Sasanian Babylonia*. E. J. Brill: Leiden.

GRABBE, L. (2001): The Law of Moses in the Ezra Tradition. *Persia and Torah. The Theory of Imperial Authorization of the Pentateuch* (ed. WATTS, W.), 91–113. Society of Biblical Literature No. 17. Atlanta.

HAKIM, B. S. (1993): The Role of 'Urf in Shaping the Traditional Islamic City. *Islam and Public Law. Classical and Contemporary Studies* (ed. MALLAT, CH.), 141–59. Arab and Islamic Laws Series. Graham & Trotman: London and Boston.

HALIVNI, D. W. (1986): *Midrash, Mishnah, and Gemara. The Jewish Predilection for Justified Law*. Harvard University Press: Cambridge, MA.

HALIVNI, D. W. (1991): *Peshat and Derash. Plain and Applied Meaning in Rabbinic Exegesis*. Oxford University Press: New York.

HALLAQ, W. B. (1984): Was the gate of ijtihad closed? *International Journal of Middle East Studies* 16, 3–41. New York.

HALLAQ, W. B. (1986): On the authoritativeness of Sunni consensus. *International Journal of Middle East Studies* 18, 427–54. New York.

HALLAQ, W. B. (1993): Was al-Shafī'i the master architect of Islamic jurisprudence? *International Journal of Middle East Studies* 25, 587–605. New York.

HALLAQ, W. B. (1994): From Fatwās to Furūᶜ: Growth and change in Islamic substantive law *Islamic Law and Society* 1/1, 29–65. E. J. Brill Leiden.

HALLAQ, W. B. (1996): Ifta' and Ijtihad in Sunni Legal Theory: A Developmental Account. *Islamic Legal Interpretation. Muftis and their Fatwas* (ed. MASUD–MESSICK–POWERS), 33–44. Harvard University Press: Cambridge, MA, and London.

HALLAQ, W. B. (1997): *A History of Islamic Legal Theories*. Cambridge University Press: Cambridge.

HALLAQ, W. B. (2001): From Regional to Personal Schools of Law? *Islamic Law and Society* 8/1, 1–26. E. J. Brill: Leiden.

Hallaq W. B. (2001a): *Authority, Continuity, and Change in Islamic Law*. Cambridge University Press: Cambridge.

Hallaq W. B. (2009): *Sharī'a. Theory, Practice, Transformations*. Cambridge University Press: Cambridge.

Hecht–Jackson–Passamaneck–Piatelli–Rabello (1996): *An Introduction to the History and Sources of Jewish Law*. Clarendon Press: Oxford.

Hefner, R. W. (2007): Introduction: The Culture, Politics, and Future of Islamic Education. In: Hefner, R. W.–Zaman, M. Q: *Schooling in Islam. The Culture and Politics of Modern Muslim Education*, 1–40. Princeton University Press: Princeton.

Hefner, R. W.–Zaman, M. Q (2007): *Schooling in Islam. The Culture and Politics of Modern Muslim Education*. Princeton University Press: Princeton.

Hennigan, P. (2004): *The Birth of a Legal Institution*. E. J. Brill: Leiden.

Hjerrild, B. (1992): The Parsees in Bombay and their Present Problems. *The Middle East – Unity and Diversity. Papers from the Second Nordic Conference on Middle Eastern Studies* (ed. Palva–Vikor). Copenhagen.

Hourani, G. F. (1964): The Basis of Authority of Consensus in Sunnite Islam. *Studia Islamica* 21, 13–60.

Hurvitz, N. (2000): Schools of law and historical context: Re-examining the formation of the Ḥanbalī *Madhhab*. *Islamic Law and Society* 7/1, 37–64. E. J. Brill: Leiden.

Huxley, A. (2002): *Religion, Law and Tradition. Comparative Studies in Religious Law*. RoutledgeCurzon: London.

Jackson, B. (2002): Judaism as a Religious Legal System. In: *Religion, Law and Tradition. Comparative Studies in Religious Law* (ed. Huxley, A.). RoutledgeCurzon: London.

Jany, J. (2001): Judicial contradictions in Ardakhšēr's succession. *Acta Orintalia* 54, 203–9. Budapest.

Jany, J. (2004): The idea of a trust in Zoroastrian law. *Journal of Legal History* 25/3, 269–86.

Jany, J. (2004a): The 'Ghost Marriage' in Zoroastrian Law. *Transeuphraténe 28. Recherches pluridisciplinaires sur une province de l'empire achéménide*, 117–31. Gabalda: Paris.

Jany, J. (2005): The four sources of law in Zoroastrian and Islamic jurisprudence. *Islamic Law and Society* 12/3, 293–334. E. J. Brill: Leiden.

Jany, J. (2006): The jurisprudence of the Sasanian sages. *Journal Asiatique* 294/2, 291–323. Paris.

Jany, J. (2007): Criminal law in Sasanian Persia. *Iranica Antiqua* 42, 347–86. Peeters Publishers: Gent.

Jany, J (2008): Persian influence on the Islamic office of *qāḍī al quḍāt*: A reconsideration. *Jerusalem Studies in Arabic and Islam* 34, 149–69. The Hebrew University of Jerusalem: Jerusalem.

Jany, J (2009): The legal status of slaves in Sasanian and Talmudic law. *With Wisdom as a Robe. Qumran and other Jewish Studies in Honour of Ida Fr*öhlich (ed. Dobos–Kőszeghy). Phoenix Press: Sheffield.

Jany, J (2010): Private litigation in Sasanian law. *Iranica Antiqua* 45, 395–419. Peeters Publishers: Gent.

Jany, J (2011): Sasanian law. e-Sasanika 14, 35 (www.humanities.uci.edu/sasanika/pdf/e-sasanika14.pdf).

Johansen, B. (1993): Legal Literature and the Problem of Change: The Case of the Land Rent. *Islam and Public Law. Classical and Contemporary Studies* (ed. Mallat, Ch.), 29–47. Arab and Islamic Laws Series. Graham & Trotman: London and Boston.

Johansen, B. (2002): Signs as Evidence: The Doctrine of Ibn Taymiyya (1263–1328) and Ibn Qayyim al-Jawziyya (D. 1351) on Proof. *Islamic Law and Society* 9/2, 168–93. E. J. Brill: Leiden.

Juynboll, G. H. A. (1983): *Muslim Tradition. Studies in Chronology, Provenance, and Authorship of Early Ḥadith.* Cambridge University Press: Cambridge.

Kamali, M. (1993): Appellate Review and Judicial Independence in Islamic Law. *Islam and Public Law. Classical and Contemporary Studies* (ed. Mallat, Ch.), 49–84. Arab and Islamic Laws Series. Graham & Trotman: London.

Kirschenbaum, A. (1991): The role of punishment in Jewish criminal law: A chapter in rabbinic penological thought. *The Jewish Law Annual* 9, 123–43.

Knoppers, G. (2001): An Achaemenid Imperial Authorization of Torah in Yehud? *Persia and Torah. The Theory of Imperial Authorization of the Pentateuch* (ed. Watts, W.), 41–62. Society of Biblical Literature No. 17. Atlanta.

Kramer, D. (1990): *The Mind of the Talmud. An Intellectual History of the Bavli.* Oxford University Press: Oxford and New York.

Kreyenbroek, Ph. (1994): On the concept of spiritual authority in Zoroastrianism. *Jerusalem Studies in Arabic and Islam* 17, 1–15. The Hebrew University of Jerusalem: Jerusalem.

Libson, G. (1996): The Age of the Geonim. *An Introduction to the History and Sources of Jewish Law* (ed. Hecht et al.), 197–244. Clarendon Press: Oxford.

Libson, G. (2003): *Jewish and Islamic Law. A Comparative Study of Custom during the Geonic Period.* Harvard Series in Islamic Law, vol. 1. Harvard University Press: Cambridge, MA.

Lifshitz, B. (1996): The Age of the Talmud. *An Introduction to the History and Sources of Jewish Law* (ed. Hecht et al.), 169–96. Clarendon Press: Oxford.

Lightstone, J. (1993): The institutionalization of the rabbinic Academy in late Sassanid Babylonia and the redaction of the Babylonian Talmud. *Studies in Religion* 22/2. Waterloo, Ontario.

Lentz, W. (1970): The 'Social Function' of the Old Iranian Mithra. *W. B. Henning Memorial Volume*, 245–55. Lund Humphries: London.

Lowry, J. (2002): Does Shāfiʿī Have a Theory of Four Sources of Law? *Studies in Islamic Legal Theory* (ed. Weiss, B. G.). E. J. Brill: Leiden.

LÖSCHNER, H. (1971): *Die dogmatischen Grundlagen des šī'itischen Rechts. Eine Untersuchung zur modernen imāmitischen Rechtsquellenlehre.* Erlanger Juristische Abhandlungen, Vol. 9. Carl Heymanns Verlag KG: Cologne.

MACKENZIE, D. N. (1971): *A Concise Pahlavi Dictionary.* Oxford University Press: London, New York, Toronto.

MACUCH, M. (1985): Die Zeitehe im Sasanidischen Recht – ein Vorläufer der Šīᶜitischen Mutᶜa-Ehe in Iran? *Archeologische Mitteilungen aus Iran* 18, 187–203. Dietrich Reimer Verlag: Berlin.

MACUCH, M. (1994): Die sasanidische Stiftung 'für die Seele' – Vorbild für den islamischen waqf? *Iranian and Indo-European Studies. Memorial Volume of Otakar Klima* (ed. VAVROUSEK, P.), 163–80. Enigma Corporation: Prague.

MACUCH, M. (1995): Herrschaftskonsolidierung und zoroastrisches Familienrecht: Zum Verhältnis von Kirche und Staat unter den Sasaniden. *Iran und Turfan. Beiträge Berliner Wissenschaftler, Werner Sundermann zum 60. Geburtstag gewidmet* (ed. RECK, Ch.–ZIEME, P.). Harrassowitz: Wiesbaden.

MACUCH, M. (1999): Iranian legal terminology in the Babylonian Talmud in the light of Sasanian jurisprudence. *Irano-Judaica* 4, 91–101. Ben-Zvi Institute: Jerusalem.

MACUCH, M. (2002): The Talmudic expression 'servant of the fire' in the light of Pahlavi legal sources. *Jerusalem Studies in Arabic and Islam* 26, 109–29. The Hebrew University of Jerusalem: Jerusalem.

MACUCH, M. (2003): An Iranian Legal Term in the Babylonian Talmud and in Sasanian Law. (Lecture at a conference, 16 September 2003, Piliscsaba.)

MAKDISI, G. (1981): *The Rise of Colleges.* Edinburgh University Press: Edinburgh.

MALLAT, CH. (1993): *The Renewal of Islamic Law. Muhammad Baqer as-Sadr, Najaf and the Shi'i International.* Cambridge Middle East Library 29. Cambridge University Press: Cambridge.

MANTEL, H. (1965): *Studies in the History of the Sanhedrin.* Harvard University Press: Cambridge, MA.

MASUD, M. K.–MESSICK, B.–POWERS, D. S. (1996): Muftis, Fatwas and Islamic legal Interpretation. *Islamic Legal Interpretation* (ed. MASUD, M. K.–MESSICK, B.–POWERS, D. S.), 3–32. Harvard University Press: Cambridge, MA and London.

MELCHERT, CH. (1997): *The Formation of the Sunni Schools of Law. 9th–10th Centuries C. E.* E. J. Brill: Leiden.

MELCHERT, CH. (1999): How Hanafism came to originate in Kufa and traditionalism in Medina. *Islamic Law and Society* 6/3, 319–47. E. J. Brill: Leiden.

MELCHERT, CH. (2001): Traditionist-jurisprudents and the framing of Islamic law. *Islamic Law and Society* 8/3, 383–406. E. J. Brill: Leiden.

MENSKI, W. (2002): *Hindu Law as 'Religious' System. Religion, Law and Tradition. Comparative Studies in Religious Law* (ed. HUXLEY, A.), 108–26. RoutledgeCurzon: London.

MESSICK, B. (1996): Media Muftis: Radio Fatwas in Yemen. *Islamic Legal Interpretation* (ed. MASUD, M. K.–MESSICK, B.–POWERS, D. S.), 310–20. Harvard University Press: Cambridge, MA and London.

MIRSKY, S. K. (1959): Types of Lectures in the Babylonian Academies. *Essays on Jewish Life and Thought Presented in Honour of Salo Wittmayer Baron.* Columbia University Press: New York.

MILLER, M.–HAYES, J. (1986): *A History of Ancient Israel and Judah.* The Westminster Press: Philadelphia.

MOTZKI, H. (2002): *The Origins of Islamic Jurisprudence. Meccan Fiqh before the Classical Schools.* Leiden: Brill.

MÜLLER, CHR. (1999): *Gerichtspraxis im Stadtstaat* Córdoba. *Zum Recht der Gesellschaft in einer mālikitisch–islamischen Rechtstradition des 5./11. Jahrhunderts.* E. J. Brill: Leiden, Boston, Cologne.

NEUSNER, J. (1965): *History of the Jews in Babylonia I.* E. J. Brill: Leiden.

NEUSNER, J. (1966): *History of the Jews in Babylonia II.* E. J. Brill: Leiden.

NEUSNER, J. (1968): *History of the Jews in Babylonia III.* E. J. Brill: Leiden.

NEUSNER, J. (1969): *History of the Jews in Babylonia IV.* E. J. Brill: Leiden.

NEUSNER, J. (1970): *History of the Jews in Babylonia V.* E. J. Brill: Leiden.

NEUSNER, J. (1971): *The Rabbinic Traditions about the Pharisees before 70* (3 vols). E. J. Brill: Leiden.

NEUSNER, J. (1981): *Method and Meaning in Ancient Judaism.* Scholars Press: Chico, CA.

NEUSNER, J. (1984): *Israel and Iran in Talmudic Times.* University Press of America: Lanham, MD.

NEUSNER, J. (1990): *Judaism, Christianity, and Zoroastrianism in Talmudic Babylonia.* Scholars Press: Atlanta.

NEUSNER, J. (1993): *Judaism and Zoroastrianism at the Dusk of late Antiquity. How Two Ancient Faiths Wrote Down Their Great Traditions.* Scholars Press: Atlanta.

NEUSNER, J.–SONN, T. (1999): *Comparing Religions through Law. Judaism and Islam.* Routledge: London and New York.

NIELSEN, J. S. (1991): Maẓālim. *The Encyclopaedia of Islam*, vol. VI, 933–5. E. J. Brill: Leiden.

OLMSTEAD, A. T. (1948): *History of the Persian Empire.* The University of Chicago Press: Chicago.

PERRY, J. R. (1978): Justice for the underprivileged: The ombudsman tradition in Iran. *Journal of Near Eastern Studies* 37, 203–15.

PIATTELLI, D.–JACKSON, B. (1996): Jewish Law during the Second Temple Period. *An Introduction to the History and Sources of Jewish Law* (ed. HECHT et al.), 19–56. Clarendon Press: Oxford.

POWERS, D. (1986): *Studies in Qur'an and Hadīth. The Formation of the Islamic Law of Inheritance.* University of California Press: Berkeley.

POWERS, D. (1992): On Judicial Review in Islamic Law. *Law & Society Review* 26, 314–41.

POWERS, D. (1993): Futyā in Medieval Spain and North Africa. *Islam and Public Law. Classical and Contemporary Studies* (ed. MALLAT, CH.), 85–106. Arab and Islamic Laws Series. Graham & Trotman: London and Boston.

POWERS, D. (1994): Kadijustiz or qāḍī-justice? A paternity dispute from fourteenth-century Morocco. *Islamic Law and Society* 1/3, 332–66. E. J. Brill: Leiden.

POYA, A. (1998): Iğtihad und Glaubensfreiheit. Darstellung einer islamisch-glaubensfreiheitlichen Idee anhand sunnitisch-rechtsmethodologischer Diskussion. *Der Islam* 75/2, 226–58. Walter de Gruyter: Berlin.

RABELLO, M. (1996): Jewish and Roman Jurisdiction. *An Introduction to the History and Sources of Jewish Law* (ed. HECHT et al.), 141–67. Clarendon Press: Oxford.

REBSTOCK, U. (1999): A qāḍī's errors. *Islamic Law and Society* 6/1, 1–37. E. J. Brill: Leiden.

ROBERTS, R. (1925): *The Social Laws of the Qoran. Considered, and Compared with Those of the Hebrew and Other Ancient Codes.* Curzon Press: London.

ROSEN, L. (1980): Equity and discretion in a modern islamic legal system. *Law and Society Review* 15/2, 217–45.

ROSEN, L. (1989): *The Anthropology of Justice. Law as Culture in Islamic Society.* Lewis Henry Morgan Lectures Series. Cambridge University Press: Cambridge.

ROSEN, L. (2000): *The Justice of Islam. Comparative Perspectives on Islamic Law and Society.* Oxford University Press: Oxford.

SANDERS, E. P. (1990): *Jewish Law from Jesus to the Mishnah. Five Studies.* SCM Press: London.

SCHACHT, J. (1925): Die arabische *hijal*-Literatur. *Der Islam* 15, 211–32. Walter de Gruyter: Berlin.

SCHACHT, J. (1934): Zur sozilogischen Betrachtung des islamischen Rechts. *Der Islam* 22, 207–38. Walter de Gruyter: Berlin.

SCHACHT, J. (1950): *The Origins of Muhammadan Jurisprudence.* Oxford University Press: Oxford.

SCHACHT, J. (1964): *Introduction to Islamic Law.* Oxford University Press: Oxford.

SCHACHT, J. (1970): Law and Justice. *The Cambridge History of Islam*, vol. 2B, 539–68. Cambridge University Press: Cambridge.

SCHACHT, J. (1986): Hiyal. *The Encyclopaedia of Islam*, vol. III, 510–13. E. J. Brill: Leiden.

SCHACHT, J. (1991): Maḥkama. *The Encyclopaedia of Islam*, vol. VI, 1–3. E. J. Brill: Leiden.

SCHNEIDER, I. (1990): *Das Bild des Richters in der 'Adab al-Qāḍī' Literatur.* Islam und Abendland, vol. 4. Peter Lang: Frankfurt, New York, Paris.

SCHNEIDER, I. (1993): Die Merkmale der Idealtypischen qāḍī-Justiz – Kritische Anmerkungen zu Max Webers Kategorosierung der islamischen Rechtsprechung. *Der Islam* 70/1, 145–59. Walter de Gruyter: Berlin.

SCHNEIDER, I. (1995): Imprisonment in pre-classical and classical Islamic law. *Islamic Law and Society* 2/2, 157–73. E. J. Brill: Leiden.

SCHWARTZ, M (1989): Pers. Saugand Xurdan, etc. 'To Take An Oath' (Not To Drink Sulphur). Études *Irano-Aryannes offertes a Gilbert Lazard*, 293–5. Paris.
SECALL, M. (2000): Rulers and Qāḍīs: Their relationship during the Nasrid Kingdom. *Islamic Law and Society* 7/2, 235–55. E. J. Brill: Leiden.
SEGAL, P. (1996): Jewish Law during the Tannaitic Period. *An Introduction to the History and Sources of Jewish Law* (ed. HECHT et al.), 101–39. Clarendon Press: Oxford.
SERJEANT, R. B. (1991): The Caliph ᶜUmar's Letters to Abū Mūsā al-Ashᶜarī and Muᶜāwiya. *Customary and Shariᶜah Law in Arabian Society*. Variorum Reprints: London.
SERJEANT, R. B. (1995): Sunnah, Qur'ān, ᶜUrf. *Law and the Islamic World. Past and Present* (ed. TOLL–PEDERSEN), 33–49. The Royal Danish Academy of Sciences and Letters: Copenhagen.
SERRANO, D. (1996): La practica legal ('amal) en el-Andalus durante los siglos X–XII, a traves de los Maḏāhib al-ḥukkām fī nawāzil al-aḥkām de Muḥammad Ibn ᶜIyāḍ. *Qurtuba* 1, 171–92.
SERRANO, D. (2000): Legal practice in an Andalusī-Maghrebī source from the twelfth-century CE. *Islamic Law and Society* 7/2, 187–234. E. J. Brill: Leiden.
SHAHAR, I. (2008): Legal pluralism and the study of Shariᶜa courts. *Islamic Law and Society* 15, 112–41. E. J. Brill: Leiden.
SHAKED, SH. (1990): Administrative Functions of Priests in the Sasanian Period. *Proceedings of the First European Conference of Iranian Studies* Part I–II (ed. GNOLI–PANNAINO), 261–73. Rome.
SHAPIRO, M. (1980): Islam and Appeal. *California Law Review* 68, 350–80.
SHILO, SH. (1974): Dina demalkhuta dina. In: ELON, M. (1974): *The Principles of Jewish Law*. Keter Publishing House: Jerusalem.
SHILO, SH. (1982): The contrast between Mishpat Ivri and Halakhah. *Tradition* 20, 91–100.
SIMONSEN, J. B. (1995): The Development of Doctrine and Law Schools. *Law and the Islamic World. Past and Present* (ed. TOLL, CH.–PETERSEN, J. S.), 75–80. The Royal Danish Academy of Sciences and Letters: Copenhagen.
SMITH, M. (1971): *Palestinian Parties and Politics that Shaped the Old Testament*. Columbia University Press: New York and London.
STAUSBERG, M. (2002): *Die Religion Zarathustras*, vols 1–2: Geschichte, Gegenwart. Kohlhammer: Stuttgart.
STAUSBERG, M (2004): *Die Religion Zarathustras*, vol. 3: Rituale. Kohlhammer: Stuttgart.
STEMBERGER, G. (1996): *Introduction to the Talmud and Midrash*. Second edition. T&T Clark: Edinburgh.
STEWART, D. (2008): The students' representative in the law colleges of 14th-century Damascus. *Islamic Law and Society* 15, 185–218. E. J. Brill: Leiden.
TALBI, M (1996): Sahnūn. *The Encyclopaedia of Islam*, vol. VIII, 843. E. J. Brill: Leiden.
TURNER, B. (1974): *Weber and Islam*. Routledge: London.

TRITON, A. S. (1957): *Muslim Education in the Middle Ages*. Luzac and Co. Ltd: London.

TYAN, E. (1960): *Histoire de l'organisation judiciaire en pays d'Islam*. E. J. Brill: Leiden.

TYAN, E. (1962): L'autorité de la chose jugée en droit musulman. *Studia Islamica* 17, 81–90.

URBACH, E. (1975): *The Sages. Their Concepts and Beliefs*. Harvard University Press: Cambridge, MA and London.

VANDERLINDEN, J. (2002): Religious laws as systems of law – a comparatist's view. *Religion, Law and Tradition. Comparative Studies in Religious Law* (ed. HUXLEY, A.), 165–84. RoutledgeCurzon: London.

VARGA, CS. (2005): *Theatrum legale mundi* avagy a jogrendszerek osztályozásáról (*Theatrum legale mundi* or On the Classification of Legal Systems.) *Ius Unum, Lex Multiplex. Liber Amicorum Studia Z. Péteri Dedicata*. Jogfilozófiák-Bibliotheca Iuridica, Libri Amicorum 13. Szent István Társulat: Budapest.

VESEY–FITZGERALD (1955): Nature and Sources of the Shari'a. *Law in the Middle East* (ed. KHADDURI–LIEBESNY): Middle East Institute: Washington DC.

VIKOR, K. (2006): *Between God and the Sultan. A History of Islamic Law*. Oxford University Press: Oxford.

VÖÖBUS, A. (1965): *History of the School of Nisibis*. Corpus Scriptorum Christianorum Orientalium, vol. 266. Louvain.

WADĀD AL-QĀDĪ (2009): The salaries of judges in early Islam: The evidence of the documentary and literary sources. *Journal of Near Eastern Studies* 68/1, 9–30.

WATSON, A. (1999): *Ancient Law and Modern Understanding. At the Edges*. The University of Georgia Press: Athens and London.

WEBER, M. (1972): *Wirtschaft und Gesellschaft. Grundriß der verstehenden Soziologie*. Fünfte, revidierte Ausgabe (ed. WINCKELMANN, J.). J. C. B. Mohr: Tübingen.

WEBER, M. (1978): *Economy and Society. An outline of Interpretive Sociology* (ed. ROTH, G.–WITTICH, C.). University of California Press: Berkeley, Los Angeles, London.

WEGNER, J. R. (1982): Islamic and Talmudic jurisprudence: the four roots of Islamic law and their Talmudic counterparts. *The American Journal of Legal History* 26, 25–71.

WEISS, B. G. (1978): Interpretation in Islamic Law: The Theory of Ijtihād. *The American Journal of Comparative Law* 26, 199–212.

WEISS, B. G. (1990): Covenant and Law in Islam. *Religion and Law. Biblical-Judaic and Islamic Perspectives* (ed. FIRMAGE–WEISS–WELCH), 49–85. Eisenbrauns: Winona Lake, IN.

WEISS, B. G. (1992): *The Search for God's Law. Islamic Jurisprudence in the Writing of Sayf al-Dīn al-Āmidī*. University of Utah Press: Salt Lake City.

WESTBROOK, R. (1988): *Studies in Biblical and Cuneiform Law*. Cahiers de la revue Biblique 26. Gabalda: Paris.

WESTBROOK, R. (1996): Biblical Law. *An Introduction to the History and Sources of Jewish Law* (ed. HECHT et al.), 1–18. Clarendon Press: Oxford.

WHEELER, B. M. (1996): *Applying the Canon is Islam. The Authorization and Maintenance of Interpretive Reasoning in Ḥanafī Scholarship*: State University of New York Press: New York.

ZAEHNER, R. C. (1965): *Down and Twilight of Zoroastrianism*. Oxford University Press: Oxford.

ZAMAN, M. Q (2002): *The Ulama in Contemporary Islam. Custodians of Change*. Princeton University Press: Princeton.

ZIADEH, F. J. (1990): Integrity (ᶜAdālah) in Classical Islamic Law. *Islamic Law and Jurisprudence* (ed. HEER, N.), 73–93. University of Washington Press: Seattle and London.

ZIADEH, F. J. (1996): Compelling defendant's appearance at court in Islamic law. *Islamic Law and Society* 3/3, 306–15. E. J. Brill: Leiden.

ZWEIGERT, K.–KÖTZ, H. (1971): *Einführung in die Rechtsvergleichung auf dem Gebiete des Privatrechts*. J. C. B. Mohr: Tübingen.

Index

Note: page numbers in bold type refer to Tables

For Product Safety Concerns and Information please contact our
EU representative GPSR@taylorandfrancis.com Taylor & Francis
Verlag GmbH, Kaufingerstraße 24, 80331 München, Germany